Praise for SUPERCRASH

'Crisp, clever graphics, symbols and examples demystify the complexities. He challenges the way we think and resist change, even when the alternative is disaster. *Supercrash* is a hugely readable, revelatory condemnation and call to arms.'
The Independent

'A remarkable read, visually clever and inventive…eminently readable. He shows all sides of a problem in a way the reader can understand, while never losing track of the human aspect in the complex issues involved… Darryl's unique comic art takes the reader easily into the heart of complex matters that have important influences on everyone's lives and makes them understandable visually as well as with words.'
Forbidden Planet

'Cunningham's pithy prose and funky art tell a complex, important tale. He connects the dots from Ayn Rand to Alan Greenspan to the mess we're in today, tackling tangled subjects with clarity and zing.'
Michael Goodwin, author of *Economix*

'Remarkable, informed, accurate and incisive… At last there is a single, readable, beautiful book that explains to the generation that came of age after 2008 what happened, why it happened, and why it will happen again.'
Danny Dorling, author of *Inequality and the 1%*

'A provocative, thoughtful, visual essay that tackles the language of ideas. *Supercrash* will leave you better informed and, more than that, it will leave you angry.'
Teddy Jamieson, *Herald Scotland*

'*Supercrash* is nothing short of Darryl's masterpiece.'
Bradford Telegraph & Argus

'Decodes the ideas with virtuosity…stylish and effective text, supported by simple outlines and flat colours, plays with the rhetoric of graphic symbols.'
L'Humanité

'A truly outstanding piece of work, illustrated so intelligently in his wonderful no-nonsense informative style.'
Page 45

Praise for SCIENCE TALES

'Deals with some of the most urgent debates in science…sorting facts from fiction and presenting complex information in a highly accessible way.'
The Observer

'Cunningham's charming artwork complements his concise arguments…his stark lines and simple layouts give his comic the feel of a scientific analysis.'
New Scientist

'Cunningham's art has clean lines and a continuity that is often graceful, charming and endearing. He speaks with quiet authority on his subjects.'
The Independent

'Brilliantly presented, and customarily classy…Cunningham delivering his message with style, great art, even moments of outright comedy.'
Forbidden Planet

'Both succinct and substantive, and a fierce and intelligent promoter of the scientific process over blind superstition and baseless supposition.'
Broken Frontier

Praise for GRAPHIC SCIENCE

'Rich, rewarding, fascinating and warmly personable… A wonderful read.'
Forbidden Planet

'Darryl Cunningham's simplicity of style is deceptive. I never fail to learn from his work, always educational and deeply human too. This is the sort of book you think you have bought for your child, then refuse to give up until you have finished it first. Buy two copies to be on the safe side.'
Robin Ince

'In a time when the scientific enterprise itself is under attack by self-serving, know-nothing yahoos, it's good to be reminded of the scientist's virtues: careful observation, patience, and depth of thought – the same combination that Cunningham brings to his work.'
Larry Gonick

'An essential purchase…undoubtedly some of the most crucially important practice to have emerged in UK comics in the last decade.'
Broken Frontier

DARRYL CUNNINGHAM
BILLIONAIRES
THE LIVES OF THE RICH AND POWERFUL

First published in 2019 by
Myriad Editions
www.myriadeditions.com

A CIP catalogue record for this book is available from
the British Library

ISBN: 978-1-912408-22-1
E-ISBN: 978-1-912408-61-0

Printed in Poland on paper sourced from sustainable forests

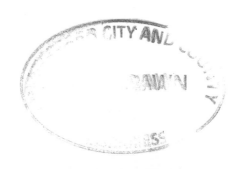

CONTENTS:

INTRODUCTION

WE ARE LIVING THROUGH WHAT HAS BEEN CALLED A NEW GILDED AGE. A TERM COINED BY MARK TWAIN THAT REFERRED TO A PERIOD IN THE UNITED STATES THAT LASTED ROUGHLY FROM THE 1870s TO ABOUT 1900, FUELLED BY A GREAT BURST OF INDUSTRIAL ACTIVITY AND CORPORATE GROWTH.

THE ENTREPRENEURS WHO DROVE THIS ECONOMIC EXPANSION GREW RICH THROUGH THE MONOPOLIES THEY CREATED IN THE STEEL, PETROLEUM AND RAILWAY INDUSTRIES. AMONG THE MOST WELL KNOWN OF THESE BUSINESSMEN WERE JOHN D. ROCKEFELLER, ANDREW CARNEGIE, CORNELIUS VANDERBILT, J.P. MORGAN AND LELAND STANFORD.

THE GLITTERING FACADE HID GRINDING POVERTY, RACIAL HATRED, VIOLENT LABOUR STRIKES AND CORRUPT POLITICS. IT WAS A TIME OF GROSS MATERIALISM, WHEN A YAWNING GAP OPENED BETWEEN RICH AND POOR, AND POLITICAL INFLUENCE WAS AVAILABLE FOR ANYONE ABLE TO PAY.

THE PARALLELS WITH OUR OWN TIME ARE OBVIOUS. OUR NEW GILDED AGE IS NOT CONFINED TO THE USA. THERE ARE FEW GEOGRAPHIC BARRIERS TO ENORMOUS WEALTH, AND ALMOST EVERYWHERE THE SUPER-RICH HAVE QUIETLY ADVANCED UNPOPULAR, INEQUALITY-EXACERBATING, HIGHLY CONSERVATIVE POLICIES. THEY ARE OPPOSED TO GOVERNMENT REGULATION OF THE ENVIRONMENT OR OF BIG BANKS, AND ARE UNENTHUSIASTIC ABOUT GOVERNMENT PROGRAMMES TO HELP WITH JOBS, INCOMES, HEALTHCARE OR RETIREMENT PENSIONS.

RUPERT MURDOCH

KOCH BROTHERS

JEFF BEZOS AND AMAZON

THIS BOOK IS DIVIDED UP INTO THREE SECTIONS, EACH TRACING THE LIFE STORY OF A PARTICULAR BILLIONAIRE: RUPERT MURDOCH (MEDIA), CHARLES AND DAVID KOCH (OIL AND GAS) AND JEFF BEZOS (ONLINE RETAIL AND TECHNOLOGY). I WANTED TO LOOK AT THESE PEOPLE IN SOME DETAIL. ALL ARE WHITE AND MALE, BECAUSE THE RICHEST PEOPLE IN THE WORLD ARE LARGELY WHITE AND MALE.

A BOOK ABOUT FEMALE BILLIONAIRES AND SUPER-RICH PEOPLE OF COLOUR WOULD BE INTERESTING (AND I MIGHT ONE DAY DO SUCH A BOOK) BUT AS THE VALUES OF OUR SOCIETY TEND TO BE THOSE OF WHITE MALES – THEY ARE THE ONES WHO HOLD ALL THE LEVERS OF POWER THROUGH OWNERSHIP OF THE MEDIA, POLITICAL INFLUENCE AND CONTROL OF THE ECONOMY – I WANTED TO FOCUS ON THEIR STORIES.

ALSO NOT FEATURED IS DONALD TRUMP (ALTHOUGH HE DOES CAMEO HERE AND THERE). THERE ARE ALREADY MANY TRUMP BOOKS OUT THERE, AND THE CONSTANT FOCUS ON TRUMP MEANS THAT OTHER POWERFUL PEOPLE ARE ESCAPING SCRUTINY. THIS BOOK IS MY SMALL ATTEMPT TO CORRECT THAT IMBALANCE. NOW READ ON.

RUPERT MURDOCH

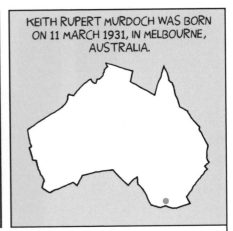

KEITH RUPERT MURDOCH WAS BORN ON 11 MARCH 1931, IN MELBOURNE, AUSTRALIA.

RUPERT MURDOCH'S GLOBAL MEDIA EMPIRE DIDN'T APPEAR FULLY FORMED FROM NOWHERE. ITS STRUCTURE AND FOUNDATION ALREADY EXISTED WHEN MURDOCH WAS A BOY. HIS FATHER, SIR KEITH ARTHUR MURDOCH, WAS AN AUSTRALIAN JOURNALIST WHO BY THE MID-1930s HAD ESTABLISHED A NATIONAL CHAIN OF MEDIA OUTLETS BASED AROUND NEWSPAPERS AND COMMERCIAL RADIO STATIONS.

THE POPULAR IMAGE OF RUPERT MURDOCH IS OF A ROUGH AND READY MAN, UNPRETENTIOUS AND SCEPTICAL OF THE ELITE. YET MURDOCH HIMSELF IS FROM AN ELITE BACKGROUND. HIS WEALTHY FAMILY OWNED A LARGE FARM ON THE OUTSKIRTS OF MELBOURNE AS WELL AS A LAVISH CITY MANSION. MURDOCH'S FATHER SUPPORTED THE POLITICAL RIGHT, AND HIS HANDFUL OF AUSTRALIAN NEWSPAPERS REFLECTED THIS VIEW. THIS PATTERN OF USING THE MEDIA TO INFLUENCE POLITICIANS AND POLICY WAS TO BE REPLICATED BY HIS SON ON A GLOBAL SCALE, BUT THE IDEA BEGAN WITH THE FATHER.

DAME ELISABETH JOY MURDOCH, MOTHER

YOUNG RUPERT WAS EDUCATED AT GEELONG GRAMMAR – A PRIVATE SCHOOL FOR THE SONS OF AUSTRALIA'S RICH FARMERS AND INDUSTRY CHIEFS, SOMETIMES STYLED 'THE ETON OF AUSTRALIA'. THEN OXFORD, ENGLAND IN 1950, WHERE HE READ PHILOSOPHY, POLITICS AND ECONOMICS AT WORCESTER COLLEGE.

MURDOCH'S POLITICAL VIEWS AT THIS TIME WERE OF CONCERN TO HIS FATHER. THE ELDER MURDOCH WROTE IN A LETTER TO THE JOURNALIST HUGH CUDLIPP IN 1952...

I'M WORRIED ABOUT MY SON, RUPERT. HE'S AT OXFORD AND IS DEVELOPING THE MOST ALARMING LEFT-WING VIEWS.

RUPERT MURDOCH WROTE TO ROHAN RIVEH, THE EDITOR OF HIS FATHER'S ADELAIDE PAPER, *THE NEWS*...

YESTERDAY WAS THE ANNIVERSARY OF THE GREAT TEACHER (LENIN). WE STOOD TO ATTENTION FOR ONE MINUTE IN FRONT OF THE BUST (OF LENIN) AND DRANK SEVERAL TOASTS.

THESE POLITICAL LEANINGS WERE NOT JUST A POSE. DURING ELECTIONS, MURDOCH TOOK PART IN CAMPAIGNING, KNOCKING ON DOORS, SEEKING TO CONVINCE VOTERS TO SUPPORT THE LOCAL LABOUR PARTY CANDIDATE.

WAS THIS PERHAPS WAS A RESPONSE TO THE ENGLISH CLASS SNOBBERY HE SAW ALL AROUND HIM IN OXFORD? AS AN AUSTRALIAN HE MAY HAVE FELT LIKE AN OUTSIDER ANYWAY. WHATEVER THE REASONS FOR THIS LEFT-WING STANCE, IT WAS SHORT-LIVED.

WHEN MURDOCH WAS 21, HIS FATHER DIED FROM CANCER. HE RETURNED TO AUSTRALIA TO TAKE CHARGE OF THE FAMILY BUSINESS. SIR KEITH'S FORTUNE HAD BEEN DEPLETED BY DEBT, TAXES ON HIS ESTATE, AND REVERSALS IN BUSINESS WHICH HAD TAKEN PLACE IN THE YEAR BEFORE HIS DEATH.

BUT THERE WERE ENOUGH ASSETS LEFT TO ALLOW THE YOUNGER MURDOCH A CHANCE TO BUILD HIS OWN BUSINESS EMPIRE.

I DON'T KNOW OF ANY SON OF ANY PROMINENT MEDIA FAMILY WHO HASN'T WANTED TO FOLLOW IN THE FOOTSTEPS OF HIS FOREBEARS.

THESE ASSETS INCLUDED *THE NEWS*.

IT'S JUST TOO GOOD A LIFE.

MURDOCH IMMERSED HIMSELF IN ALL ASPECTS OF THE PAPER'S OPERATIONS. HE WROTE HEADLINES, REDESIGNED PAGE LAYOUTS AND LABOURED IN THE TYPESETTING AND PRINTING ROOMS. HIS CONVERSION OF *THE NEWS* INTO A CHRONICLE OF CRIME, SEX AND SCANDAL SENT THE CIRCULATION SOARING. OVER THE NEXT TEN YEARS MURDOCH ACQUIRED MAJOR NEWSPAPERS IN EVERY AUSTRALIAN STATE.

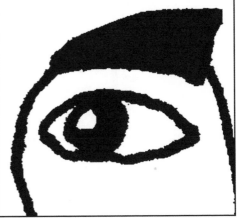

MURDOCH DIDN'T STOP AT BUYING NEWSPAPERS. HE ALSO BOUGHT TV STATIONS ALONG WITH THE RIGHTS TO BROADCAST SHOWS FROM THE AMERICAN ABC TV NETWORK.

HE ESTABLISHED THE COUNTRY'S FIRST NATIONAL DAILY, *THE AUSTRALIAN.* THE LAUNCH OF THIS PAPER GAVE HIM CONSIDERABLE KUDOS AND POLITICAL LEVERAGE.

THROUGHOUT THIS TIME, MURDOCH USED HIS BURGEONING EMPIRE TO INFLUENCE AUSTRALIAN POLITICS.

HE SOMETIMES SUPPORTED THE LABOR PARTY AND AT OTHER TIMES THE POLITICAL RIGHT.

JOHN MENADUE, WHO WAS FORMALLY A SENIOR PUBLIC SERVANT UNDER LABOR LEADER GOUGH WHITLAM, WORKED AS AN EXECUTIVE FOR MURDOCH.

HE WAS AND STILL IS A FRUSTRATED POLITICIAN. HE CAN'T LEAVE POLITICS ALONE.

WORKING WITH HIM FOR SEVEN YEARS, I SAW WHAT DROVE HIM. IT WAS NOT MAKING MONEY, AS USEFUL AS THAT WAS, BUT GAINING ACCEPTANCE BY AND THEN INFLUENCE WITH PEOPLE.

IN 1969, MURDOCH TOOK HIS FIRST STEPS TOWARDS GLOBAL EXPANSION...

WITH THE PURCHASE OF THE *NEWS OF THE WORLD* – THEN BRITAIN'S BIGGEST-SELLING SUNDAY NEWSPAPER. IT WAS A SENSATIONALIST TABLOID THAT ALREADY USED THE FORMULA OF SEX, SCANDAL AND SPORT THAT WORKED SO WELL FOR MURDOCH. SO THE PAPER NATURALLY APPEALED TO HIM.

FOUNDED IN 1843, THE *NEWS OF THE WORLD* HAD BEEN CONTROLLED BY THE CARR FAMILY FOR 60 YEARS, BUT CONFLICT WITHIN THE FAMILY HAD LEFT IT VULNERABLE TO A TAKEOVER.

MURDOCH'S COMPETITOR FOR THE *NEWS OF THE WORLD* WAS THE CZECH-BORN BRITISH CITIZEN ROBERT MAXWELL.

YOU ARE AS SAFE WITH ME AS YOU WOULD BE IN THE BANK OF ENGLAND.

MURDOCH ENTERED THE FIGHT AS AN ALLY OF THE CHAIR SIR WILLIAM CARR, WITH THE HELP OF FINANCIAL ADVISOR LORD CATTO.

CATTO HAD FIRST MET MURDOCH WHILE WORKING IN AUSTRALIA FOR AN ASSOCIATE COMPANY OF THE BRITISH BANK MORGAN GRENFELL.

I WANT TO BUY THE UK PAPER THE *DAILY MIRROR*.

THERE'S NO CHANCE OF THAT. IPC, THE MIRROR'S OWNERS, WILL NEVER SELL.

THEN I'LL BUY IPC.

THIS MAN IS SLIGHTLY MAD.

I'M GOING TO HAVE TO SEE SOME SERIOUS MONEY BEFORE THAT IDEA CAN PROCEED FURTHER.

MURDOCH PROMPTLY TRANSFERRED TWO MILLION POUNDS TO MORGAN GRENFELL, WHICH BEGAN BUYING SHARES IN IPC.

Cha-ching!

CATTO SOON SPOTTED A BETTER OPTION FOR MURDOCH IN THE *NEWS OF THE WORLD*. A MEMBER OF THE CARR FAMILY WANTED TO SELL A 25-PER-CENT STAKE AND HAD PLEDGED IT TO ROBERT MAXWELL.

I'M SELLING.

THIS HAD NOT GONE DOWN WELL WITH THE REST OF THE FAMILY, OR WITH THE EDITOR OF THE PAPER, STAFFORD SOMERFIELD.

YOU'RE DOING WHAT?

?

ROBERT MAXWELL'S FOREIGN ORIGINS AND SOCIALIST VIEWS (HE WAS AT THAT TIME A LABOUR MEMBER OF PARLIAMENT) HORRIFIED THEM.

IN AN EDITORIAL, STAFFORD SOMERFIELD RAILED AGAINST MAXWELL IN XENOPHOBIC TERMS.

IT WOULD NOT BE A GOOD THING FOR MR MAXWELL, FORMERLY JAN LUDWIG HOCH, TO GAIN CONTROL OF THIS NEWSPAPER...

WHICH IS AS BRITISH AS ROAST BEEF AND YORKSHIRE PUDDING... THIS IS A BRITISH NEWSPAPER. LET'S KEEP IT THAT WAY.

MAXWELL'S BID VALUED THE PAPER FIRST AT £26 MILLION AND THEN AT £34 MILLION – A PRICE BEYOND MURDOCH'S REACH.

HMMPH!

LORD CATTO HAD A PROPOSAL.

I SUGGEST A SHARE SWAP WITH THE CARR FAMILY. TURN SOME OF YOUR AUSTRALIAN ASSETS IN MINOR VENTURES INTO SHARES IN THE NEWS OF THE WORLD GROUP.

DO IT.

BY DECEMBER 1968, MURDOCH'S NEWS LIMITED CONTROLLED 40 PER CENT OF NEWS OF THE WORLD STOCK.

WHAT!

IN JANUARY 1969, MAXWELL'S BID WAS REJECTED AT A SHAREHOLDERS' MEETING, WHERE HALF OF THOSE PRESENT WERE COMPANY STAFF TEMPORARILY GIVEN VOTING SHARES.

MURDOCH HAD WON. BY JUNE, ILLNESS HAD OBLIGED SIR WILLIAM CARR TO STEP DOWN AS CHAIRMAN, AND MURDOCH SUCCEEDED HIM.

THERE WAS INSTANT FRICTION BETWEEN THE NEW PROPRIETOR AND STAFFORD SOMERFIELD, WHO WAS USED TO FAR MORE INDEPENDENCE AS EDITOR.

HE WANTED TO READ PROOFS, WRITE LEADERS IF HE FELT LIKE IT, CHANGE THE PAPER ABOUT AND GIVE INSTRUCTIONS TO STAFF.

I DIDN'T COME ALL THIS WAY NOT TO INTERFERE.

YOU'RE FIRED.

THAT SAME YEAR, IPC (INTERNATIONAL PUBLISHING COMPANY) WERE LOOKING TO OFFLOAD THEIR DAILY BROADSHEET *THE SUN*. ORIGINALLY KNOWN AS *THE DAILY HERALD*. IT HAD BEEN RELAUNCHED BY IPC AS *THE SUN* IN 1964, BUT IT HAD NEVER THRIVED. ONCE AGAIN, ROBERT MAXWELL WAS FRONTRUNNER TO BUY THE PAPER, BUT THE COMPANY DIDN'T BELIEVE HE HAD THE FUNDS. MURDOCH ASSURED IPC THAT HE WOULD PUBLISH A 'STRAIGHTFORWARD, HONEST NEWSPAPER', WHICH WOULD CONTINUE TO SUPPORT THE BRITISH LABOUR PARTY. THIS WAS GOOD NEWS FOR THE POWERFUL PRINT UNION, WHO HAD PUT PRESSURE ON IPC TO REJECT MAXWELL'S OFFER.

MURDOCH BOUGHT *THE SUN* FOR £800,000, TO BE PAID IN INSTALMENTS.

I AM CONSTANTLY AMAZED AT THE EASE WITH WHICH I ENTERED BRITISH NEWSPAPERS.

HE PROMPTLY SWITCHED *THE SUN* INTO A TABLOID FORMAT AND REDUCED COSTS BY PRINTING BOTH THE *NEWS OF THE WORLD* AND *THE SUN* ON THE SAME PRINTING PRESS.

MURDOCH TOLD THE EDITOR OF *THE SUN*, LARRY LAMB, THAT...

I WANT A TEARAWAY PAPER WITH LOTS OF TITS IN IT.

THE SUN PUBLISHED ITS FIRST BARE-BREASTED MODEL IN 1970.

MURDOCH'S TRIED AND TESTED FORMULA OF GOSSIP, SCANDAL, SPORTS, AND COMPETITIONS TO WIN CARS AND TV SETS BOOSTED THE PAPER'S CIRCULATION FROM 1 MILLION TO 3.5 MILLION BY 1975. THREE YEARS LATER IT PASSED THE *DAILY MIRROR*, WHICH HAD BEEN THE COUNTRY'S BIGGEST-SELLING NEWSPAPER SINCE 1949.

IN THE BRITISH ELECTION OF 1970 *THE SUN* TOOK A LEFT-WING STANCE. IN AN EDITORIAL, IT EXPLAINED THAT THE LABOUR PARTY CARED MORE ABOUT ORDINARY PEOPLE AND SOCIAL JUSTICE AND EXPRESSED ITS OPPOSITION TO THE CONSERVATIVE PARTY'S SCARE TACTICS ON IMMIGRATION AND LAW AND ORDER.

THE CONSERVATIVES WENT ON TO WIN, BUT THE PAPER CONTINUED TO SUPPORT LABOUR. WHEN PRIME MINISTER EDWARD HEATH DECLARED A STATE OF EMERGENCY DURING THE COAL MINERS' STRIKE OF 1972, *THE SUN* SUPPORTED THE MINERS, AND OPPOSED THE RESTRICTIONS ON TRADE UNION LAWS.

MURDOCH'S DRIFT TO THE POLITICAL RIGHT BEGAN IN 1975. THAT YEAR AUSTRALIA SUFFERED A CONSTITUTIONAL CRISIS. GOUGH WHITLAM'S LABOR GOVERNMENT'S SMALL MAJORITY MEANT THAT IT WAS UNABLE TO PASS A BUDGET THROUGH THE SENATE. THE CONSERVATIVE OPPOSITION BLOCKED THE BILL, LEAVING THE RULING PARTY UNABLE TO FINANCE ANY GOVERNMENT OPERATIONS.

AS THE CRISIS DEEPENED, SIR JOHN KERR, THE GOVERNOR GENERAL APPOINTED BY THE QUEEN, RESOLVED THE IMPASSE BY DISMISSING THE LABOR GOVERNMENT AND APPOINTING OPPOSITION LEADER MALCOLM FRASER AS CARETAKER PRIME MINISTER.

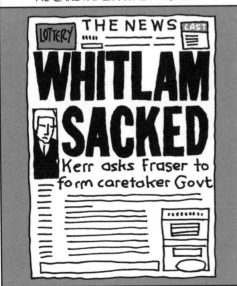

MURDOCH HAD ORIGINALLY BACKED WHITLAM BUT HAD COME TO OPPOSE HIM ONCE HE WAS IN POWER, BECAUSE HE WAS INTRODUCING...

A EUROPEAN TYPE OF SOCIALISM WHICH CAUSED RUIN AND MISERY IN OTHER COUNTRIES.

MURDOCH'S CAMPAIGN VILIFYING WHITLAM COST HIM MONEY. SALES OF *THE AUSTRALIAN* FELL WHEN A BOYCOTT WAS ORGANISED AGAINST THE PAPER.

WHARF LABOURERS REFUSED TO HANDLE THE PAPER'S SUPPLIES.

MURDOCH'S OWN JOURNALISTS WALKED OUT IN THE FIRST STRIKE OVER NEWSPAPER BIAS IN THEIR HISTORY. SEVENTY-FIVE SIGNED A LETTER TO MURDOCH, STATING...

'WE CAN BE LOYAL TO *THE AUSTRALIAN*, NO MATTER HOW MUCH ITS STYLE, THRUST AND READERSHIP CHANGES, AS LONG AS IT RETAINS THE PRINCIPLES AND INTEGRITY OF A RESPONSIBLE NEWSPAPER...

HMMPH!

'WE CANNOT BE LOYAL TO A PROPAGANDA SHEET.'

CRUMPLE!

UNTIL THIS TIME, MURDOCH'S GROWING MEDIA EMPIRE HAD BEEN RELATIVELY EVEN-HANDED POLITICALLY, BUT FROM THE 1980s ONWARD, THIS CHANGED. A NEW KIND OF CONSERVATISM ARRIVED THAT WOULD TRANSFORM BRITISH AND AMERICAN POLITICS – PERSONIFIED BY MARGARET THATCHER IN THE UK AND RONALD REAGAN IN THE USA. MURDOCH BECAME THE POPULARISER, THE ADVOCATE AND ULTIMATELY THE BENEFICIARY OF THE PHILOSOPHY OF FREE MARKETS, LOW TAXES, DEREGULATION AND GLOBALISATION.

I WAS PRETTY MUCH TURNED INTO A STRONG CONSERVATIVE BY... THE MOST SEARING EXPERIENCE OF MY LIFE (WHICH WAS) HAVING 17 YEARS OF DEALING WITH THE FLEET STREET CHAPELS.

FLEET STREET: THE AREA OF LONDON DOMINATED AT THAT TIME BY THE NATIONAL PRESS AND RELATED INDUSTRIES.

A CHAPEL: A BRANCH OR MEMBERS OF A PRINT OR NEWSPAPER UNION.

A SECRET MEETING BETWEEN MURDOCH AND UK PRIME MINISTER MARGARET THATCHER TOOK PLACE IN EARLY 1981. THE SUBJECT OF THE MEETING WAS MURDOCH'S WISH TO BUY *THE TIMES* AND THE *SUNDAY TIMES*.

CHEQUERS COURT – THE PRIME MINISTER'S COUNTRY RESIDENCE.

AS THE NEWSPAPER TYCOON ALREADY OWNED *THE SUN* AND THE *NEWS OF THE WORLD*, THIS BID SHOULD PROPERLY HAVE BEEN REFERRED TO THE MONOPOLIES AND MERGERS COMMISSION, FOR REVIEW.

BOTH PARTIES WANTED TO AVOID THIS.

THE DECISION TO REFER THE BID WAS ONE TO BE TAKEN BY THE THEN SECRETARY OF STATE FOR TRADE, JOHN NOTT.

RING! RING!

ON HER RETURN TO LONDON THAT SUNDAY, MARGARET THATCHER SUMMONED NOTT TO A MEETING AT 9PM IN HER FLAT AT DOWNING STREET.

NOTT WAS AN EXPERIENCED POLITICIAN WITH A BACKGROUND IN LAW AND ECONOMICS WHO HAD SERVED PREVIOUSLY AS SECRETARY TO THE TREASURY UNDER PRIME MINISTER TED HEATH.

YES, PRIME MINISTER.

WHEN I GOT THERE, I WAS SURPRISED THAT THE PRIME MINISTER'S HUSBAND AND TWO OF HIS PRIVATE SECRETARIES WERE ALSO PRESENT.

THE ATMOSPHERE WAS VERY FRIENDLY AND INFORMAL AND I WAS OFFERED A DRINK.

IT STILL SEEMS A LITTLE ODD TO ME THAT IT WAS WAS NOT A PRIVATE MEETING WITH THE PRIME MINISTER ALONE.

THATCHER OFFERED NOTT THE POSITION OF SECRETARY OF DEFENCE, WHICH HE HAPPILY ACCEPTED.

THE PRIME MINISTER THEN TELEPHONED THE CHIEF SECRETARY TO THE TREASURY, JOHN BIFFEN, AND OFFERED HIM NOTT'S JOB.

RING! RING!

THATCHER TOLD BIFFEN THAT IT WOULD WIDEN HIS EXPERIENCE. SHE WAS ABSOLUTELY DELIGHTED WHEN HE ACCEPTED.

BIFFEN WAS IMMEDIATELY OUT OF HIS DEPTH. IN HIS DIARY HE WROTE...

THE EPISODE CAME AT ME WITH GREAT SPEED. I HAD NO PARTICULAR KNOWLEDGE OF THE NEWSPAPER INDUSTRY.

I AM CERTAINLY ENCOUNTERING THE STRAINS OF OFFICE. I HAD A RESTLESS NIGHT AND GOT TO THE OFFICE LADEN WITH ANXIETY.

THE ONLY WAY A MURDOCH TAKEOVER OF THE TIMES NEWSPAPER GROUP COULD BE EXEMPT FROM SCRUTINY BY THE MONOPOLIES AND MERGERS COMMISSION WAS IF BIFFEN COULD SATISFY HIMSELF THAT THE PUBLICATIONS WERE NOT MAKING A PROFIT.

THE BID RELIED ON BOTH *THE TIMES* AND THE *SUNDAY TIMES* BEING LOSS-MAKING. THERE WAS NO DOUBT ABOUT THE FORMER, BUT THE *SUNDAY TIMES* WAS A CLOSE-RUN THING.

IN FACT, ACCORDING TO THE THEN *SUNDAY TIMES* EDITOR HAROLD EVANS, SOME FANCY ACCOUNTING FOOTWORK TOOK PLACE IN ORDER TO MAKE THE *SUNDAY TIMES* LOOK LESS VIABLE.

MR MURDOCH IS HERE, MINISTER.

IN A MEETING WITH BIFFEN, MURDOCH TOOK AN AGGRESSIVE STANCE.

GRR!

HE WAS REPORTED TO HAVE SAID...

BEFORE YOU BEGIN, I HEAR YOU ARE CONSIDERING A REFERRAL TO THE MONOPOLIES COMMISSION. IF YOU DO THAT AND IT ENDS UP ALLOWING ME TO GO AHEAD, IT WILL MEAN A LONG DELAY. IF I DON'T GET AN ANSWER NOW, I'LL NOT PAY A PENNY IN REDUNDANCIES.

BY WHICH HE MEANT REDUNDANCY MONEY FOR THE WORKERS HE WOULD HAVE TO LET GO IN ORDER TO PUT THE TIMES GROUP BACK ON A SECURE FINANCIAL FOOTING.

THE DEAL WENT AHEAD. MARGARET THATCHER LEFT NOTHING TO CHANCE. SHE IMPOSED A THREE-LINE WHIP ON THE COMMONS VOTE ON 27 JANUARY – A STRICT INSTRUCTION FOR MEMBERS OF HER PARTY TO VOTE – THE BREACH OF WHICH WOULD HAVE SERIOUS CONSEQUENCES.

CRACK!

MURDOCH HAD TO GIVE STRICT, LEGALLY BINDING GUARANTEES THAT THE NEWSPAPERS WOULD HAVE EDITORIAL INDEPENDENCE. HAROLD EVANS WAS LURED FROM THE SUNDAY TIMES TO BE EDITOR OF THE TIMES.

NO EDITOR OR JOURNALIST COULD ASK FOR WIDER GUARANTEES OF EDITORIAL INDEPENDENCE ON NEWS OR POLICY THAN THOSE MR MURDOCH HAS ACCEPTED.

A YEAR LATER EVANS WAS FORCED TO RESIGN.

I WAS SO ABSOLUTELY DISGUSTED, DISMAYED AND DEMORALISED BY LIVING IN A VINDICTIVE ATMOSPHERE. NOTHING IN MY EXPERIENCE COMPARED TO THE ATMOSPHERE OF INTRIGUE, FEAR AND SPITE ON THE PAPER BY MURDOCH'S LIEUTENANTS.

DESPITE THE WIDESPREAD USE OF NEW PRINTING TECHNOLOGY ACROSS THE WORLD, IN THE EARLY 1980s FLEET STREET NEWSPAPERS WERE STILL BEING PRODUCED BY THE LABOUR-INTENSIVE HOT-METAL LINOTYPE METHOD, RATHER THAN BEING COMPOSED ELECTRONICALLY.

UNIONS HAD ENORMOUS POWER IN A BUSINESS WHERE EVEN A SHORT INDUSTRIAL ACTION COULD DISRUPT TIGHT PRODUCTION AND DISTRIBUTION SCHEDULES AND SO INFLICT GREAT FINANCIAL DAMAGE.

MURDOCH TOOK ON THE UNIONS. HE WANTED TO INTRODUCE TECHNOLOGICAL INNOVATION THAT WOULD PUT 90 PER CENT OF THE OLD-FASHIONED TYPESETTERS OUT OF WORK. THE COMPANY OFFERED REDUNDANCY PAYMENTS OF £2,000 TO £3,000 TO EACH PRINTER TO GIVE UP THEIR JOBS. MURDOCH ALSO DEMANDED THE UNIONS ACCEPT A NO STRIKE CLAUSE AND ABANDON THEIR CLOSED SHOP POLICY (A PLACE OF WORK WHERE ALL EMPLOYEES MUST BELONG TO A UNION).

THE UNIONS REFUSED AND WENT ON STRIKE. THIS WAS EXACTLY WHAT MURDOCH WANTED. ON 24 JANUARY 1986, DISMISSAL NOTICES WERE SERVED ON ALL THOSE TAKING PART IN THE INDUSTRIAL ACTION, SACKING 6,000 EMPLOYEES. THEY HAD FALLEN INTO A TRAP.

MURDOCH HAD BUILT A NEW HIGH-TECH PRINTING PLANT AT WAPPING IN THE LONDON DOCKLANDS, WHICH HE HAD LED THE UNIONS TO BELIEVE WAS FOR A NEW NEWSPAPER, CALLED THE *LONDON POST*. THIS WAS UNTRUE.

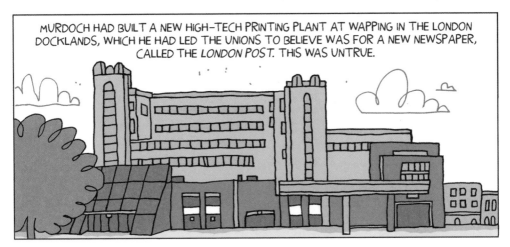

THE INTENTION WAS TO MOVE ALL FOUR MURDOCH TITLES TO WAPPING – *THE TIMES*, *THE SUN*, THE *SUNDAY TIMES*, AND THE *NEWS OF THE WORLD*. A SECRET DEAL HAD BEEN MADE WITH THE ELECTRICAL, ELECTRONIC, TELECOMMUNICATIONS AND PLUMBERS' UNION (EETPU) TO REPLACE THE SACKED EMPLOYEES WITH THEIR WORKERS. THE NEW SITE, WITH ITS SPIKED STEEL RAILINGS TOPPED BY BARBED WIRE, WAS LABELLED FORTRESS WAPPING.

THE BATTLE OF WAPPING

IN THE YEAR-LONG DISPUTE THAT FOLLOWED, THOUSANDS OF UNION PICKETS TRIED TO BLOCK SHIPMENTS OUT OF THE PLANT.

THE PICKETING WAS EXCEPTIONALLY VIOLENT, WITH 1,262 ARRESTS AND 410 POLICE INJURIES.

THE POLICE IN TURN WERE ACCUSED OF BRUTALITY AND AGGRESSIVENESS IN THEIR DEALINGS WITH BOTH STRIKERS AND LOCAL RESIDENTS.

ANYONE IN THE VICINITY OF THE PLANT, INCLUDING LOCALS, WERE ASSUMED BY THE POLICE TO BE SYMPATHETIC TO THE UNIONS. THE RESIDENTS OF WAPPING WERE SOMETIMES DENIED ACCESS TO THEIR OWN STREETS AND HOMES. THEIR CARS WERE TOWED AWAY FROM LEGITIMATE PARKING SPACES TO ALLOW DELIVERY TRUCKS TO EXIT THE AREA.

I'D BEEN INVOLVED IN QUITE A FEW DISPUTES, STRIKES AND PICKETS. I'D ALWAYS GOT ON QUITE WELL WITH THE POLICE AND I'D SEEN THE MINERS THE PREVIOUS YEAR, AND THOUGHT THEY'RE OVER THE TOP, OVERREACTING. BUT THEN I SAW THE WAY THE POLICE TREATED US AT WAPPING, THE WOMEN TOO, SECRETARIES AND THE LIKE, AND SAW SOMETHING HAD CHANGED. THE POLICE WERE USING VIOLENCE TO DISCOURAGE PEOPLE FROM DEMONSTRATING.

RON GARNER, SACKED WAREHOUSE WORKER

I PERSONALLY SAW MANY PEOPLE VICIOUSLY ASSAULTED BY THE POLICE OR ARRESTED ON TRUMPED-UP CHARGES, AND WITNESSED A SUCCESSION OF POLICEMEN COMMITTING PERJURY ON AN ALMOST INDUSTRIAL SCALE.

NIC OATRIDGE, WITNESS

ON AT LEAST THREE OCCASIONS I AND OTHER PHOTOGRAPHERS WERE CHASED BY THE POLICE WITH TRUNCHEONS WHO WERE DELIBERATELY PREVENTING US FROM PHOTOGRAPHING OTHER OFFICERS INDISCRIMINATELY TRUNCHEONING DEMONSTRATORS.

JOHN STURROCK, PHOTOGRAPHER

ACCORDING TO GOVERNMENT ESTIMATES AT THE TIME, THERE WERE AT LEAST 130 POLICE ON DUTY EACH NIGHT, WITH A PEAK OF OVER 1,800 ON ONE OCCASION.

THE POLITICIAN AND JOURNALIST WOODROW WYATT – A FRIEND OF BOTH MURDOCH AND THATCHER – CLAIMED THAT A GOVERNMENT MINISTER PRIVATELY COMPLAINED TO MURDOCH THAT SIX MONTHS OF POLICE SUPPORT HAD COST THE TAXPAYER £5 MILLION. SHORTLY AFTER THIS, MURDOCH ASKED FOR AND THEN RECEIVED A PERSONAL ASSURANCE FROM THE PRIME MINISTER THAT SHE WOULD 'SQUASH' ANY WEAKENING BY HER MINISTERS.

NONE OF THIS COULD HAVE HAPPENED WITHOUT GOVERNMENT BACKING. THE WAPPING DISPUTE TOOK PLACE AGAINST A BACKGROUND OF NEW LEGISLATION TO CURB THE POWER OF THE UNIONS.

MURDOCH'S NEWS INTERNATIONAL DID NOT LOSE A SINGLE NIGHT OF PRODUCTION DURING THE YEAR–LONG INDUSTRIAL ACTION. IN FEBRUARY 1987 THE STRIKE ENDED IN TOTAL DEFEAT FOR THE PRINT UNIONS, WHO WERE NEAR BANKRUPTCY AND UNDER THREAT OF COURT PROCEEDINGS.

TECHNOLOGICAL CHANGE HAD TO HAPPEN, BUT IT WAS DONE IN A MANNER THAT WAS BRUTAL AND UNFAIR TO WORKERS. NEWS INTERNATIONAL WANTED A BUSINESS THAT WAS FREE OF UNION CONSTRAINTS AND ANY REAL NEED TO CONCERN THEMSELVES WITH EMPLOYEES' RIGHTS.

THE EETPU HEAD, ERIC HAMMOND, WHO HAD ASSISTED THE MOVE TO WAPPING IN THE EXPECTATION THAT HIS UNION WOULD BE THE ONLY REPRESENTATIVE OF THE WORKERS THERE, FOUND HIMSELF BETRAYED. WAPPING REMAINED NON-UNION.

HAMMOND, IN HIS AUTOBIOGRAPHY, STATED THAT MURDOCH HAD NOT SHOWN...

ONE SPARK OF GRATITUDE.

FROM THIS TIME, MURDOCH'S CHEERY, GIVE-THE-PEOPLE-WHAT-THEY-WANT APPROACH BEGAN, IN SOME AREAS OF HIS ORGANISATION, TO HARDEN INTO A MORE UNPLEASANT, ETHICS-FREE PURSUIT OF PROFIT, REGARDLESS OF THE HARM IT CAUSED.

ON 15 APRIL 1987, 95 LIVERPOOL FOOTBALL FANS WERE CRUSHED TO DEATH AND HUNDREDS MORE INJURED ON THE STEEL FENCES OF SHEFFIELD WEDNESDAY'S HILLSBOROUGH STADIUM...

WHICH WAS HOSTING THE FA CUP SEMI-FINAL BETWEEN LIVERPOOL AND NOTTINGHAM FOREST. THE 96TH VICTIM, TONY BLAND, DIED IN 1993 AFTER FOUR YEARS IN A PERSISTENT VEGETATIVE STATE.

ALMOST IMMEDIATELY AFTER THE DISASTER, POLICE SPOKESMEN BEGAN TO LEAK STORIES TO THE MEDIA...

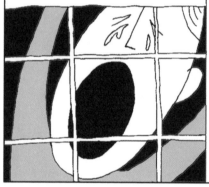

IN AN ATTEMPT TO DIVERT ATTENTION AWAY FROM THE DECISIONS THEY MADE THAT HAD LED TO THE CRUSH. MOST PAPERS REPORTED THESE STATEMENTS AS ALLEGATIONS...

BUT NOT *THE SUN*.

KELVIN MACKENZIE, THEN EDITOR OF *THE SUN*, PERSONALLY WROTE THE HEADLINE, 'THE TRUTH' WHICH WOULD BE A DISASTER FOR THE PAPER'S REPUTATION AND SALES.

THE STORY CLAIMED THAT SOME DRUNKEN LIVERPOOL FANS HAD 'VICIOUSLY ATTACKED RESCUE WORKERS', URINATED ON 'BRAVE COPS' AND PICKED THE POCKETS OF VICTIMS.

ALL UNTRUE AND EASILY REFUTED. THE PAPER'S SALES IN LIVERPOOL DROPPED BY 40 PER CENT AND REMAINED LOWER THAN ELSEWHERE FOR MORE THAN A DECADE.

MACKENZIE DID NOT APOLOGISE FOR MORE THAN 20 YEARS AND EVEN THEN HIS CONCESSION APPEARED GRUDGING.

THE SUN DID NOT ACCUSE ANYBODY OF ANYTHING. WE WERE THE VEHICLE OF OTHERS.

DURING HIS TIME AT *THE SUN*, MACKENZIE WAS WIDELY CRITICISED FOR HIS PERCEIVED CRUELTY TO THE TARGETS OF HIS NEWSPAPER STORIES – PEOPLE WHO WERE NOT JUST CELEBRITIES OR LEFT-WING POLITICIANS, BUT PREVIOUSLY UNKNOWN MEMBERS OF THE PUBLIC.

MACKENZIE FELT NO NEED TO DO SERIOUS JOURNALISM AT *THE SUN*.

YOU JUST DON'T UNDERSTAND READERS, DO YOU, EH? HE'S THE BLOKE YOU SEE IN THE PUB, A RIGHT OLD FASCIST, WANTS TO SEND THE WOGS BACK, BUY HIS POXY COUNCIL HOUSE, HE'S AFRAID OF THE UNIONS, AFRAID OF THE RUSSIANS, HATES THE QUEERS AND THE WEIRDOS AND DRUG DEALERS. HE DOESN'T WANT TO HEAR ABOUT THAT STUFF (SERIOUS NEWS).

DID RUPERT MURDOCH APPROVE OF SUCH VILE OPINIONS? WE HAVE SEEN THAT EDITORS WHO DIDN'T SHARE HIS WORLD VIEW WERE SOON SHOWN THE DOOR, SO THE ANSWER HAS TO BE YES.

ANOTHER FORMER *SUN* EDITOR, DAVID YELLAND, WROTE...

ALL MURDOCH EDITORS...END UP AGREEING WITH EVERYTHING RUPERT SAYS BUT YOU DON'T ADMIT TO YOURSELF THAT YOU'RE BEING INFLUENCED. MOST MURDOCH EDITORS WAKE UP IN THE MORNING, SWITCH ON THE RADIO, HEAR THAT SOMETHING HAS HAPPENED AND THINK: WHAT WOULD RUPERT THINK ABOUT THIS? IT'S LIKE A MANTRA INSIDE YOUR HEAD, IT'S LIKE A PRISM. YOU LOOK AT THE WORLD THROUGH RUPERT'S EYES.

ANDREW NEIL, FORMER EDITOR OF THE *SUNDAY TIMES*...

DURING THE 11 YEARS I WAS EDITOR, RUPERT FIRED OR EASED OUT EVERY CHIEF EXECUTIVE OF REAL TALENT OR INDEPENDENT MINDSET. THIS REFLECTS RUPERT'S GENERAL DISDAIN FOR INDIVIDUALS. HE HAS NEVER EXPRESSED REGRET ABOUT THOSE HE HAS AXED AND HAS REPEATEDLY SAID THAT EVERY INDIVIDUAL CAN BE REPLACED.

IN THEIR BOOK, *STICK IT UP YOUR PUNTER: THE UNCUT STORY OF THE SUN NEWSPAPER*, CHRIS HORRIE AND PETER CHIPPENDALE RELATE HOW, UNDER MACKENZIE, SOME JOURNALISTS WERE TOLD TO THEIR FACES THAT THEY HAD NO FUTURE IN THE PLACE, AND WERE THEN GIVEN IMPOSSIBLE JOBS, HUGE WORKLOADS, AND WERE PERSONALLY INSULTED.

ARE YOU STILL HERE?

MACKENZIE'S DOMINANCE WAS SO TOTAL THAT THERE WAS NO ONE TO CHALLENGE HIM WHEN HE WROTE HIS DISASTROUS AND INSULTING HILLSBOROUGH FRONT PAGE.

I QUIT.

A SIMILAR CULTURE OF AGGRESSION AND BULLYING EXISTED AT OTHER NEWS INTERNATIONAL PAPERS.

MATT DRISCOLL, FORMER SPORTS WRITER, *NEWS OF THE WORLD*

DRISCOLL WAS AWARDED £792,736 IN COMPENSATION FOR BEING THE VICTIM OF A CONSISTENT PATTERN OF BULLYING BEHAVIOUR.

IN MY YEARS AT NEWS INTERNATIONAL, I CAME TO BELIEVE – ALONG WITH OTHER JOURNALISTS...

THAT THE NEWSPAPER GROUPS WERE INDEED CONFIDENT THAT THEY WERE UNTOUCHABLE BECAUSE THEY WERE SURE THEY HAD THE GOVERNMENT AND POLICE FIGHTING THEIR CORNER.

THUS THEY FELT THEY WERE ALMOST BEYOND THE REACH OF THE LAW. THESE POWERFUL CONTACTS WERE THE REASON WHY SOME ON THE *NEWS OF THE WORLD* COULD LEAVE THEIR MORALS AND RESPECT AT THE DOOR WHEN THEY CLOCKED ON EACH MORNING.

THE NEXT FRONT PAGE WAS ALL THAT MATTERED, HOWEVER IT WAS OBTAINED.

WHILE ALL THIS WAS HAPPENING, MURDOCH WAS EXPANDING HIS BUSINESS BEYOND NEWSPAPERS INTO OTHER MEDIA.

HE ACQUIRED A CONTROLLING INTEREST IN 20TH CENTURY FOX. MURDOCH WAS BUYING NOT JUST A MOVIE STUDIO, BUT A FILM LIBRARY AND PRODUCTION FACILITIES THAT WOULD HELP HIM IN HIS TELEVISION AMBITIONS.

HE BOUGHT THE US COMPANY METROMEDIA WHICH OWNED SIX TELEVISION STATIONS. THIS WOULD FORM THE BACKBONE OF MURDOCH'S FOX BROADCASTING COMPANY.

IN 1985 MURDOCH WAS OBLIGED TO BECOME AN AMERICAN CITIZEN TO SATISFY THE LEGAL REQUIREMENTS THAT ONLY US CITIZENS WERE PERMITTED TO OWN US TELEVISION STATIONS.

APART FROM A SHORT TIME IN CALIFORNIA HE HAS LIVED IN NEW YORK EVER SINCE.

IN 1989, MURDOCH PURCHASED THE PUBLISHER COLLINS. THIS COMPANY WAS THEN COMBINED WITH HARPER AND ROW, WHICH HE HAD BOUGHT THE YEAR BEFORE. THIS MADE THE NEWLY NAMED HARPER COLLINS ONE OF THE WORLD'S LARGEST PUBLISHING COMPANIES.

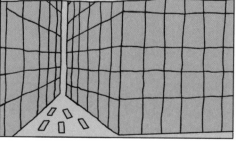

THE BIRTH OF SKY TV

IN THE 1980s, THE UK GOVERNMENT WAS KEEN TO SEE THE DEVELOPMENT OF SATELLITE TELEVISION. NO TAXPAYER MONEY WAS TO BE SPENT ON THIS. ALL THE COSTS WERE TO BE BORNE BY THE PRIVATE SECTOR.

IN 1986 THE FRANCHISE WAS AWARDED TO BRITISH SATELLITE BROADCASTING (BSB), A CONSORTIUM OF FIVE MEDIA COMPANIES THAT DID NOT INCLUDE MURDOCH.

ABOVE ALL THE GOVERNMENT WANTED A HIGH-QUALITY SERVICE. SO, UNDER THE TERMS OF ITS FRANCHISE, BSB WAS COMPELLED TO USE A NEW, UNTRIED AND VERY EXPENSIVE TRANSMISSION SYSTEM CALLED D-MAC, OPERATED FROM A YET TO BE LAUNCHED NEW SATELLITE, NAMED MARCO POLO.

ALL THIS WOULD PRODUCE A BETTER PICTURE THAN THE OLD PAL (PHASE ALTERNATING LINE) COLOUR ENCODING SYSTEM.

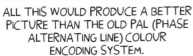

IN ORDER TO HAVE TIME TO DEVELOP THIS TECHNOLOGY AND GET ON TO A FIRM FINANCIAL FOOTING, BSB WAS TOLD IT WOULD HAVE A MONOPOLY FOR THE FIRST FEW YEARS.

IN 1988, MURDOCH ANNOUNCED PLANS FOR SKY, A TELEVISION SERVICE AIMED AT BRITISH VIEWERS AND USING THE ESTABLISHED PAL TECHNOLOGY...

BUT OPERATING ON THE ALREADY EXISTING LUXEMBOURG—BASED ASTRA SATELLITE.

HA HA HA!

IT WAS A CHEAP ROUTE INTO SATELLITE TELEVISION. THE BULK OF THE PROGRAMMING ON THE FOUR CHANNELS WAS REPEATS AND US MATERIAL.

I'VE SEEN THIS.

THE DIRECTORS OF BSB WERE APPALLED. THEY HAD BEEN BETRAYED.

WHEN THEY MET MRS THATCHER TO AIR THEIR GRIEVANCES, SHE GAVE THEM A LECTURE ON THE VIRTUES OF COMPETITION...

AND SENT THEM PACKING.

CRACK!

BY SUMMER 1990, BOTH COMPANIES WERE HAEMORRHAGING MONEY. BSB WERE THOUGHT TO BE LOSING £8 MILLION A WEEK AND SKY £2 MILLION.

A MERGER WAS INEVITABLE. SO BSKYB WAS BORN.

MRS THATCHER WAS TOLD ABOUT THE MERGER A FEW DAYS BEFORE THE OFFICIAL ANNOUNCEMENT, BUT FAILED TO INFORM HER CABINET COLLEAGUES.

THANK YOU, RUPERT.

PETER LLOYD, THE MINISTER IN CHARGE OF BROADCASTING AT THE HOME OFFICE, ONLY LEARNED OF IT WHEN HE READ HIS MORNING PAPER.

UNDER UK GOVERNMENT RULES, NEWSPAPER OWNERS WERE LIMITED TO 20 PER CENT OF DOMESTIC SATELLITE BROADCASTING.

BUT SKY, AND LATER BSKYB, WERE JUDGED NOT TO BE DOMESTIC, SO MURDOCH WAS ALLOWED TO EXCEED THAT NUMBER. THIS HELPED ENSURE THAT HE WOULD ALWAYS BE THE LARGEST SHAREHOLDER.

THANK YOU, PRIME MINISTER.

ALL THIS EXPANSION CAME AT THE PRICE OF IMMENSE DEBT. BY DECEMBER 1990, NEWS CORP NEEDED TO RESCHEDULE $7.6 BILLION OF DEBT HELD BY 146 BANKS ALL AROUND THE WORLD. WHAT SAVED MURDOCH WAS THE DIFFICULTY AND COST TO HIS CREDITORS OF LETTING HIS COMPANY COLLAPSE. THE STRUCTURE OF NEWS CORP WAS SO COMPLICATED, SPREAD THROUGH SO MANY COUNTRIES, WITH SO MANY COMPETING CLAIMS, THAT ALL PARTIES WOULD HAVE SPENT YEARS IN COURT UNTANGLING THE MESS.

MURDOCH WAS TOO BIG TO FAIL WITHOUT DAMAGING HIS CREDITORS, SO THEY HAD TO SAVE HIM. BY 10 JANUARY 1991 THE BIGGEST BANKS HAD BROKERED A DEAL.

ALL EARLIER DEBTS WERE RESCHEDULED TO BE PAID OVER A LONGER PERIOD. SOME ASSETS WERE SOLD OFF. NEWS CORP HAD TO RAISE AROUND ONE BILLION DOLLARS A YEAR TO KEEP UP WITH REPAYMENTS.

BUT ALL THIS WAS MANAGEABLE. MURDOCH HAD BET THE COMPANY AND WON.

MURDOCH HAS NOT ALWAYS BEEN THE GREAT BUSINESSMAN HE WOULD HAVE US ALL BELIEVE.

SINCE THE DEBT CRISIS OF THE EARLY 1990s THE OVERALL PERFORMANCE OF NEWS CORP HAS BEEN SOLID...

BUT THERE ARE THREE AREAS WHERE MURDOCH HAS FAILED.

IN CHINA, WHERE, DESPITE SPENDING MILLIONS, HE WAS ULTIMATELY STOPPED BY THE CHINESE GOVERNMENT.

SECOND WAS THE FAILURE TO KEEP OWNERSHIP OF THE US BROADCAST PROVIDER DIRECTV.

MURDOCH SPENT ALMOST TEN YEARS STRIVING TO BUY THIS PROVIDER.

GOTCHA!

BUT THEN LOST IT IN AN INTERNAL NEWS CORP BATTLE WITH ANOTHER SHAREHOLDER – JOHN MALONE...

WHOSE BUYING OF SHARES IN NEWS CORP THREATENED THE MURDOCH FAMILY'S CONTROL OF THE COMPANY. IN ORDER TO GET MALONE OUT OF THE PICTURE, MURDOCH WAS OBLIGED TO SELL HIM DIRECTV.

THANKS.

MURDOCH'S THIRD FAILURE WAS WITH THE INTERNET.

MYSPACE

HE BOUGHT MYSPACE, THE SOCIAL NETWORKING WEBSITE, FOR $580 MILLION IN 2005, ONLY TO SELL IT FOR A MERE $35 MILLION IN 2011.

CRASH!

WHAT WAS A HUGE SUCCESS FOR MURDOCH WAS...

LAUNCHED ON 7 OCTOBER 1996 TO 17 MILLION SUBSCRIBERS, FOX NEWS HAS GROWN TO BE THE DOMINANT CABLE NEWS NETWORK IN AMERICA. THE MAN MURDOCH CHOSE TO HEAD FOX NEWS WAS ROGER AILES.

AS A TV EXECUTIVE, AILES HAD WON EMMY AWARDS FOR HIS WORK ON THE TALK-VARIETY PROGRAMME *THE MIKE DOUGLAS SHOW*. IT WAS HERE IN 1967 THAT AILES MET RICHARD NIXON. THE FORMER VICE-PRESIDENT WAS ON A MEDIA TOUR TO REHABILITATE HIS IMAGE.

NIXON DISLIKED BEING ON TELEVISION. HIS SWEATY AND UNCOMFORTABLE DEBATE PERFORMANCE AGAINST JOHN F. KENNEDY, HAD HELPED SINK HIS CHANCES IN THE 1960 PRESIDENTIAL RACE.

THE CAMERA DOESN'T LIKE YOU.

IT'S A SHAME A MAN HAS TO USE GIMMICKS LIKE TELEVISION TO GET ELECTED.

TELEVISION IS NOT A GIMMICK, AND IF YOU THINK IT IS THEN YOU WILL LOSE AGAIN.

NIXON WAS IMPRESSED ENOUGH WITH AILES TO HIRE HIM. IN THE YEARS THAT FOLLOWED, AILES WOULD BECOME ONE OF THE MOST FEARED AND SKILLED POLITICAL OPERATIVES IN THE HISTORY OF THE REPUBLICAN PARTY. AS A CONSULTANT, AILES REPACKAGED NIXON FOR TELEVISION, PAPERED OVER RONALD REAGAN'S ENCROACHING ALZHEIMER'S IN 1984...

STOKED RACIAL FEARS TO ELECT GEORGE H.W. BUSH IN 1988, AND WAGED A SECRET CAMPAIGN ON BEHALF OF THE TOBACCO INDUSTRY TO DERAIL HEALTH-CARE REFORM IN 1993. MURDOCH AND AILES WERE THE PERFECT PARTNERSHIP FOR FOX NEWS. THEY SHARED THE SAME RIGHT-WING BELIEFS AND EXTENSIVE POLITICAL CONTACTS.

HA HA!

HEH!

BOTH THOUGHT MAINSTREAM JOURNALISM DULL AND BIASED TOWARDS THE LEFT.

I HONESTLY CANNOT DISTINGUISH ONE TV NEWS PROGRAMME FROM ANOTHER. IT'S LIKE EVERY NEWS DIRECTOR IN THE MARKETPLACE GRADUATED FROM THE SAME DUMB JOURNALISM CLASS.

WE THINK IT'S ABOUT TIME CNN WAS CHALLENGED, ESPECIALLY AS IT TENDS TO DRIFT FURTHER AND FURTHER TO THE LEFT. WE THINK IT'S TIME FOR A TRULY OBJECTIVE NEWS CHANNEL.

AILES COINED TWO SLOGANS FOR FOX NEWS...

WE REPORT, YOU DECIDE.

AND...

FAIR AND BALANCED.

FOX NEWS WAS CREATED TO BE AN ALTERNATIVE TO THE ESTABLISHED TV NEWS NETWORKS. ITS AIM WAS TO REACH AN AUDIENCE OUTSIDE THE NEW YORK-WASHINGTON MEDIA AXIS AND SPEAK TO PEOPLE WHO BELIEVED THAT TRADITIONAL AMERICAN VALUES WERE BEING ABANDONED AND THAT GOVERNMENT INTERFERED TOO MUCH IN THEIR LIVES.

AILES TOOK THE SHOCK-JOCK FORMULA OF CONSERVATIVE TALK RADIO AND PUT IT ON TV. GRAPHICS WERE DESIGNED TO BE COLOURFUL AND ATTENTION-GRABBING.

Breaking NEWS

A TICKER WAS INTRODUCED ACROSS THE BOTTOM OF THE SCREEN...

A DEVICE THAT OTHER NEWS CHANNELS SOON COPIED. AFTER THE 11 SEPTEMBER ATTACKS OF 2001, FOX NEWS ADDED THE US FLAG TO ITS LOGO.

PRESENTERS WORE US FLAGS IN THEIR LAPELS, BLENDING PATRIOTISM WITH VIEWERSHIP OF THE CHANNEL.

FOX NEWS VIEWERS ARE MORE CONSERVATIVE THAN ITS CABLE COMPETITORS.

FULLY 60 PER CENT OF THE FOX NEWS AUDIENCE DESCRIBE THEMSELVES AS CONSERVATIVE, ACCORDING TO A 2012 SURVEY BY THE PEW RESEARCH CENTRE.

BY CONTRAST ONLY 32 PER CENT OF CNN AND MSNBC VIEWERS DESCRIBE THEMSELVES AS BEING CONSERVATIVE.

THE FOX NEWS AUDIENCE IS ALSO OLDER THAN THAT OF OTHER TV NEWS NETWORKS, WITH AN AVERAGE AGE OF 68.

ADS ON FOX NEWS CATER TO THE INFIRM, THE IMMOBILE AND THE INCONTINENT, WITH APPEALS TO CLASS ACTION HIP REPLACEMENT LAW-SUITS.

THE AUDIENCE IS ALMOST ENTIRELY WHITE. ONLY 1.38 PER CENT OF VIEWERS ARE AFRICAN-AMERICAN.

FOX NEWS STATS

THE TYPICAL VIEWER OF POPULAR HOST SEAN HANNITY IS PRO-BUSINESS (86 PER CENT), WITH NO COLLEGE DEGREE (66 PER CENT), CHRISTIAN CONSERVATIVE (78 PER CENT)...

FOX NEWS STATS

IS A TEA-PARTY BACKER (75 PER CENT), SUPPORTS THE NATIONAL RIFLE ASSOCIATION (77 PER CENT), AND DOESN'T BACK GAY RIGHTS (84 PER CENT).

IT IS A NICHE AUDIENCE THAT DISPLAYS A CULT-LIKE DEVOTION TO THE NETWORK.

FOX NEWS TELLS THE TRUTH. YOU CAN'T TRUST THE LEFTIE LAMESTREAM MEDIA.

IN SURVEYS, FOX NEWS VIEWERS SHOW REPEATEDLY THAT THEY ARE THE MOST MISINFORMED OF ALL TV NEWS AUDIENCES.

I ONLY WATCH FOX NEWS.

THEY ARE SIGNIFICANTLY MORE LIKELY THAN NON-FOX NEWS VIEWERS TO BELIEVE THAT MUSLIMS WANT TO ESTABLISH SHARIA LAW IN AMERICA...

CHRISTIANITY IS UNDER ATTACK IN THIS COUNTRY.

MORE LIKELY TO THINK THAT CLIMATE CHANGE IS A HOAX...

IT'S A PLOT TO DESTROY THE US ECONOMY

AND STRONGLY DOUBT THAT BARACK OBAMA WAS BORN IN THE USA.

HE'S A SECRET MUSLIM. HE HATES AMERICA.

ROGER AILES WAS NOT INTERESTED IN PROVIDING PEOPLE WITH INFORMATION, OR EVEN A BALANCED RANGE OF SPECULATION.

THE CONFLATION OF NEWS WITH OPINION ON THE FOX NEWS NETWORK BLURS THE LINE BETWEEN NEWS AND ENTERTAINMENT.

IT HAS HELPED POLARISE US AUDIENCES, BY PUSHING THOSE WHO ARE ALREADY EXTREME EVEN FURTHER TO THE RIGHT.

THEY'RE COMING FOR OUR GUNS,

THE FOX NEWS AUDIENCE MAY BE SMALL COMPARED TO THE US POPULATION AS A WHOLE...

BUT THOSE WHO WATCH THE NETWORK ARE MORE PARTISAN AND POLITICALLY INVOLVED.

THESE ARE PEOPLE WHO ARE MORE LIKELY TO GET THEIR VOICES HEARD IN THE HALLS OF POWER.

FOX NEWS DOES MORE THAN REPORT AND ANALYSE THE NEWS. IT DIRECTLY SEEKS TO SHAPE POLITICAL OUTCOMES.

IT HAS HEIGHTENED THE CONSERVATIVE ABILITY TO MOBILISE OUTRAGE AND OPPOSE SOCIAL REFORM...

AND CONTRIBUTED TO BRINGING EXTREME VIEWS INTO THE MAINSTREAM.

I CHALLENGE ANYBODY TO SHOW ME AN EXAMPLE OF BIAS IN THE FOX NEWS CHANNEL.

USING HIS TV STATIONS AND NEWSPAPERS IS NOT THE ONLY WAY MURDOCH ACHIEVES POLITICAL INFLUENCE.

HATE

BUILDING CLOSE RELATIONSHIPS WITH POLITICIANS IS ALSO A TACTIC HE USES.

NONE OF THESE FRIENDSHIPS WAS AS ODD AS THE ONE HE FORMED WITH BRITISH PRIME MINISTER TONY BLAIR.

HEH!

WHEN BLAIR BECAME LEADER OF THE LABOUR PARTY IN 1994, HE WAS DETERMINED TO AVOID THE FATE OF ONE OF HIS PREDECESSORS, NEIL KINNOCK.

A MAN WHOSE SAVAGING BY THE MURDOCH PRESS IN THE LEAD-UP TO THE 1992 GENERAL ELECTION CONTRIBUTED TO THE PARTY'S DEFEAT.

ON ELECTION DAY *THE SUN'S* FRONT–PAGE HEADLINE READ...

BLAIR PLANNED TO MOVE THE LABOUR PARTY FROM THE LEFT INTO THE CENTRE GROUND OF POLITICS. IF HE WANTED TO WIN, AND NOT BE TREATED LIKE KINNOCK, IT WAS ESSENTIAL THAT HE DEVELOP A GOOD RELATIONSHIP WITH MURDOCH.

I HAD TO COURT MURDOCH. IT IS BETTER TO BE RIDING THE TIGER'S BACK THAN LET IT RIP YOUR THROAT OUT.

AN OPPORTUNITY EXISTED, AS MURDOCH'S ASSOCIATION WITH THE CONSERVATIVE PARTY HAD SOURED SINCE MRS THATCHER HAD LEFT OFFICE IN 1990. HER SUCCESSOR, PRIME MINISTER JOHN MAJOR, WAS FAR LESS ENAMOURED OF THE MEDIA TYCOON.

MAJOR'S BROADCASTING BILL OF 1996 ALLOWED NEWSPAPER PUBLISHERS TO EXPAND INTO NON–SATELLITE, TERRESTRIAL TELEVISION, EXCEPT FOR THOSE WHO HELD MORE THAN 20-PER-CENT MARKET SHARE. THIS WAS SQUARELY AIMED AT NEWS CORP AND WAS A RARE EXAMPLE OF A PRIME MINISTER STANDING UP TO MURDOCH. THE BILLIONAIRE WAS REPORTEDLY FURIOUS.

BLAIR LET IT BE KNOWN THAT HE WAS PREPARED TO RAISE THE 20-PER-CENT LIMIT. IN MAY 1995 HE AND HIS MEDIA ADVISOR, ALASTAIR CAMPBELL, FLEW TO AUSTRALIA TO ATTEND A NEWS CORP EDITORIAL CONFERENCE.

INTRODUCING BLAIR TO HIS SENIOR STAFF, MURDOCH SAID...

IF THE BRITISH PRESS IS TO BE BELIEVED, TODAY IS ALL PART OF A BLAIR-MURDOCH FLIRTATION.

IF THAT FLIRTATION IS EVER CONSUMMATED, TONY, I SUSPECT WE WILL END UP MAKING LOVE LIKE TWO PORCUPINES...

VERY CAREFULLY.

HA HA HA HA HA!

HA HA!

WHEN NEIL KINNOCK HEARD ABOUT THIS TRIP, HE WAS NOT PLEASED. HE RAGED AT ALASTAIR CAMPBELL...

YOU IMAGINE WHAT IT'S LIKE HAVING YOUR HEAD STUCK IN A FUCKING LIGHTBULB...

THEN YOU TELL ME HOW I'M SUPPOSED TO THINK WHEN I SEE YOU SET OFF HALFWAY AROUND THE WORLD TO GREASE HIM UP.

WHAT MURDOCH MOST WANTED FROM BLAIR WAS TO PROTECT HIS MEDIA EMPIRE AND HAVE INFLUENCE ON BRITISH FOREIGN POLICY.

HE WAS ESPECIALLY CONCERNED THAT THERE SHOULD BE NO FURTHER DEEPENING OF BRITAIN'S RELATIONSHIP WITH THE EUROPEAN UNION.

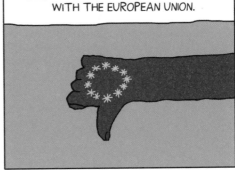

ASKED ONCE WHY HE WAS SO AGAINST THE EU, MURDOCH REPLIED...

WHEN I GO INTO DOWNING STREET THEY DO WHAT I SAY. WHEN I GO INTO BRUSSELS THEY TAKE NO NOTICE.

MURDOCH BACKED BLAIR, WHO WENT ON TO WIN THE 1997 GENERAL ELECTION.

THE SUN CLAIMED THEY HAD 'WON IT' FOR THE NEW PRIME MINISTER, BUT BLAIR HAD BEEN AHEAD IN THE POLLS LONG BEFORE THE PAPER ENDORSED HIM.

MURDOCH HAD UNIQUE ACCESS TO THE BRITISH PRIME MINISTER ALL THROUGH THE BLAIR YEARS.

LANCE PRICE, A FORMER BLAIR ADVISOR, DESCRIBED MURDOCH AS...

THE 24TH MEMBER OF THE CABINET. HIS VOICE WAS RARELY HEARD, BUT HIS PRESENCE WAS ALWAYS FELT.

RUPERT MURDOCH COULD ALMOST CLICK HIS FINGERS AND SEE TONY BLAIR WHENEVER HE WANTED.

THE RELATIONSHIP DID NOT ALWAYS GENERATE SUCCESS FOR MURDOCH. THE MONOPOLIES AND MERGERS COMMISSION STOPPED BSKYB'S BID TO BUY MANCHESTER UNITED FOOTBALL CLUB.

BAH!

BUT HE DID ACHIEVE HIS MAIN AIMS OF LOOSENING MEDIA OWNERSHIP RULES AND HALTING ANY FURTHER INTEGRATION WITH EUROPE.

HAHA!

IN 2003, MURDOCH URGED BLAIR TO SUPPORT THE US INVASION OF IRAQ. THE BRITISH PEOPLE NEEDED TO BE CONVINCED, SO *THE SUN* HELPED GALVANISE POPULAR BACKING FOR THE WAR.

THE RESULTING CONFLICT KILLED, DIRECTLY AND INDIRECTLY, HALF A MILLION PEOPLE AND FOREVER TARNISHED BLAIR'S REPUTATION.

MEANWHILE, AT FORTRESS WAPPING, THE POISONOUS ETHICS–FREE, ULTRA–COMPETITIVE CULTURE OF HEADLINES AT ALL COSTS HAD DEGENERATED EVEN FURTHER.

THE ATMOSPHERE WAS DRENCHED IN FEAR AND REPRESSION. DREAD SO POWERFUL, AT TIMES, SO TANGIBLE...

GRAHAM JOHNSON, *NEWS OF THE WORLD* JOURNALIST

THAT IT WEIGHED DOWN ON THE BODIES OF REPORTERS LIKE THE ATMOSPHERIC PRESSURE UNDER THE OCEAN, OFTEN CRUSHING THEM.

THIS PRESSURE, WHICH CAME FROM THE TOP, ENCOURAGED REPORTERS TO TAKE EXTREME MEASURES TO GET STORIES.

FOR EXAMPLE, WHEN THE SPORTS REPORTER MATT DRISCOLL WAS WORKING AT THE *NEWS OF THE WORLD*, HE RECEIVED A TIP THAT SIR ALEX FERGUSON – THEN MANAGER OF MANCHESTER UNITED – WAS HAVING HEALTH PROBLEMS.

I SEE.

BUT DRISCOLL WAS UNABLE TO CONFIRM THE STORY AS NO ONE WOULD GO ON RECORD.

I'M STUCK ON THIS ONE.

SPORTS EDITOR

LEAVE IT WITH ME. I'LL SEE WHAT I CAN COME UP WITH.

LATER...

YOU'RE RIGHT. THE STORY IS TRUE. I HAVE HIS MEDICAL RECORDS.

SPORTS EDITOR

I WAS TOLD THAT SOMETIMES YOU'D GET A SITUATION WHERE IF AN INVESTIGATOR SENT A FAX TO A GP OR A HOSPITAL, SAYING...

'I'M HIS SPECIALIST. I NEED THESE DETAILS.' IT WAS INCREDIBLE HOW MANY TIMES THEY WOULD JUST GET STRAIGHT BACK.

THEY THEN USED 'LEVERAGE', OFFERING TO KEEP FERGUSON'S HEALTH PROBLEMS A SECRET IN RETURN FOR A STEADY STREAM OF STORIES.

GREAT RESULT.

BECAUSE OF THAT HE THEN STARTED CO-OPERATING WITH THE PAPER. A FEW MONTHS LATER HE GAVE US SOME STORIES.

BY THE LATE 1990s MANY UK TABLOIDS HAD REPLACED THEIR TRADITIONAL TECHNIQUES OF GATHERING NEWS WITH FAR MORE SINISTER METHODS.

REPORTERS OUTSOURCED WORK TO PRIVATE DETECTIVES WHO COULD INSTANTLY, AND ILLEGALLY, ACCESS INFORMATION ON COMPUTER DATABASES.

THESE INVESTIGATORS HAD CONTACTS WITHIN THE POLICE AND WITH CORRUPT OFFICIALS IN VEHICLE AND TAX OFFICES.

THEY WERE SKILLED IN EXTRACTING INFORMATION FROM DOCTORS' RECEPTIONISTS AND PHONE NUMBERS FROM PHONE COMPANIES.

BY 2002, BLACKMAIL, ENTRAPMENT, BURGLARIES, THEFT OF MOBILE PHONES AND BRIBERY WERE ALL WIDESPREAD METHODS IN THE NEW INDUSTRY, THAT HAD DEVELOPED IN BRITAIN TO SERVICE TABLOID NEWSPAPERS.

ONE PARTICULAR TRICK, USED BY PRIVATE DETECTIVES AND REPORTERS ALIKE, WAS PHONE HACKING.

HERE'S HOW IT WORKED. A REPORTER PHONED A TARGETED INDIVIDUAL AND, IF THE LINE WAS ENGAGED, THE CALL WOULD GO THROUGH TO A VOICEMAIL INBOX. THESE INBOXES HAD THEIR OWN NUMBER, AND, IF THAT WAS KNOWN, IT COULD BE RUNG DIRECTLY.

ONCE THE INBOX HAD BEEN ACCESSED, THE VOICEMAIL COULD BE UNLOCKED BY USING A PERSONAL IDENTIFICATION NUMBER (PIN).

THIS IS WHERE A MAJORITY OF PEOPLE PROVED CARELESS, LEAVING THE MANUFACTURER'S DEFAULT CODE IN PLACE, INSTEAD OF CHANGING IT TO A NEW ONE KNOWN ONLY TO THEM.

BUT EVEN IF THE PIN NUMBER HAD BEEN CHANGED, INVESTIGATORS COULD GET THE CODE FROM CROOKED PHONE COMPANY EMPLOYEES.

GET ME PIN NUMBERS.

OK!

LISTENING IN ON PEOPLE'S PRIVATE PHONE MESSAGES COULD REAP POLITICAL SECRETS, EXTRAMARITAL AFFAIRS AND MUCH ELSE.

WE'VE GOT A GOOD ONE HERE.

TARGETS INCLUDED ROYALTY, HOLLYWOOD ACTORS, FOOTBALLERS, POLITICIANS, AND ORDINARY PEOPLE WHO WERE UNFORTUNATE ENOUGH TO BE PART OF NEWS EVENTS.

NEWS OF THE WORLD

BECKHAM SECRET AFFAIR

BETWEEN 1999 AND 2011 THE LONDON METROPOLITAN POLICE (THE MET) CONDUCTED SEVERAL INVESTIGATIONS INTO THE TRADE IN CONFIDENTIAL INFORMATION.

YOU'RE NICKED.

BY 2006, SEVEN MEN HAD BEEN FOUND GUILTY (INCLUDING PRIVATE INVESTIGATOR GLENN MULCAIRE AND *NEWS OF THE WORLD* ROYAL REPORTER CLIVE GOODMAN) BUT NO FURTHER ARRESTS WERE MADE UNTIL 2011.

THE SCOPE OF THESE INVESTIGATIONS APPEARED DELIBERATELY LIMITED. THE MET WERE CRITICISED FOR NOT PURSUING ALL LEADS, FOR NOT INFORMING ALL INDIVIDUALS WHO WERE VICTIMS OF PHONE HACKING...

AND FOR ALLEGEDLY MISLEADING THE PUBLIC AND PARLIAMENT ABOUT THE EXTENT OF THE PROBLEM.

IN 2003, WHILE GIVING EVIDENCE AT AN INQUIRY BY THE HOUSE OF COMMONS CULTURE, MEDIA AND SPORT COMMITTEE...

REBEKAH BROOKS (*NEWS OF THE WORLD* EDITOR AND LATER EDITOR OF *THE SUN* AND CHIEF EXECUTIVE OF NEWS INTERNATIONAL) MADE A REVEALING COMMENT...

WE HAVE PAID THE POLICE FOR INFORMATION IN THE PAST.

HOW CLOSE WERE NEWS INTERNATIONAL EXECUTIVES TO HIGH-RANKING OFFICERS IN THE MET? HERE ARE TWO EXAMPLES. PAUL STEPHENSON, THE METROPOLITAN COMMISSIONER DURING THIS PERIOD, WAS KNOWN TO HAVE DINED WITH NEWS INTERNATIONAL EXECUTIVES 18 TIMES, INCLUDING EIGHT TIMES WITH NEAL WALLIS (DEPUTY EDITOR OF *THE SUN*, ARRESTED IN CONNECTION WITH THE PHONE-HACKING SCANDAL). STEPHENSON RESIGNED IN 2011 AFTER ACCEPTING AN £11,000 FREE STAY AT CHAMPNEYS HEALTH SPA – WHOSE PUBLIC RELATION'S ADVISOR WAS NEIL WALLIS.

ANDY HAYMAN WAS ASSISTANT COMMISSIONER FOR SPECIALIST OPERATIONS BETWEEN 2005 AND 2007, DURING WHICH HE LED THE INQUIRY INTO THE PHONE HACKING OF THE ROYAL HOUSEHOLD. HE ATTENDED FOUR DINNERS WITH *NEWS OF THE WORLD* EDITORS, INCLUDING ONE WHILE HIS OFFICERS WERE GATHERING EVIDENCE ON THE CASE. HAYMAN RESIGNED HIS JOB IN LATE 2007 OVER THIS AND OTHER SCANDALS. HE WAS SOON HIRED TO WRITE A LUCRATIVE COLUMN FOR *THE TIMES* – OWNED, OF COURSE, BY RUPERT MURDOCH.

BY 2011 IT LOOKED AS IF THE PHONE-HACKING SCANDAL HAD BLOWN OVER. AT THE NEWS CORP ANNUAL MEETING IN NEW YORK IN OCTOBER, RUPERT MURDOCH TOLD INVESTORS...

WE HAVE VERY STRICT RULES. THERE WAS AN INCIDENT MORE THAN FIVE YEARS AGO. THE PERSON WHO BOUGHT A BUGGED PHONE CONVERSATION WAS IMMEDIATELY FIRED, AND IN FACT WENT TO JAIL.

THERE HAVE BEEN TWO PARLIAMENTARY INQUIRIES WHICH HAVE FOUND NO FURTHER EVIDENCE OF ANYTHING AT ALL. IF ANYTHING WAS TO COME TO LIGHT, WE CHALLENGE PEOPLE TO GIVE US EVIDENCE, AND NO ONE HAS BEEN ABLE TO.

BACK IN THE UK, NEWS CORP HAD LAUNCHED ITS LONG-AWAITED BID TO TAKE FULL CONTROL OF SKY TV. MURDOCH ALREADY OWNED 39 PER CENT OF SKY AND WANTED 100 PER CENT. THE SCANDAL WAS NOW BEHIND THEM. WHAT COULD POSSIBLY GO WRONG?

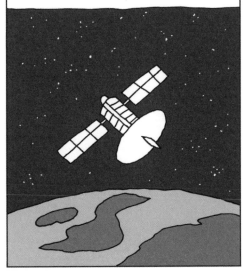

AFTER THE ELECTION OF 2010, MURDOCH HAD FORMED A CLOSE ASSOCIATION WITH THE CONSERVATIVE-LED COALITION GOVERNMENT. THE NEW PRIME MINISTER, DAVID CAMERON, MADE ANDY COULSON, AN EX-*NEWS OF THE WORLD* EDITOR, THE GOVERNMENT'S DIRECTOR OF COMMUNICATION ON A SALARY OF £140,000. THIS WAS MORE THAN ANY OF CAMERON'S OTHER OFFICIALS, INCLUDING HIS CHIEF OF STAFF.

ONE OF CAMERON'S FIRST VISITORS WAS RUPERT MURDOCH, WHO ENTERED DOWNING STREET BY THE BACK DOOR, AT CAMERON'S REQUEST.

OVER THE FIRST THREE MONTHS OF THE NEW GOVERNMENT, REBEKAH BROOKS (BY THEN PROMOTED TO CHIEF EXECUTIVE OF NEWS INTERNATIONAL) STAYED THREE TIMES AT THE PRIME MINISTER'S COUNTRY RESIDENCE OF CHEQUERS. RUPERT MURDOCH'S SON, JAMES (BROOKS' IMMEDIATE BOSS) WAS ALSO A GUEST.

BROOKS, CAMERON AND ELISABETH MURDOCH (RUPERT MURDOCH'S DAUGHTER) WERE ALL MEMBERS OF WHAT BECAME KNOWN AS THE 'CHIPPING NORTON SET' – A GROUP OF MEDIA, POLITICIANS AND SHOW BUSINESS ACQUAINTANCES WHO LIVED AND SOCIALISED TOGETHER AROUND THE MARKET TOWN OF CHIPPING NORTON IN OXFORDSHIRE, ENGLAND.

SO, WITH A PASSIVE GOVERNMENT BACKING HIM, MURDOCH MUST HAVE BEEN SURE HE WOULD GET THE REGULATORY APPROVAL NEEDED FOR THE DEAL TO GO THROUGH.

BUT, AT THE 11TH HOUR, NEW REVELATIONS IN THE PHONE-HACKING SCANDAL SANK THE TAKEOVER.

BACK IN MARCH 2002, AMANDA JANE 'MILLY' DOWLER, A 13-YEAR-OLD SURREY SCHOOLGIRL, HAD GONE MISSING.

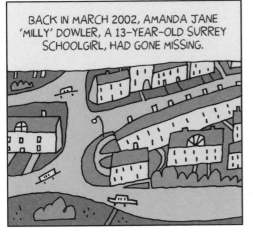

MONTHS LATER HER BODY WAS DISCOVERED IN A WOOD IN HAMPSHIRE.

ON 4 JULY 2011, *THE GUARDIAN* REPORTED THAT MILLY DOWLER'S VOICEMAIL HAD BEEN ACCESSED BY *NEWS OF THE WORLD* JOURNALISTS SHORTLY AFTER HER DISAPPEARANCE.

POLICE LINE DO NOT CROSS

IT WAS FURTHER REPORTED THAT SURREY POLICE AND OTHER POLICE FORCES KNEW THAT DOWLER'S MOBILE PHONE HAD BEEN HACKED, BUT DID NOTHING ABOUT IT. INSTEAD A SENIOR SURREY OFFICER INVITED *NEWS OF THE WORLD* STAFF TO A MEETING TO DISCUSS THE CASE.

POLICE

THERE HAD BEEN LITTLE PUBLIC SYMPATHY FOR THE RICH CELEBRITY VICTIMS OF PHONE HACKING, BUT THE TARGETING OF A MURDERED SCHOOLGIRL CAUSED AN OUTCRY. MARK LEWIS, THE SOLICITOR REPRESENTING THE DOWLER FAMILY, HAD THIS TO SAY...

THE PARENTS WERE GETTING THROUGH THE MOST AWFUL EXPERIENCE FOR ANY PARENT. IT'S UNIMAGINABLE, AND YET PEOPLE IN THE *NEWS OF THE WORLD* HAD NO COMPUNCTION, NO FEAR OF ANYTHING: NO SENSE OF MORAL RIGHT.

THE GOVERNMENT WAS RELUCTANTLY FORCED TO ACT. ON 6 JULY DAVID CAMERON ANNOUNCED TO PARLIAMENT THAT THERE WOULD BE A PUBLIC INQUIRY INTO THE AFFAIR.

CAMERON NAMED LORD JUSTICE LEVESON AS CHAIRMAN OF THE INQUIRY WITH A REMIT TO LOOK INTO PHONE HACKING, THE INITIAL POLICE INVESTIGATION, AND ALLEGATIONS OF ILLICIT PAYMENTS TO POLICE BY THE PRESS.

ON 7 JULY JAMES MURDOCH ANNOUNCED THAT THE 10 JULY EDITION OF THE *NEWS OF THE WORLD* WOULD BE THE 168-YEAR-OLD PAPER'S LAST EDITION.

NEWS OF THE WORLD

THANK YOU & GOODBYE

ON 13 JULY NEWS CORPORATION WITHDREW ITS BID TO TAKE OVER SKY. ON 15 JULY, REBEKAH BROOKS, EDITOR OF THE *NEWS OF THE WORLD* WHEN MILLY DOWLER'S PHONE WAS HACKED, RESIGNED AS CHIEF EXECUTIVE OF NEWS INTERNATIONAL.

BROOKS LEFT WITH A REPORTED PAY-OFF OF £7 MILLION, A FREE OFFICE AND A CAR.

ON 17 JULY SHE WAS ARRESTED ON SUSPICION OF PHONE HACKING AND CORRUPTION.

YOU'RE NICKED.

THIS WAS THE SAME DAY THAT PAUL STEPHENSON, COMMISSIONER OF THE METROPOLITAN POLICE, RESIGNED.

THE NEXT DAY ASSISTANT COMMISSIONER JOHN YATES ALSO RESIGNED.

NO COMMENT.

YATES HAD COME UNDER FIRE FOR NOT REOPENING THE PHONE-HACKING INVESTIGATION BACK IN 2009, DESPITE NEW EVIDENCE COMING TO LIGHT.

ON 19 JULY RUPERT MURDOCH AND HIS SON JAMES WERE CALLED BEFORE THE HOUSE OF COMMONS' CULTURE, MEDIA AND SPORT COMMITTEE.

MURDOCH AND SON WERE GRILLED BY MEMBERS OF THE COMMITTEE FOR TWO HOURS. THE ELDER MURDOCH HAD HIS EXCUSES READY.

THE *NEWS OF THE WORLD* IS LESS THAN ONE PER CENT OF OUR COMPANY.

I EMPLOY 53,000 PEOPLE AROUND THE WORLD. I WORK A 10– OR 12-HOUR DAY AND I CANNOT TELL YOU THE MULTITUDE OF ISSUES I HAVE TO HANDLE EVERY DAY. THE *NEWS OF THE WORLD*, PERHAPS I LOST SIGHT OF. MAYBE BECAUSE IT WAS SO SMALL IN THE GENERAL FRAME OF OUR COMPANY.

MURDOCH'S BIOGRAPHER, MICHAEL WOLFF, HAS SINCE MADE THE CLAIM THAT MURDOCH MISLED THE MEMBERS OF PARLIAMENT. IT WAS HIS OBSERVATION THAT THE MEDIA TYCOON WOULD SPEND UP TO HALF A DAY SPEAKING TO THE EDITORS OF HIS NEWSPAPERS IN LONDON.

HIS INVOLVEMENT WITH THE PAPER IS TOTAL. RUPERT SAT UP THERE AND THEY (HIS ADVISORS) SAID, 'YOU HAVE TO SAY YOU ARE NOT INVOLVED WITH THE NEWSPAPERS,' AND THAT'S WHAT HE SAID AND THAT'S A LIE.

NO ONE NAMED MURDOCH HAS EVER BEEN HELD ACCOUNTABLE FOR THE CRIMINALITY THAT TOOK PLACE AT FORTRESS WAPPING.

ALTOGETHER 38 NEWS INTERNATIONAL STAFF WERE ARRESTED, INCLUDING REPORTER NEVILLE THURLBECK AND NEWS EDITOR GREG MISKIW, WHO RECEIVED SHORT PRISON SENTENCES.

ANDY COULSON, THE EX-*NEWS OF THE WORLD* EDITOR AND PRIME MINISTER DAVID CAMERON'S DIRECTOR OF COMMUNICATION, WAS SENTENCED TO 15 MONTHS' IMPRISONMENT.

BUT NO SENIOR EXECUTIVE AT NEWS INTERNATIONAL WAS CONVICTED OF ANY CRIME, AND THAT INCLUDES REBEKAH BROOKS, WHO WAS FOUND NOT GUILTY OF ALL CHARGES AT HER TRIAL.

IN MARCH 2012 JAMES MURDOCH WAS OBLIGED TO RESIGN AS EXECUTIVE CHAIR OF NEWS INTERNATIONAL AND CHAIR OF BSKYB.

CONTINUAL RUMOURS THAT HE WAS FULLY AWARE OF ALL THAT WAS HAPPENING AT THE *NEWS OF THE WORLD* HAD DAMAGED HIS POSITION.

THE LEVESON INQUIRY INTO THE PHONE-HACKING SCANDAL HELD A SERIES OF PUBLIC HEARINGS THROUGHOUT 2011 AND 2012.

THE INQUIRY PUBLISHED ITS REPORT IN NOVEMBER 2012. IT REVIEWED THE GENERAL CULTURE AND ETHICS OF BRITISH MEDIA.

IT'S HERE, PRIME MINISTER.

IT MADE RECOMMENDATIONS FOR A NEW BODY TO REPLACE THE EXISTING PRESS COMPLAINTS COMMISSION.

HMM!

PRIME MINISTER DAVID CAMERON SAID THAT HE WELCOMED MANY OF THE FINDINGS, BUT DECLINED TO ENACT THE REQUIRED LEGISLATION.

PART TWO OF THE INQUIRY WAS TO BE DELAYED UNTIL AFTER THE CRIMINAL PROSECUTIONS WERE OVER.

BUT THE CONSERVATIVE PARTY'S 2017 MANIFESTO STATED THAT THE SECOND PART OF THE INQUIRY WOULD BE DROPPED ALTOGETHER.

THE COST TO THE BRITISH TAXPAYER FOR THE LEVESON INQUIRY WAS £5.4 MILLION.

JAMES MURDOCH'S FALL DIDN'T LAST LONG. IN 2015 HE WAS MADE CHIEF EXECUTIVE OF 20TH CENTURY FOX...

AND IN 2016 HE WAS REAPPOINTED AS CHAIRMAN OF BSKYB.

IN 2015 REBEKAH BROOKS GOT HER OLD JOB BACK AS CHIEF EXECUTIVE OF NEWS INTERNATIONAL (NOW RENAMED NEWS UK).

WELCOME BACK.

ALTHOUGH NO SENIOR PEOPLE IN THE NEWS CORPORATION GROUP WERE IMPRISONED DUE TO THE PHONE-HACKING SCANDAL...

INTEG-RITY

NEWS OF THE WORLD 1843 TO 2011

TRUTH

THE PRICE PAID BY THE COMPANY AS A WHOLE WAS A HIGH ONE. FIRSTLY, THE CLOSURE OF A BEST-SELLING NEWSPAPER WITH THE LOSS OF 150 JOURNALISTS...

NEWS CORPORATION

SECONDLY, FAILURE TO TAKE OVER BRITAIN'S LARGEST TELEVISION NETWORK. THEN THE PAYMENT OF OVER £200 MILLION IN COMPENSATION TO PHONE-HACKING VICTIMS...

AND SOME OF THE WORST PUBLICITY IMAGINABLE FOR A MAJOR COMPANY. FINALLY, NEWS CORP HAD LOST MOST OF ITS INFLUENCE ON BRITISH POLITICS WHEN THE NAME MURDOCH BECAME TOXIC TO THE UK ESTABLISHMENT.

ON 28 JUNE 2013, NEWS CORP ANNOUNCED THAT IT WOULD SPLIT ITSELF INTO TWO COMPANIES. ONE COMPANY, NAMED 20TH CENTURY FOX, WOULD CONTAIN THE MORE PROFITABLE ENTERTAINMENT DIVISION, WHICH INCLUDED THE MOVIE STUDIO, SKY, FOX, AND OTHER TV NETWORKS. WHILE THE SLUGGISH PUBLISHING ARM, RETAINING THE NAME NEWS CORPORATION, WOULD INCLUDE HARPERCOLLINS, NEWS INTERNATIONAL, AND THE AMERICAN AND AUSTRALIAN PAPERS.

THERE WERE TWO REASONS FOR THE SPLIT. THE LAGGING REVENUES OF THE PRINT PROPERTIES WERE DRAGGING DOWN THE OVERALL PROFITABILITY OF NEWS CORP, AND THE FILM AND TV BRANDS NEEDED TO BE INSULATED AGAINST THE PHONE-HACKING SCANDAL.

MEANWHILE BACK AT FOX NEWS

IN 2016 ANOTHER SCANDAL ROCKED THE MURDOCH EMPIRE.

NOW WHAT?

ROGER AILES, THE CHAIR OF FOX NEWS, WAS FORCED TO RESIGN AFTER MULTIPLE ACCUSATIONS OF SEXUAL HARASSMENT WERE MADE AGAINST HIM.

MORE THAN 20 WOMEN ACCUSED AILES, INCLUDING FOX NEWS ANCHORS GRETCHEN CARLSON AND MEGAN KELLY.

ME TOO.

AILES HAD BEEN THE KING OF FOX NEWS FOR TWO DECADES, BUILDING THE NETWORK UP INTO THE MOST INFLUENTIAL MEDIA FORCE IN AMERICA.

HIS DOWNFALL WAS ABRUPT, BUT LUCRATIVE. HE RECEIVED AN EXIT PAYMENT OF $40 MILLION.

THEN A SECOND SCANDAL BROKE AT FOX NEWS WHEN TOP-RATED HOST BILL O'REILLY WAS ALSO ACCUSED OF SEXUAL HARASSMENT.

OH REALLY?

FOR DECADES O'REILLY HAD BEEN A POPULIST CONSERVATIVE VOICE, FIGHTING POLITICAL CORRECTNESS, WHILE INFUSING HIS SHOW WITH PATRIOTISM AND SCORN FOR FEMINISTS.

BUT IT WAS REVEALED IN 2016 THAT THERE HAD BEEN MULTIPLE ACCUSATIONS OF SEXUAL HARASSMENT AGAINST O'REILLY, LEADING TO AT LEAST EIGHT FINANCIAL SETTLEMENTS.

THE LAST SETTLEMENT, PAID BY O'REILLY PERSONALLY RATHER THAN BY FOX, ENDED IN A $32 MILLION AGREEMENT WITH LIS WIEHL, A LEGAL ANALYST AND PERIODIC GUEST ON O'REILLY'S SHOW. THIS WAS AN EXTRAORDINARY AMOUNT FOR SUCH A SETTLEMENT. THE NEW YORK TIMES REPORTED THAT THE LAWSUIT ALLEGED NON-CONSENSUAL SEX AND THE SENDING OF GAY PORNOGRAPHY AND OTHER EXPLICIT MATERIAL TO WIEHL. LIKE AILES BEFORE HIM, O'REILLY WAS FORCED TO RESIGN AND RECEIVED A $40 MILLION EXIT PAYMENT.

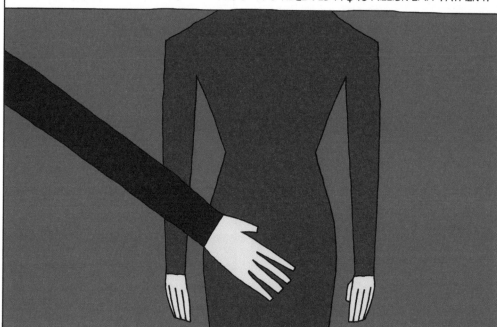

ANOTHER CASUALTY OF THE SEXUAL HARASSMENT SCANDAL WAS FOX'S CO-PRESIDENT BILL SHINE, WHO WAS IN CHARGE OF THE NETWORK'S NEWS AND PROGRAMMING OPERATIONS. HE WAS FORCED OUT OF FOX IN MAY 2017 AFTER HE WAS NAMED IN MULTIPLE LAWSUITS AND COMPLAINTS, ALLEGING THAT HE HAD IGNORED OR SOUGHT TO SUPPRESS ALLEGATIONS AGAINST AILES AND O'REILLY. BY 2018 HE HAD JOINED THE TRUMP WHITE HOUSE AS DIRECTOR OF COMMUNICATIONS AND DEPUTY CHIEF OF STAFF.

IN AN INTERVIEW ON SKY NEWS, RUPERT MURDOCH SPOKE DISMISSIVELY ABOUT THE ALLEGATIONS.

IT'S ALL NONSENSE... THAT WAS POLITICAL BECAUSE WE ARE CONSERVATIVE.

HE SEEMED TO FORGET THAT THE MAJORITY OF COMPLAINANTS WERE FEMALE FOX NEWS EMPLOYEES WHO WERE CONSERVATIVE THEMSELVES.

AFTER ROGER AILES LEFT FOX NEWS HE BECAME AN ADVISOR TO THE DONALD TRUMP 2016 PRESIDENTIAL CAMPAIGN, ASSISTING WITH DEBATE PREPARATION. AILES DIED IN MAY 2017, AGED 77, FROM COMPLICATIONS FROM A FALL AT HIS HOME IN PALM BEACH, FLORIDA, BUT HE LIVED TO SEE TRUMP ELECTED PRESIDENT.

FOR DECADES AILES, WITH MURDOCH'S BACKING, HAD SOLD AN IMAGE OF A DISINTEGRATING AMERICA TO AN ELDERLY WHITE CONSERVATIVE AUDIENCE, FEEDING THEM STORIES OF RAMPANT CRIME, TERRORISM, OUT-OF-CONTROL IMMIGRATION AND AN IMMINENT LEFT-WING DICTATORSHIP.

TRUMP, WITH HIS RACIALLY INFLAMMATORY STATEMENTS, CRASS SEXISM AND ANTI-POLITICALLY CORRECT VIEWS, WAS THE PERFECT PRESIDENTIAL CANDIDATE FOR THE NETWORK AND ITS VIEWERS. THEY EMBRACED HIM WHOLEHEARTEDLY AND THE LOVE AFFAIR WAS MUTUAL.

ONCE IN OFFICE, TRUMP SOON SETTLED INTO A ROUTINE OF WATCHING SEVERAL HOURS OF CABLE NEWS TV A DAY. MANY OBSERVERS NOTED HOW CLOSELY HIS TWEETS MATCHED THE SUBJECTS COVERED BY FOX NEWS, ESPECIALLY THE MORNNG SHOW 'FOX AND FRIENDS', ON WHICH, PRIOR TO HIS POLITICAL LIFE TRUMP HAD BEEN A REGULAR GUEST.

THIS MADE THE SHOW HUGELY INFLUENTIAL ON THE NEWS CYCLE. OTHER NEWS MEDIA WOULD HAVE TO SCRAMBLE TO COVER TRUMP'S TWEETS AFTER 'FOX AND FRIENDS' HAD SET THE NEWS AGENDA FOR THE DAY. BUT WHAT IS MORE DISTURBING IS THAT A MAN WITH ACCESS TO THE WORLD'S MOST POWERFUL INFORMATION-GATHERING MACHINE, WITH AN INTELLIGENCE BUDGET ESTIMATED AT $37 BILLION, PREFERRED TO RELY ON CONSERVATIVE NEWS HOSTS TO UNDERSTAND EVENTS.

ALTHOUGH FOR DECADES RUPERT MURDOCH HAD ESTABLISHED CLOSE CONNECTIONS WITH UK AND AUSTRALIAN LEADERS, HE HAD LARGELY FAILED TO CULTIVATE TIES WITH ANY AMERICAN PRESIDENT, BUT THIS CHANGED WHEN TRUMP ENTERED THE WHITE HOUSE. MURDOCH HAD ORIGINALLY BACKED JEB BUSH IN THE REPUBLICAN PRIMARIES, BUT PRAGMATICALLY SWITCHED ALLEGIANCE WHEN TRUMP BECAME FRONT RUNNER.

MURDOCH WOULD HAVE HAD TO SMOOTH OVER OLD COMMENTS HE'D MADE ABOUT TRUMP, SUCH AS CALLING THE REAL-ESTATE DEVELOPER A 'PHONEY' AND ACCUSING HIM OF EXAGGERATING HIS WEALTH. IN THE END DIFFERENCES BETWEEN THE TWO MEN WERE SWEPT ASIDE. TRUMP NEEDED FOX NEWS TO REACH OUT TO HIS BASE. WHILE MURDOCH NEEDED TRUMP TO PROTECT AND EXPAND HIS BUSINESS INTERESTS.

AFTER INAUGURATION DAY, MURDOCH BEGAN REGULAR WEEKLY CALLS TO THE PRESIDENT. THE MEDIA TYCOON OFFERED TRUMP ADVICE THAT PERHAPS OTHERS WOULD HAVE BEEN RELUCTANT TO GIVE, SUCH AS URGING TRUMP TO STOP TWEETING, ENCOURAGING HIM TO IMPROVE HIS RELATIONSHIP WITH SECRETARY OF STATE REX TILLERSON, AND SUGGESTING HE FIRE CHIEF STRATEGIST STEVE BANNON (WHICH TRUMP EVENTUALLY DID). MURDOCH ALSO HAD WEEKLY CONVERSATIONS WITH TRUMP'S SON-IN-LAW AND SENIOR ADVISOR, JARED KUSHNER.

TRUMP ALSO DEVELOPED A CLOSE RELATIONSHIP WITH FOX NEWS PRESENTER, SEAN HANNITY, THE HOST OF THE MOST WIDELY WATCHED PROGRAMME ON CABLE NEWS IN 2018 (FOR THE SECOND YEAR RUNNING), DRAWING IN 32 MILLION VIEWERS. HANNITY CLAIMED THAT HE SPOKE TO PRESIDENT TRUMP MOST NIGHTS AFTER HIS SHOW.

HE WOULD RING THE GENERAL NUMBER, WHERE THE OPERATOR SAW HE WAS ON A LIST OF CLEARED CALLERS, AND THEY'D PUT HIM THROUGH ON A LINE THAT WENT DIRECTLY TO TRUMP. THE TWO REPORTEDLY TRADED MEDIA GOSSIP AND DISCUSSED ROBERT MUELLER'S SPECIAL COUNSEL INVESTIGATION INTO THE RUSSIAN GOVERNMENT'S EFFORTS TO INTERFERE IN THE 2016 PRESIDENTIAL ELECTION.

JANE MEYER, AUTHOR OF A *NEW YORKER* ARTICLE ON THE FEEDBACK LOOP BETWEEN FOX NEWS AND THE OVAL OFFICE, BELIEVES THAT THE NETWORK HAS AS MUCH INFLUENCE ON THE PRESIDENT'S DECISIONS AS HIS CLOSE ADVISORS.

AS THE PRESIDENT HAS BEEN BESET BY SCANDALS, CONGRESSIONAL HEARINGS AND EVEN TALK OF IMPEACHMENT, FOX HAS BEEN HIS SHIELD AND HIS SWORD. THE WHITE HOUSE AND FOX ACT SO SEAMLESSLY THAT IT CAN BE HARD TO DETERMINE DURING A NEWS CYCLE WHICH ONE IS FOLLOWING THE OTHER'S LEAD.

ALL THIS WAS HAPPENING OVER A PERIOD WHEN MURDOCH WAS ATTEMPTING TO COMPLETE ONE OF HIS BIGGEST DEALS EVER. IN DECEMBER 2017 IT WAS ANNOUNCED THAT NEWS CORP WAS SELLING 20TH CENTURY FOX TO DISNEY. THE DEAL DID NOT JUST INCLUDE THE MOVIE AND TV STUDIO, BUT CABLE NETWORKS, INCLUDING FX, STAR INDIA, AND STAKES IN NATIONAL GEOGRAPHIC, HULU AND SKY TV, IN EXCHANGE FOR $52 BILLION IN DISNEY STOCK. THIS DEAL MADE RUPERT MURDOCH THE LARGEST DISNEY SHAREHOLDER.

THE ACQUISITION WAS COMPLETED ON 20 MARCH 2019. RUPERT MURDOCH RETAINED OWNERSHIP OF FOX NEWS, THE DIVISION'S BIGGEST PROFIT DRIVER, AS WELL AS FOX SPORTS, FOX BUSINESS AND ITS BROADCAST TV NETWORK OF 28 LOCAL STATIONS IN THE US. ALL THIS WAS RECOMBINED WITH NEWS CORPORATION ASSETS, INCLUDING *THE SUN*, *THE TIMES*, *THE WALL STREET JOURNAL*, DOW JONES AND TALKSPORT.

THEN IN HIS EIGHTIES, RUPERT MURDOCH PERHAPS CONSIDERED THE DISNEY DEAL AS PART OF HIS MASTER PLAN OF SUCCESSION, WHICH WOULD KEEP NEWS INTERNATIONAL IN MURDOCH FAMILY CONTROL ONCE HE WAS NO LONGER IN CHARGE.

IN 2015 HE'D NAMED HIS ELDER SON, LACHLAN, EXECUTIVE CO-CHAIR, GIVING FATHER AND SON EQUAL STANDING.

OVER A SPAN OF 60 YEARS MURDOCH HAD TAKEN TWO NEWSPAPERS IN SOUTH AUSTRALIA AND BUILT HIS COMPANY INTO A GLOBAL MEDIA EMPIRE. AN ENORMOUS ACHIEVEMENT, BUT ONE CREATED WITH A RUTHLESSNESS THAT HAD LITTLE ROOM FOR EMPATHY OR COMPASSION.

IT'S WORTH CONTRASTING RUPERT'S LIFE WITH THAT OF HIS PHILANTHROPIC MOTHER, DAME ELISABETH MURDOCH, WHO DIED IN DECEMBER 2012, AGED 103. SHE WAS RENOWNED FOR HER CHARITABLE WORKS AND HELPED CREATE THE ROYAL CHILDREN'S HOSPITAL IN AUSTRALIA AND THE MURDOCH CHILDREN'S INSTITUTE. SHE WAS CHAIR OF THE COMMITTEE WHICH ESTABLISHED THE VICTORIAN TAPESTRY WORKSHOP; TRUSTEE OF THE REGIONAL MCLELLAND GALLERY AND A BENEFACTOR OF ORGANISATIONS RANGING FROM THE AUSTRALIAN BALLET AND OPERA AUSTRALIA TO THE BELL THEATRE COMPANY.

THE MORAL CONTRAST COULDN'T BE MORE STARK.

FOR MORE THAN HALF A CENTURY, MURDOCH HAD RUTHLESSLY BULLDOZED OVER COMPETITORS, CAST FRIENDS AND BUSINESS ALLIES ASIDE WHEN THEY WERE NO LONGER OF USE, INTERFERED THROUGH BULLYING AND INTIMIDATION IN AUSTRALIAN, UK AND US POLITICS, AND ALLOWED HIS NEWSPAPERS TO BREAK NUMEROUS LAWS AND DESTROY LIVES.

FOR BETTER OR WORSE, (NEWS CORP) IS A REFLECTION OF MY THINKING, MY CHARACTER, MY VALUES.

THE LAST WORD SHOULD BE LEFT TO RUPERT MURDOCH'S MOTHER, DAME ELISABETH.

I DO SOMETIMES FEEL UNCOMFORTABLE WHEN PEOPLE SAY, 'OH YOU KNOW, RUPERT'S SO WONDERFUL. YOU MUST BE SO PROUD. HE'S A GREAT MAN.' A LOT OF THOSE PEOPLE THINK IT'S BECAUSE HE'S MADE MONEY. THAT'S NOT GREATNESS. THE POINT IS WHAT YOU DO WITH IT.

END

WHO ARE THE KOCH BROTHERS?

CHARLES AND DAVID KOCH OWN VIRTUALLY ALL OF WHAT HAS BECOME, UNDER THEIR LEADERSHIP, THE SECOND-LARGEST PRIVATE COMPANY IN AMERICA. KOCH INDUSTRIES IS NOT REALLY A SINGLE COMPANY, BUT A CONGLOMERATE OF COMPANIES THEY OWN AND OPERATE. THESE COMPANIES INCLUDE...

KOCH PIPELINE COMPANY. THIS COMPANY OWNS PIPELINES THROUGHOUT TEXAS, MINNESOTA, MISSOURI, IOWA, WISCONSIN AND ILLINOIS, THROUGH WHICH THEY TRANSPORT OIL, REFINED PETROLEUM AND NATURAL GAS.

FLINT HILLS RESOURCES IS A FUEL-PRODUCING COMPANY. IT OFFERS PETROLEUM PRODUCTS, GASOLINE, DIESEL FUELS, JET FUELS AND OTHER OIL PRODUCTS.

KOCH AG AND ENERGY SOLUTIONS OPERATE THREE KOCH INDUSTRY COMPANIES THAT MANUFACTURE AND MARKET A WIDE VARIETY OF FERTILISER PRODUCTS USED IN THE AGRICULTURE INDUSTRY.

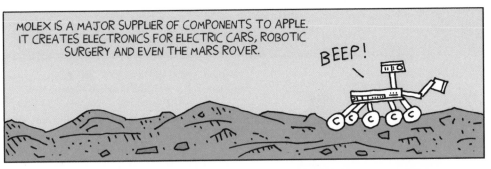

MOLEX IS A MAJOR SUPPLIER OF COMPONENTS TO APPLE. IT CREATES ELECTRONICS FOR ELECTRIC CARS, ROBOTIC SURGERY AND EVEN THE MARS ROVER.

BEEP!

GUARDIAN INDUSTRIES IS A GLASS MANUFACTURER, MAKING FIBREGLASS INSULATION, AND GLASS FOR CARS AND BUILDINGS.

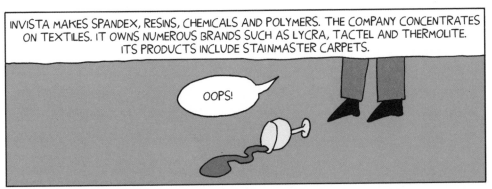

INVISTA MAKES SPANDEX, RESINS, CHEMICALS AND POLYMERS. THE COMPANY CONCENTRATES ON TEXTILES. IT OWNS NUMEROUS BRANDS SUCH AS LYCRA, TACTEL AND THERMOLITE. ITS PRODUCTS INCLUDE STAINMASTER CARPETS.

OOPS!

THE KOCHS OWN GEORGIA-PACIFIC, A PAPER COMPANY THAT INCLUDES THE BRANDS QUILTED NORTHERN TISSUE, BRAWNEY PAPER TOWELS AND DIXIE CUPS. KOCH INDUSTRIES IS ALSO INVOLVED IN RANCHING (MATADOR CATTLE COMPANY), FINANCE, COMMODITIES TRADING, MINERALS, PUBLISHING AND MANY OTHER VENTURES AND INVESTMENTS. THE CONGLOMERATE EXISTS ON SUCH A VAST SCALE THAT IT IS HARD TO GRASP ITS FULL SIZE.

I'M CHARLES.

I'M DAVID.

ORIGIN OF THE KOCH FORTUNE

CHARLES AND DAVID KOCH'S FATHER, FRED C. KOCH, WAS BORN IN QUANAH, TEXAS IN 1900.

A CHEMICAL ENGINEER, FRED KOCH DEVELOPED A MORE EFFICIENT THERMAL CRACKING PROCESS FOR TURNING CRUDE OIL INTO PETROL.

BUT LARGE OIL COMPANIES SUED HIM AND HIS CUSTOMERS FOR PATENT INFRINGEMENT, KEEPING HIM EMBROILED IN LITIGATION FOR YEARS.

LOCKED OUT OF THE US OIL INDUSTRY, KOCH AND HIS BUSINESS PARTNER, LEWIS WINKLER, TURNED TO THE SOVIET UNION, WHERE THEY SIGNED CONTRACTS TO BUILD PETROLEUM DISTILLATION PLANTS. BETWEEN 1929 AND 1932 THE WINKLER-KOCH COMPANY TRAINED SOVIET ENGINEERS AND HELPED STALIN'S REGIME SET UP 15 OIL REFINERIES.

FRED WAS PROFOUNDLY AFFECTED BY HIS EXPERIENCES IN THE SOVIET UNION.

IT WAS A LAND OF HUNGER, MISERY AND TERROR.

CITIZENS WERE ALLOTTED A MONTHLY RATION OF FOOD THAT WAS BARELY ENOUGH TO LIVE ON.

EVERYONE WORE BLAND, ILL-FITTING CLOTHING. HALF A BAR OF SOAP A MONTH WAS ALL THEY HAD FOR WASHING.

INFORMERS LURKED EVERYWHERE. EXECUTION OR A TRIP TO THE SIBERIAN MINES AWAITED ANYONE SUSPECTED OF DISLOYALTY.

A DAUGHTER OF A RUSSIAN FAMILY THAT FRED HAD BEFRIENDED BEGGED HIM TO TAKE A LETTER OUT OF THE COUNTRY FOR HER.

YOU CAN GET IT PAST THE SOVIET CENSORS FOR ME.

FRED AGREED, BUT COULDNT RESIST READING THE THE LETTER.

SHE HAD WRITTEN...

WE ARE HERE JUST LIKE SLAVES. WE CANNOT DO ANYTHING WE WANT, BUT ...DO WHAT THEY TELL US TO DO. I CANNOT WRITE IT TO YOU HOW TERRIBLE IT IS HERE.

FRED WROTE IN A LETTER TO THE *WASHINGTON POST* IN 1964...

I WAS NAIVE ENOUGH TO THINK IN THAT FARAWAY DAY THAT I COULD HELP THE RUSSIAN PEOPLE BY WHAT I WAS DOING. WHAT I SAW IN RUSSIA CONVINCED ME OF THE UTTER EVIL NATURE OF COMMUNISM...AND I MUST DO EVERYTHING IN MY POWER TO FIGHT IT.

BACK IN 1938 HE'D SEEN SOMETHING POSITIVE IN FASCISM AS A FORCE TO FIGHT COMMUNISM. HE WROTE TO A FRIEND...

I AM OF THE OPINION THAT THE ONLY SOUND COUNTRIES IN THE WORLD ARE GERMANY, ITALY AND JAPAN.

DURING THE 1930s, FRED KOCH TRAVELLED FREQUENTLY TO NAZI GERMANY ON OIL BUSINESS. ARCHIVAL RECORDS SHOW THAT WINKLER-KOCH ENGINEERING PROVIDED THE PLANS AND BEGAN OVERSEEING THE CONSTRUCTION OF A HUGE OIL REFINERY IN HAMBURG.

THIS REFINERY, THE THIRD LARGEST IN GERMANY, WAS ONE OF THE FEW INSTALLATIONS THE THIRD REICH HAD THAT COULD PRODUCE THE HIGH-OCTANE FUEL NEEDED FOR FIGHTER PLANES. HOWEVER, WHEN THE SECOND WORLD WAR BROKE OUT, KOCH TRIED TO ENLIST IN THE US MILITARY (ACCORDING TO THE FAMILY), BUT WAS DIRECTED TO USE HIS CHEMICAL ENGINEERING PROWESS TO HELP REFINE FUEL FOR AMERICAN WARPLANES. THE HAMBURG FACILITY WAS DESTROYED ON 18 JUNE 1944 BY AMERICAN B17 BOMBERS.

AFTER THE WAR FRED KOCH FOUNDED, ALONG WITH THE CANDY MANUFACTURER ROBERT WELSH AND OTHERS, THE JOHN BIRCH SOCIETY. THIS WAS A RADICAL FAR–RIGHT ORGANISATION CREATED TO DEFEND THE US AGAINST A PERCEIVED CLANDESTINE COMMUNIST TAKEOVER OF AMERICA.

THE MOVEMENT WAS NAMED AFTER A BAPTIST PREACHER AND ARMY CAPTAIN WHO WAS SHOT DEAD BY CHINESE COMMUNISTS IN 1945.

BY THE EARLY 1960s THE JOHN BIRCH SOCIETY HAD OVER 60,000 MEMBERS, AND AN ANNUAL REVENUE OF $1.6 MILLION. *THE SATURDAY EVENING POST* REPORTED THAT ITS MEMBERS, 'ARE SAID TO HAVE INFILTRATED REPUBLICAN ORGANISATIONS, DISRUPTED SCHOOL BOARDS, HARASSED CITY COUNCILS AND LIBRARIANS AND SUBVERTED PARENT TEACHERS ORGANISATIONS'.

THE SOCIETY TARGETED ISSUES RANGING FROM US PARTICIPATION IN THE UNITED NATIONS, WATER FLUORIDATION (SEEN AS A TOOL OF COMMUNIST DOMINATION), AND THE CIVIL RIGHTS ACT OF 1964 (A COMMUNIST CREATION INTENDED TO DIVIDE AND CONQUER AMERICA.) BIRCH SOCIETY PARANOIA OVER COMMUNISM OFTEN REACHED LUDICROUS LEVELS. THERE WERE NO AREAS OF SOCIETY WHERE THEY DIDN'T SEE COMMUNIST SUBVERSION.

THE SONS OF WICHITA

FRED KOCH MARRIED MARY ROBINSON, DAUGHTER OF A KANSAS PHYSICIAN, A MONTH AFTER HE MET HER AT A POLO MATCH. THEY HAD FOUR SONS: FREDERICK (1933), CHARLES (1935) AND TWINS DAVID AND WILLIAM (1940).

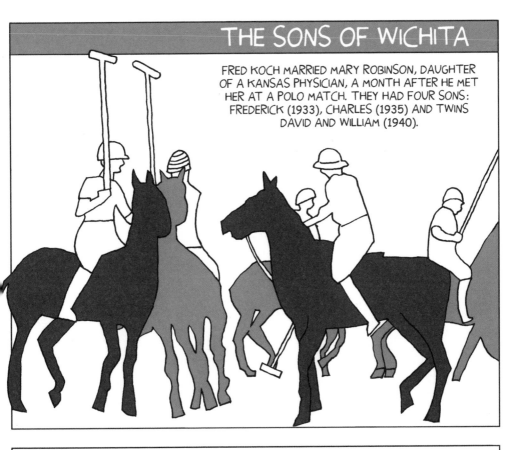

FRED WAS A TOUGH FATHER. HE DID NOT WANT HIS BOYS TO TURN OUT LIKE THE SPOILED SONS OF MANY OF THE OTHER OIL MOGULS HE KNEW. BY THE TIME THE BOYS WERE FIVE YEARS OLD THEY WERE DIGGING UP DANDELIONS, AND WHEN THEY WERE OLDER THEY SHOVELLED MANURE AT THE FAMILY RANCH IN WICHITA.

FREDERICK, THE ELDEST OF THE KOCH BROTHERS, SHOWED LITTLE INTEREST IN THE FAMILY BUSINESS, MUCH PREFERRING THE HUMANITIES. HE STUDIED AT HARVARD COLLEGE, GAINING A BACHELOR OF ARTS DEGREE (1955), AFTER WHICH HE ENLISTED IN THE US NAVY, SERVING ON THE *USS SARATOGA*.

CHARLES STUDIED AT THE MASSACHUSETTS INSTITUTE OF TECHNOLOGY (MIT). HE RECEIVED A BACHELOR OF SCIENCE IN GENERAL ENGINEERING (1957), A MASTER OF SCIENCE IN NUCLEAR ENGINEERING (1958) AND A SECOND MASTER OF SCIENCE IN CHEMICAL ENGINEERING (1960).

DAVID FOLLOWED THE SAME PATH, EARNING FIRST A BACHELOR'S DEGREE (1962) AND THEN A MASTER'S DEGREE (1963) AT THE MASSACHUSETTS INSTITUTE OF TECHNOLOGY. HE PLAYED BASKETBALL AT MIT, AVERAGING 21 POINTS PER GAME OVER A THREE-YEAR PERIOD, A SCHOOL RECORD. HE ALSO HELD THE SINGLE-GAME SCORING RECORD OF 41 POINTS FROM 1962 UNTIL 2009.

BILL, DAVID'S TWIN BROTHER, ALSO WENT TO THE MASSACHUSETTS INSTITUTE OF TECHNOLOGY. HE GRADUATED WITH BACHELOR'S, MASTER'S AND DOCTORAL DEGREES IN CHEMICAL ENGINEERING.

AFTER FREDERICK LEFT THE NAVY, HE ENROLLED IN THE YALE SCHOOL OF DRAMA, WHERE HE FOCUSED ON PLAYWRITING.

HE RECEIVED A MASTER OF FINE ARTS DEGREE IN 1961.

A COUPLE OF YEARS LATER, ACCORDING TO JANE MAYER'S BOOK *DARK MONEY*, CHARLES AND DAVID KOCH TRIED TO BLACKMAIL FREDERICK.

THE TWO BROTHERS HAD MANAGED TO SNEAK INTO HIS APARTMENT IN GREENWICH VILLAGE, NEW YORK, WHILE HE WAS OUT...

AND FOUND EVIDENCE WHICH THEY BELIEVED PROVED HE WAS GAY.

THEY CONFRONTED FREDERICK AND THREATENED TO INFORM THEIR FATHER UNLESS HE RENOUNCED HIS CLAIM ON THE FAMILY COMPANY.

YEAR'S LATER, FREDERICK TOLD DANIEL SCHULMAN, AUTHOR OF THE KOCH FAMILY BIOGRAPHY *THE SONS OF WICHITA*, THAT...

CHARLES'S HOMOSEXUAL BLACKMAIL TO GET CONTROL OF MY SHARES DID NOT SUCCEED FOR THE SIMPLE REASON THAT I AM NOT HOMOSEXUAL.

CHARLES HIMSELF RETURNED TO WICHITA IN 1961. HIS FATHER HAVING IDENTIFIED HIM AS THE FUTURE CEO OF THE COMPANY IN PREFERENCE TO HIS OTHER SONS.

PHONE CALL FROM YOUR FATHER, CHARLES.

AT FIRST HE WAS RELUCTANT TO GO, BUT FRED KOCH GAVE HIM AN ULTIMATUM.

YOU EITHER COME BACK AND TAKE OVER THE COMPANY OR I'M GOING TO SELL IT. GOT THAT?

THE BOSS

FRED'S HEALTH WAS IN DECLINE. BY THE MID-1960s HE WAS ROUTINELY IN HOSPITAL WITH HEART TROUBLE.

SLAM!

THE BOSS

17 NOVEMBER 1967. FRED WENT DUCK-HUNTING AT BEAR RIVER, UTAH.

BOY, THAT WAS A MAGNIFICENT SHOT.

MR KOCH!

FRED KOCH WAS DEAD AT 67...

AND, AT 32, CHARLES FOUND HIMSELF IN CHARGE OF A BILLION-DOLLAR COMPANY.

THE BOSS

FREDERICK WAS SHOCKED TO FIND THAT HE DIDN'T GET THE SAME INHERITANCE AS HIS YOUNGER BROTHERS.

BUT HE WAS HARDLY LEFT A PAUPER. TWO TRUST FUNDS WERE LEFT TO HIM AND HE OWNED 14.2 PER CENT OF THE COMPANY (HIS BROTHERS OWNED 20.7 PER CENT EACH).

THIS STILL AMOUNTED TO A PAYOUT OF MILLIONS BUT, COMPARED TO THE MONEY HIS SIBLINGS RECEIVED, FREDERICK FELT SHORT-CHANGED. THIS CAUSED MUCH RESENTMENT AND SOWED THE SEEDS OF FUTURE LEGAL CHALLENGES.

FUME!

ACCORDING TO CHARLES, FREDERICK RECEIVED LESS OF AN INHERITANCE BECAUSE HE HAD STOLEN FROM HIS FATHER.

HE'D TAKEN TRAVELLERS' CHEQUES, CASH AND EVEN FORGED HIS FATHER'S SIGNATURE.

I REFUTE ALL OF CHARLES'S ALLEGATIONS AS A CALCULATED CAMPAIGN OF VILIFICATION. HE WHO WOULD CAST ASPERSIONS SHOULD BE BEYOND REPROACH.

CHARLES'S FIRST MAJOR SUCCESS WAS IN GAINING CONTROL OF THE PINE BEND REFINERY IN ROSEMOUNT, MINNESOTA. FRED KOCH HAD BOUGHT A ONE-THIRD INTEREST IN THE REFINERY IN 1959, BUT CHARLES MANAGED TO ACQUIRE A MAJORITY SHARE IN 1969. PINE BEND PROVED TO BE A LUCRATIVE INVESTMENT AND ONE THAT FUELLED THE COMPANY'S GROWTH FOR YEARS.

PINE BEND WAS GEOGRAPHICALLY WELL SITUATED TO BUY CHEAP, HEAVY CRUDE OIL FROM CANADA, WHICH, AFTER BEING REFINED, COULD BE SOLD AT THE SAME PRICE AS OTHER GASOLINE. THE RESULT WAS HUGE PROFIT MARGINS FOR KOCH INDUSTRIES – GOOD FOR THE COMPANY, BUT BAD FOR THE PLANET, AS THE TAR-SAND OIL BEING USED (A COMBINATION OF SAND, WATER AND BITUMEN) CAN ONLY BE REFINED THROUGH A COMPLEX AND ENERGY-INTENSIVE PROCESS THAT CAUSES WIDESPREAD ENVIRONMENTAL DAMAGE.

THE WAR BETWEEN THE KOCHS

WHILE FREDERICK'S SHARES ENTITLED HIM TO TAKE A SEAT ON THE BOARD AT KOCH INDUSTRIES, HE DECLINED TO DO SO.

THE TWINS, DAVID AND BILL, WERE VERY INTERESTED. NOT ONLY DID THEY TAKE THEIR SEATS ON THE BOARD, BUT THEY ALSO TOOK SENIOR MANAGERIAL POSTS.

EVEN WHEN THEY WERE CHILDREN THE TWINS HAD NEVER BEEN CLOSE. DAVID'S REAL BOND HAD ALWAYS BEEN WITH HIS OLDER BROTHER, CHARLES.

WHICH LEFT BILL FEELING LIKE AN OUTSIDER. THIS RELATIONSHIP BEGAN TO PLAY OUT AGAIN IN ADULTHOOD.

OLD ANIMOSITIES RESURFACED. BILL BEGAN TO BE OPENLY CRITICAL OF CHARLES AND HIS AUTOCRATIC STYLE OF LEADERSHIP.

BILL HAD NO COMPLAINTS OVER CHARLES'S EXPANSION OF THE COMPANY. PROFITS HAD EXPLODED SINCE HIS BROTHER BECAME CEO, BUT THERE WERE A FEW AREAS OF CONCERN THAT BOTH HE AND OTHER SHAREHOLDERS WERE WORRIED ABOUT.

VARIOUS GOVERNMENT DEPARTMENTS, INCLUDING THE INTERNAL REVENUE SERVICE AND THE DEPARTMENT OF ENERGY, WERE INVESTIGATING KOCH INDUSTRIES.

CHARLES WAS PLOUGHING COMPANY MONEY INTO LIBERTARIAN POLITICAL CAUSES, WHICH BILL THOUGHT FRINGE AT BEST.

BILL WAS ONE OF THE RICHEST MEN IN AMERICA, WORTH HUNDREDS OF MILLIONS, YET NEARLY ALL HIS WEALTH WAS LOCKED UP IN A PRIVATE COMPANY. HE CONSIDERED THE $1-MILLION SALARY AND THE $4 MILLION IN DIVIDENDS HE RECEIVED FROM KOCH INDUSTRIES INADEQUATE.

WHAT IS THE PURPOSE OF WEALTH IF YOU CANNOT DO ANYTHING WITH IT, ESPECIALLY WHEN, UNDER PRESENT TAX LAW, ON DEATH THEY WILL UNDOUBTEDLY END UP IN THE HANDS OF THE GOVERNMENT AND POLITICIANS.

RICH AS HE WAS, HE HAD TO BORROW MONEY TO BUY A MANSION IN DOVER, MASSACHUSETTS.

BILL'S SOLUTION TO THESE PROBLEMS WAS TO ATTEMPT A BOARDROOM COUP WITH THE HELP OF HIS BROTHER FREDERICK AND OTHER DISGRUNTLED SHAREHOLDERS.

BILL AND FREDERICK WERE NATURAL ALLIES. BOTH WERE FRUSTRATED BY THE LACK OF CONTROL OVER THEIR WEALTH.

THEY FAVOURED TAKING KOCH INDUSTRIES PUBLIC IN ORDER TO UNLOCK ITS ASSETS – A MOVE THEY KNEW CHARLES WOULD BE AGAINST AS HE WOULD LOSE MUCH OF HIS CONTROL OF THE COMPANY.

BILL CALLED A SHAREHOLDERS' MEETING. HE BELIEVED HE HAD ENOUGH SUPPORT TO DISSOLVE THE BOARD OF DIRECTORS, OUST CHARLES FROM HIS POSITION AS CHAIR, AND ELECT A NEW BOARD THAT WOULD ALLOW HIM TO TAKE THE COMPANY IN A NEW DIRECTION.

THE BOSS

BUT THEY HAD UNDERESTIMATED CHARLES.

ONE PIECE OF ADVICE MY FATHER GAVE ME WAS THAT 'IF YOU WANT SOMEONE TO HATE YOU, MAKE HIM A LOT OF MONEY'.

THE BOSS

I DIDN'T UNDERSTAND IT AT THE TIME. I UNDERSTAND IT NOW.

AS THE CRUCIAL MEETING DREW NEAR, IT BECAME APPARENT THAT BOTH CHARLES'S AND BILL'S FACTIONS HAD AN EQUAL NUMBER OF SHAREHOLDERS ON THEIR SIDE. EVERY VOTE WAS GOING TO COUNT.

A SHAREHOLDER CHARLES KNEW HE COULD RELY ON WAS THE TEXAN OIL MAN, J. HOWARD MARSHALL II, WHO HAD HELPED KOCH INDUSTRIES IN THEIR ACQUISITION OF THE PINE BEND REFINERY. HOWARD ASSURED CHARLES THAT HE AND HIS TWO SONS, WHO TOGETHER CONTROLLED JUST OVER EIGHT PER CENT OF THE STOCK, WOULD BACK CHARLES.

HOWARD BELIEVED THAT HIS TWO BOYS WOULD NEVER CROSS THEIR FATHER, BUT THIS ASSUMPTION TURNED OUT TO BE WRONG. THE OIL MAN WAS SHOCKED AND HURT TO DISCOVER THAT HIS SON, HOWARD III, INTENDED TO VOTE WITH BILL. NO AMOUNT OF PLEADING MADE ANY DIFFERENCE.

WELL, THERE'S ONE THING THAT HOWARD III UNDERSTANDS AND THAT'S MONEY. I'M GOING TO OFFER HIM $8 MILLION FOR HIS SHARES. TAKE IT OR LEAVE IT.

WHEN BILL HEARD ABOUT THIS MOVE HE ALMOST DOUBLED MARSHALL'S OFFER.

HOWARD III HAD UNDERESTIMATED HOW DISTRESSED HIS FATHER WOULD BE AT HIS BETRAYAL OF CHARLES.

SON.

FOR THIS REASON HE DECIDED TO REFUSE BILL'S OFFER OF $14 MILLION AND TOOK HIS FATHER'S OFFER OF $8 MILLION.

THIS MEANT THAT CHARLES HAD CONTROL OF 51 PER CENT OF THE COMPANY. HE HAD WON. THE SHAREHOLDERS' MEETING WAS CANCELLED...

CLAP! CLAP!

AND BILL WAS FIRED.

IN 1983 THE DISSIDENT SHAREHOLDERS WERE BOUGHT OUT IN A DEAL WORTH $1.1 BILLION.

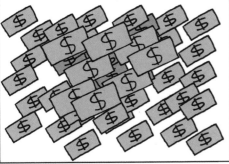

OF THIS, BILL KOCH RECEIVED $470 MILLION AND FREDERICK $330 MILLION.

THIS LEFT CHARLES AND DAVID CONTROLLING OVER 80 PER CENT OF KOCH INDUSTRIES WITH THE STOCK EVENLY SPLIT BETWEEN THEM.

DESPITE THE COLOSSAL PAYOUT, BILL AND FREDERICK WERE STILL NOT HAPPY. THEY BELIEVED THAT THE COMPANY HAD BEEN UNDERVALUED IN ORDER TO CHEAT THEM.

KOCH INDUSTRIES HAD BORROWED $800 MILLION TO FINANCE THE BUYOUT. BILL AND HIS BANKERS CALCULATED THAT THE COMPANY WOULD TAKE MANY YEARS TO PAY OFF THIS DEBT.

YET SOMEHOW THE COMPANY REPAID THE DEBT IN ONLY TWO. THE RESULTING SERIES OF LAWSUITS THAT BILL AND FREDERICK BROUGHT AGAINST THEIR BROTHERS LASTED 17 YEARS.

WHILE THE WAR BETWEEN THE KOCHS PLAYED OUT, THE BROTHERS WERE GETTING ON WITH THEIR LIVES.

IN 1980 DAVID KOCH TRIED HIS HAND AT POLITICS, BECOMING THE LIBERTARIAN PARTY'S VICE-PRESIDENTIAL CANDIDATE...

SHARING THE TICKET WITH ED CLARK. THEY RAN ON A PLATFORM THAT PROMISED TO ABOLISH SOCIAL SECURITY...

THE FEDERAL RESERVE BOARD, WELFARE, MINIMUM WAGE LAWS, CORPORATE TAXES...

HOMELESS + HUNGRY

AND THE ABOLITION OF MOST US AGENCIES, INCLUDING THE ENVIRONMENTAL PROTECTION AGENCY AND THE DEPARTMENT OF THE ENVIRONMENT.

KOFF!

THEY RECEIVED ONE PER CENT OF THE NATIONAL VOTE.

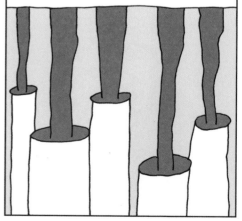

THE RISE OF THE KOCHTOPUS

FOR YEARS BOTH DAVID AND CHARLES HAD DONATED MONEY TO LIBERTARIAN CAUSES...

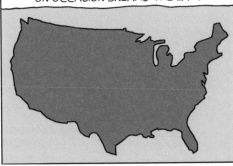

WITH THE AIM OF PROMOTING SMALL GOVERNMENT AND INDIVIDUAL RIGHTS.

CHARLES, WHO, LIKE HIS FATHER, HAD BEEN A MEMBER OF THE BIRCH SOCIETY, FELT HE WAS FIGHTING AGAINST...

ARROGANT AND INTRUSIVE TOTALITARIAN LAWS.

AS A LIBERTARIAN, HE BELIEVED THAT PEOPLE SHOULD BE FREE TO THINK AND BEHAVE AS THEY WANT AND NOT HAVE LIMITS PUT ON THEM BY GOVERNMENT.

THIS IS A USEFUL POLITICAL PHILOSOPHY IF YOU HAVE COLOSSAL WEALTH, DON'T WANT TO PAY TAXES, AND RUN A COMPANY THAT DESPOILS THE ENVIRONMENT AND ON OCCASION BREAKS THE LAW.

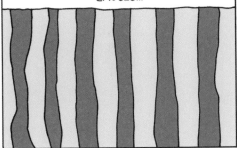

BY THE MID-1990s CHARLES AND DAVID HAD LARGELY CUT THEIR TIES WITH THE LIBERTARIAN PARTY. THEY NEEDED TO GET CLOSER TO THE LEVERS OF POWER – AND THAT MEANT THE REPUBLICAN PARTY.

WASHINGTON DC ★

THE KOCHS INTENDED TO MOVE LIBERTARIAN IDEAS FROM THE FRINGE AND INTO THE POLITICAL MAINSTREAM.

THEY WANTED TO PUSH THE REPUBLICAN PARTY, AND THEREFORE AMERICA, TOWARDS THE PRO-BUSINESS, LIMITED-GOVERNMENT POLICIES THAT WOULD BEST SERVE THEIR INTERESTS.

IN 1996, DAVID KOCH BECAME BOB DOLE'S VICE-CHAIR, FOR THE REPUBLICAN CANDIDATE'S BID AGAINST BILL CLINTON IN THE PRESIDENTIAL ELECTION.

THE KOCHS WERE DOLE'S THIRD-LARGEST FINANCIAL BACKERS. DAVID HOSTED A FUND-RAISING BIRTHDAY PARTY FOR DOLE WHERE THE CANDIDATE RAISED $150,000.

DIRECT POLITICAL FUNDING WAS NOT THE ONLY WAY THE KOCHS USED THEIR FINANCIAL MUSCLE.

SOME ASPECTS OF THE 1996 ELECTION WERE SUSPICIOUS ENOUGH THAT THE DEMOCRATS IN THE US SENATE BEGAN AN INVESTIGATION. THEY FOUND EVIDENCE OF AN ATTEMPT TO SWING LOCAL ELECTIONS IN THE FINAL DAYS OF THE CAMPAIGN.

A SHELL CORPORATION (A COMPANY THAT EXISTS ONLY ON PAPER AND HAS NO OFFICE OR EMPLOYEES) KNOWN AS TRIAD MANAGEMENT SERVICES...

PAID OUT MORE THAN $3 MILLION FOR ATTACK ADS AGAINST DEMOCRATIC CANDIDATES IN 29 RACES.

THIS JUST IN. DEMS ARE WEAK ON CRIME.

THE KANSAS REPUBLICAN SAM BROWNBACK GOT PARTICULAR HELP IN HIS RACE FOR THE US SENATE.

TRILL!

VOTERS IN THE DISTRICT HE WAS CAMPAIGNING IN WERE INUNDATED WITH PHONE CALLS INFORMING THEM THAT HIS OPPONENT, JILL DOCKING, WAS A JEW.

SHE WHAT?

BROWNBACK WON. THE HUGE INFLUX OF MONEY IS THOUGHT TO HAVE TIPPED THE SCALES IN FOUR CLOSE RACES, ENSURING THAT THE REPUBLICANS RETAINED CONTROL OF THE HOUSE, EVEN THOUGH BILL CLINTON WAS RE-ELECTED.

WE COULDN'T FIGURE OUT WHERE THE MONEY WAS COMING FROM. THE ADS CAME AT ME IN EVERY DIRECTION IN THE LAST WEEKS. THERE WERE FIVE OR SIX OF THEM TO EVERY ONE OF MINE. IT CLEARLY SWAYED THE ELECTION.

JILL DOCKING

THE KOCHS REFUSED TO BE DRAWN ON WHETHER THEY HAD PROVIDED THE MONEY.

NO COMMENT.

REPUBLICANS ARGUED THAT THEY WERE JUST BALANCING THE SCORE AGAINST SPENDING BY LABOUR UNIONS. BY 1998 BUSINESS WAS OUTSPENDING LABOUR BY TWELVE TO ONE.

THE FEDERAL ELECTION COMMISSION RULED THAT THE TRIAD SCHEME WAS ILLEGAL AND FINED ITS PRESIDENT, CAROLYN S. MALENICK, A PALTRY $5,000.

TRIAD WAS JUST THE BEGINNING. IN THE YEARS FOLLOWING, THE KOCHS FUNNELLED MILLIONS OF DOLLARS INTO CAUSES PROMOTING THEIR INTERESTS.

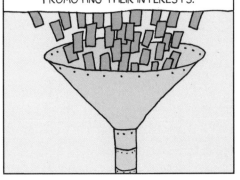

THEY DID THIS IN THREE WAYS. THEY MADE PERSONAL POLITICAL CONTRIBUTIONS TO REPUBLICAN PARTY COMMITTEES AND CANDIDATES.

THE COMPANY ITSELF, KOCH INDUSTRIES, MADE CONTRIBUTIONS THROUGH ITS POLITICAL ACTION COMMITTEE (KOCHPAC) AND EXERTED INFLUENCE BY LOBBYING.

THE THIRD WAY THE KOCHS CHANNELLED MONEY INTO POLITICAL CAUSES WAS THROUGH PRIVATE FOUNDATIONS CREATED FOR THIS PURPOSE.

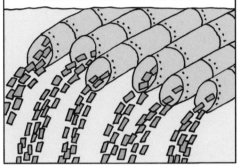

UNLIKE A CHARITABLE FOUNDATION, A PRIVATE FOUNDATION DOES NOT GENERALLY ASK FOR FUNDS FROM THE PUBLIC.

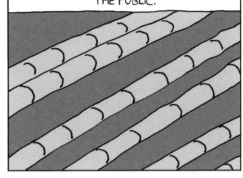

IT IS USUALLY CREATED WITH A SINGLE LARGE DONATION TO BEGIN WITH, FROM AN INDIVIDUAL OR BUSINESS. THESE FUNDS ARE THEN MANAGED BY ITS OWN DIRECTORS.

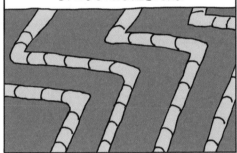

RATHER THAN FUNDING ITS OPERATIONS THROUGH DONATIONS, AS A CHARITABLE FOUNDATION WOULD, A PRIVATE FOUNDATION GENERATES ITS INCOME BY INVESTING ITS MONEY.

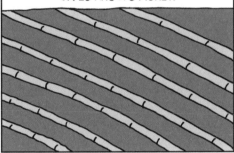

PROFITS ARE THEN DISTRIBUTED TO CHARITABLE CAUSES.

WHICH SOUNDS ALL WELL AND GOOD. WHAT COULD POSSIBLY BE WRONG IN THE WEALTHY GIVING AWAY THEIR OWN MONEY? WELL, IT TURNS OUT, QUITE A LOT.

AT LEAST FIVE PER CENT OF A FOUNDATION'S ASSETS ARE OBLIGED BY LAW TO BE GIVEN TO CHARITY. IN RETURN THE DONORS GET GENEROUS TAX DEDUCTIONS. IT'S A NICE DEAL. THE WEALTHY GET TO FEEL THEY ARE BEING PUBLIC-SPIRITED, EVEN THOUGH THEIR DONATIONS ARE BEING PAID FOR BY A LOSS IN GENERAL TAXATION. PLUS, THEY HAVE THE POWER TO USE THIS FINANCIAL MUSCLE TO IMPACT SOCIETY AS THEY PLEASE, OFTEN IN NEGATIVE WAYS.

WHY CAN'T WE REPAIR THE STATE'S INFRASTRUCTURE, SENATOR?

WE'VE HAD AN UNEXPECTED SHORTFALL IN TAX REVENUE.

PRIVATE FOUNDATIONS ARE COMMONPLACE IN MODERN TIMES AND ARE RARELY CONTROVERSIAL. BUT THIS HAS NOT ALWAYS BEEN THE CASE. THE PRACTICE BEGAN IN THE EARLY YEARS OF THE 20TH CENTURY. IN 1909, JOHN D. ROCKEFELLER SOUGHT PERMISSION FROM CONGRESS TO OBTAIN A FEDERAL CHARTER TO SET UP A GENERAL-PURPOSE PRIVATE FOUNDATION WHOSE MISSION WAS TO ALLEVIATE POVERTY AND PROMOTE KNOWLEDGE AND PROGRESS. CONGRESS DENIED ROCKEFELLER APPROVAL, SO THE OIL MAGNATE SIMPLY ASKED THE NEW YORK LEGISLATURE TO APPROVE HIS PLAN.

NOT EVERYONE AT THE TIME THOUGHT FOUNDATIONS A GOOD IDEA.

NO AMOUNT OF CHARITY IN SPENDING SUCH FORTUNES CAN COMPENSATE IN ANY WAY FOR THE MISCONDUCT IN ACQUIRING IT.

THEODORE ROOSEVELT

HUGE PHILANTHROPIC TRUSTS KNOWN AS FOUNDATIONS APPEAR TO BE A MENACE TO THE WELFARE OF SOCIETY.

FRANK WALSH

CHAIRMAN OF THE US COMMISSION ON INDUSTRIAL RELATIONS

OVER TIME THE NUMBER OF PRIVATE FOUNDATIONS GREW, SO BY 1930, THERE WERE AROUND 200 OF THEM.

BY 1950 THE NUMBER HAD GROWN TO TWO THOUSAND AND BY 1895 THERE WERE THIRTY THOUSAND.

IN 2013 THERE WERE A HUNDRED THOUSAND PRIVATE FOUNDATIONS IN THE UNITED STATES...

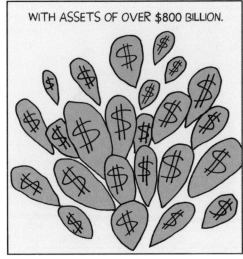

WITH ASSETS OF OVER $800 BILLION.

HERE ARE FIVE KOCH BROTHERS FOUNDATIONS...

THE FRED C. AND MARY R. KOCH FOUNDATION

THE CHARLES G. KOCH CHARITABLE FOUNDATION

THE CHARLES KOCH INSTITUTE

THE CHARLES KOCH FOUNDATION

THE DAVID H. KOCH CHARITABLE FOUNDATION

ALL HAVE DIFFERENT REMITS, BUT TEND OVERALL TO PROMOTE SMALL GOVERNMENT AND FREE-MARKET COMPETITION.

WHERE DOES ALL THE MONEY GO?

SOME OF THIS MONEY FUNDS THINK TANKS, LIKE THE CATO INSTITUTE, WHICH CHARLES KOCH FOUNDED IN 1974 WITH THE LIBERTARIAN THINKERS ED CRANE AND MURRAY ROTHBARD.

WHAT ARE THINK TANKS? A THINK TANK OR POLICY INSTITUTE IS A RESEARCH CENTRE...

STAFFED WITH INTERDISCIPLINARY GROUPS OF EXPERTS ENGAGED IN THE STUDY OF POLICY ISSUES IN BUSINESS AND GOVERNMENT. A KIND OF UNIVERSITY WITHOUT STUDENTS.

SINCE THE 1970s HUNDREDS OF TAX-EXEMPT, NON-PROFIT THINK TANKS HAVE BEEN CREATED. MANY OF THE MOST INFLUENTIAL ARE CONSERVATIVE.

FUNDED BY THE KOCH BROTHERS AND OTHER WEALTHY DONORS, THINK TANKS LIKE THE HERITAGE FOUNDATION, FREEDOMWORKS AND THE AMERICAN ENTERPRISE INSTITUTE...

HAVE HELPED SUCCESSFULLY MOVE WHAT WERE PREVIOUSLY CONSIDERED TO BE HARDLINE FRINGE CONSERVATIVE IDEAS INTO THE MAINSTREAM.

HERE'S A REPORT FROM A THINK TANK, CONCLUDING THAT THE MINIMUM WAGE SHOULD BE ABOLISHED BECAUSE IT CREATES UNEMPLOYMENT.

HERE'S ANOTHER CLAIMING THAT RENT CONTROLS REDUCE THE AMOUNT OF RENTED HOUSING AVAILABLE.

EVEN IF YOU ASSUME THAT SUCH RESEARCH IS ACADEMICALLY RIGOROUS (AND MUCH OF IT CAN BE CONTESTED), THERE'S STILL THE PROBLEM OF BIAS.

IN 2016 A *NEW YORK TIMES* ARTICLE SHOWED THAT THINK TANKS REGULARLY CONSULT WITH WEALTHY DONORS BEFORE COMPLETING THEIR STUDIES AND RELEASING FINDINGS.

IT UNCOVERED DOCUMENTS SUGGESTING THAT THINK TANKS ARE ACTIVELY PUSHING CORPORATE AGENDAS AND BLURRING THE LINE BETWEEN RESEARCH AND POLITICAL LOBBYING.

TIME AND AGAIN WE SEE CONSERVATIVE THINK TANKS SUPPORTING THE INTERESTS OF CORPORATE AMERICA OVER THAT OF ORDINARY CITIZENS.

SUCH RESEARCH IS SOON PICKED UP AS TALKING POINTS BY THE MEDIA, AND, BEFORE YOU KNOW IT, POLITICIANS HAVE MADE IT POLICY.

WELL, THAT'S WHAT I THINK ANYWAY.

ANOTHER WAY THAT THE KOCH BROTHERS HAVE ATTEMPTED TO CHANGE AMERICAN SOCIETY IS THROUGH FUNDING EDUCATION. THOSE ON THE POLITICAL RIGHT HAVE LONG BELIEVED THAT ACADEMIA INDOCTRINATES STUDENTS WITH LEFT-WING VIEWS.

BRAINWASHING

STUDIES SUGGEST OTHERWISE. FOR EXAMPLE, IN THEIR BOOK *CLOSED MINDS? POLITICS AND IDEOLOGY IN AMERICAN UNIVERSITIES,* THE THREE AUTHORS, A. FRITSCHLER, BRUCE L. R. SMITH AND JEREMY D. MAYER CAME TO A DIFFERENT CONCLUSION.

HERE'S WHAT TO THINK.

COMMUNISM IS THE ANSWER TO ALL THE WORLD'S PROBLEMS. IT WILL BRING YOU A HEAVEN ON EARTH IN WHICH EVERYONE WILL BE HAPPY.

NOPE!

THE NOTION THAT STUDENTS ARE INDUCED TO MOVE LEFTWARD...

IS A FANTASY. IT'S ACTUALLY HARD TO CHANGE THE MIND OF ANYONE OVER 15.

JEREMY D. MAYER

PARENTS AND FAMILY ARE THE MOST IMPORTANT INFLUENCES, FOLLOWED BY THE NEWS MEDIA AND PEERS. PROFESSORS ARE THE LEAST INFLUENTIAL.

SUCH RESEARCH HASN'T STOPPED THE RIGHT FROM CONTINUING TO BELIEVE IN ACADEMIC INDOCTRINATION AND BIAS.

IN 1974, CHARLES KOCH, IN HIS CAPACITY AS PRESIDENT AND CHAIR OF THE INSTITUTE OF HUMANE STUDIES (ANOTHER NON-PROFIT HE FUNDED), SPOKE TO THE BOARD OF DIRECTORS.

WE HAVE SUPPORTED THE VERY INSTITUTIONS FROM WHICH THE ATTACK ON FREE MARKETS EMANATE. ALTHOUGH MUCH OF OUR SUPPORT HAS BEEN INVOLUNTARY THROUGH TAXES, WE HAVE ALSO CONTRIBUTED VOLUNTARILY TO COLLEGES AND UNIVERSITIES ON THE ERRONEOUS ASSUMPTION THAT THIS ASSISTANCE BENEFITS BUSINESSES AND THE FREE-ENTERPRISE SYSTEM, EVEN THOUGH THESE INSTITUTIONS ENCOURAGE EXTREME HOSTILITY TO AMERICAN BUSINESSES.

WE SHOULD CEASE FINANCING OUR OWN DESTRUCTION AND FOLLOW THE COUNSEL OF DAVID PACKARD, FORMER DEPUTY SECRETARY OF DEFENSE, BY SUPPORTING ONLY THOSE PROGRAMMES, DEPARTMENTS OR SCHOOLS THAT CONTRIBUTE IN SOME WAY TO OUR INDIVIDUAL COMPANIES OR TO THE GENERAL WELFARE OF OUR FREE-ENTERPRISE SYSTEM.

IN THE DECADES SINCE, CHARLES KOCH HAS POURED MILLIONS INTO EDUCATION, TYPICALLY GIVING LARGE DONATIONS TO FREE-MARKET ECONOMIC PROGRAMMES AT HUNDREDS OF COLLEGES AND UNIVERSITIES.

GEORGE MASON UNIVERSITY   ARIZONA STATE UNIVERSITY

TEXAS TECH UNIVERSITY   GEORGE WASHINGTON UNIVERSITY

PURDUE UNIVERSITY   UNIVERSITY OF LOUISVILLE

UNIVERSITY OF TEXAS   SOUTHERN METHODIST UNIVERSITY

UTAH STATE UNIVERSITY   UNIVERSITY OF CHICAGO   BROWN UNIVERSITY

CREIGHTON UNIVERSITY   WEST VIRGINIA UNIVERSITY

MISSISSIPPI STATE UNIVERSITY   OKLAHOMA STATE UNIVERSITY

UNIVERSITY OF NORTH CAROLINA   INDIANA UNIVERSITY

AND MANY MORE.

THESE DONATIONS HAVE GROWN EXPONENTIALLY. IN 2017 THE CHARLES KOCH FOUNDATION DISTRIBUTED ROUGHLY $100 MILLION TO 350 COLLEGES AND UNIVERSITIES – A FIVEFOLD INCREASE OVER THE PREVIOUS FIVE YEARS.

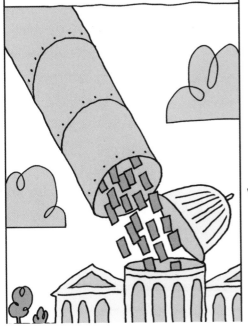

CRITICS MAINTAIN THAT THE KOCHS HAVE NOT SO MUCH ENRICHED AS CORRUPTED ACADEMIA, SPONSORING COURSES THAT WOULD OTHERWISE FAIL TO MEET THE STANDARDS OF LEGITIMATE SCHOLARSHIP.

FOR EXAMPLE, THE KOCH-FUNDED BILL OF RIGHTS INSTITUTE PROVIDES LESSON PLANS, STUDY MATERIAL AND SEMINARS GEARED TOWARDS ELEMENTARY, MIDDLE AND HIGH SCHOOL STUDENTS. EDUCATORS CAN EASILY AND FREELY DOWNLOAD MATERIAL FROM THEIR WEBSITE FOR USE IN CLASS (OR HOME SCHOOLING). THE LESSONS STRESS THE USUAL KOCH TALKING POINTS – FREE-MARKET ECONOMICS, LIMITED GOVERNMENT – BUT ALSO INCLUDED IS A WHITEWASHED HISTORY OF SLAVERY IN THE US.

ITS TUTORIAL ON 'SLAVERY AND THE CONSTITUTION' SPENDS A LOT OF TIME EXPLAINING HOW THE FOUNDING FATHERS WEREN'T RACIST, BUT JUST DIDN'T TRY HARD ENOUGH. IT NEGLECTS TO MENTION ANY DETAIL ON THE ATLANTIC SLAVE TRADE, THE ABOLITIONIST MOVEMENT OR THE PLANTATION SYSTEM. HOW SLAVERY HELPED THE US BECOME AN ECONOMIC SUPERPOWER IS COMPLETELY OVERLOOKED. IN ITS ESSAY ON THE CIVIL-RIGHTS MOVEMENT, ONLY FOUR BLACK PEOPLE ARE MENTIONED: MARTIN LUTHER KING JR, ROSA PARKS, W. E. B. DUBOIS AND THURGOOD MARSHALL.

NO MENTION IS MADE OF LYNCHINGS, BEATINGS OR CHURCH BURNINGS, BUT THERE IS MUCH DISCUSSION OF HOW SMALL-GOVERNMENT PRINCIPLES CLASH WITH FREEDOM FOR BLACK PEOPLE.

ALL SUBJECTS ARE TAUGHT FROM A RIGHT-WING PERSPECTIVE. THE LESSON PLAN CALLED 'HEALTH CARE AND THE BILL OF RIGHTS' CASTS THE AFFORDABLE CARE ACT (2010), ALSO KNOWN AS OBAMACARE, ENTIRELY AS AN INFRINGEMENT OF INDIVIDUAL RIGHTS.

THERE ARE TWO ARTICLES EXAMINING CASES WHERE THE AFFORDABLE CARE ACT IS SAID TO VIOLATE RELIGIOUS BELIEFS. STUDENTS GET TO READ ABOUT HOW THE ACT COVERS ABORTIONS, HOW INDIVIDUALS MIGHT BE CRIMINALISED IF THEY DON'T PURCHASE HEALTH COVERAGE, AND GENERALLY HOW THE ACA IS INDICATIVE OF GOVERNMENT OVERREACH.

FUNDING THE TEA PARTY

THE ELECTION OF THE DEMOCRAT BARACK OBAMA TO THE PRESIDENCY IN 2009 CAUSED OUTRAGE ON THE POLITICAL RIGHT. THIS ANGER INTENSIFIED WHEN OBAMA ANNOUNCED PROPOSALS TO HELP DISTRESSED HOMEOWNERS – PEOPLE WHO HAD BEEN VICTIMS OF THE 2008 BANKING CRISIS – WITH THE HOMEOWNER AFFORDABILITY AND STABILITY PLAN. $75 BILLION WAS TO BE FUNNELLED TO THOSE IN NEED, PLUS A FURTHER $200 BILLION TO HELP PROP UP THE FEDERAL NATIONAL MORTGAGE ASSOCIATION AND THE FEDERAL HOME LOAN MORTGAGE CORPORATION (KNOWN AS FANNIE MAE AND FREDDY MAC).

THESE WERE COLOSSAL SUMS WHICH BROUGHT INSTANT ENMITY FROM RIGHT–WING PUNDITS AND POLITICIANS – ALTHOUGH THE SAME PEOPLE HAD NOT COMPLAINED ABOUT THE $700-BILLION BAILOUT USING TAXPAYERS' MONEY THAT THE BANKS HAD RECEIVED THE PREVIOUS YEAR (THE EMERGENCY ECONOMIC STABILISATION ACT, 2008). THIS WAS FINE, APPARENTLY, EVEN THOUGH IT WAS THE FINANCIAL SYSTEM THAT HAD CAUSED THE BANKING CRISIS IN THE FIRST PLACE WITH THEIR RECKLESS, AND OFTEN CRIMINAL, BUSINESS PRACTICES. A SERIES OF MARCHES AGAINST OBAMA'S AGENDA WAS THEN ORGANISED, INCLUDING THE 2009 TAXPAYER MARCH ON WASHINGTON, WHICH COINCIDED WITH SIMILAR PROTESTS IN VARIOUS CITIES ACROSS THE USA.

THE KOCH BROTHERS POURED MONEY INTO THE NEWLY EMERGING CONSERVATIVE POPULAR MOVEMENT THAT BECAME KNOWN AS THE TEA PARTY (NAMED AFTER THE BOSTON TEA PARTY, A 1776 DEMONSTRATION BY AMERICAN COLONISTS AGAINST TAXATION BY THE BRITISH GOVERNMENT). THE ADVOCACY GROUP THE KOCHS FUNDED, AMERICANS FOR PROSPERITY (AFP), WAS NOT THE ONLY CONSERVATIVE ORGANISATION TO FUNNEL MONEY INTO TEA PARTY ACTIVITY, BUT IT WAS AMONG THE MOST EFFECTIVE.

AMERICANS FOR PROSPERITY BOUGHT POLITICAL ADVERTISEMENTS, SPONSORED A NATIONWIDE BUS TOUR TO RECRUIT ORGANISERS AND CANVASSERS, ORGANISED VOTER REGISTRATION DRIVES, PROVIDED TEA PARTY ACTIVISTS WITH EDUCATION ON POLICY TRAINING IN METHODS, AND GAVE OUT LISTS OF POLITICIANS TO TARGET. BY 2010 AFP WAS ONE OF THE MOST POWERFUL CONSERVATIVE ORGANISATIONS IN THE TEA PARTY MOVEMENT AND THE LARGEST IN TERMS OF MEMBERSHIP AND SPENDING. THE AFP CLAIMED IT SPENT $40 MILLION ON RALLIES, PHONE BANKS AND CANVASSING DURING THE 2010 ELECTION CYCLE, AND YET KOCH SPOKESPEOPLE CONSISTENTLY DENIED THEY HAD SUPPLIED FUNDING SPECIFICALLY FOR THE TEA PARTY MOVEMENT.

FROM THE BEGINNING THE TEA PARTY PORTRAYED PRESIDENT OBAMA AS UNIQUELY DANGEROUS TO THE AMERICAN WAY OF LIFE.

THESE ATTACKS WENT FAR BEYOND THE USUAL CRITICISMS OF POLITICAL OPPONENTS INTO OUTRIGHT RACISM.

THESE ARE ACTUAL TEA PARTY SIGNS.

DAVID KOCH, IN AN INTERVIEW, THOUGHT OBAMA...

THE MOST RADICAL PRESIDENT WE'VE EVER HAD AS A NATION.

HIS FATHER WAS A HARDCORE ECONOMIC SOCIALIST IN KENYA. OBAMA DIDN'T REALLY INTERACT WITH HIS FATHER FACE TO FACE VERY MUCH...

BUT APPARENTLY FROM WHAT I'VE READ, A GREAT ADMIRER OF HIS FATHER'S POINT OF VIEW. SO HE HAD A SORT OF ANTI-BUSINESS, ANTI-FREE-ENTERPRISE INFLUENCE AFFECTING HIM ALMOST ALL HIS LIFE.

IT JUST SHOWS WHAT A PERSON WITH A SILVER TONGUE CAN ACHIEVE.

BILL BURTON, WHO WAS DEPUTY WHITE HOUSE PRESS SECRETARY IN THE EARLY OBAMA YEARS, BELIEVED THAT...

YOU CAN'T UNDERSTAND OBAMA'S RELATIONSHIP WITH THE RIGHT WING WITHOUT TAKING INTO ACCOUNT HIS RACE.

THEY TREATED HIM IN A WAY THEY NEVER WOULD HAVE IF HE'D BEEN WHITE. THE LEVEL OF DISRESPECT WAS JUST DIALLED UP TO ELEVEN.

THIS HATE BEGAN IMMEDIATELY. RUSH LIMBAUGH, TALK-SHOW RADIO HOST AND ONE OF THE MOST POWERFUL VOICES IN THE CONSERVATIVE MOVEMENT, TOLD HIS LISTENERS...

I HOPE HE FAILS.

FOX NEWS, WITH ITS STABLE OF MILLIONAIRE PRESENTERS SUCH AS SEAN HANNITY, GLENN BECK AND BILL O'REILLY, BECAME THE FOCAL POINT AND CHIEF PROMOTER OF THE TEA PARTY.

OBAMA HATES AMERICA.

THE FURY INCREASED WHEN OBAMA MADE ATTEMPTS TO MITIGATE THE AFFECTS OF CLIMATE CHANGE.

THE KOCHS VERSUS CLIMATE CHANGE

CLIMATE CHANGE, ALSO KNOWN AS GLOBAL WARMING, IS THE OBSERVED CENTURIES-SCALE RISE IN THE AVERAGE TEMPERATURE OF THE EARTH'S CLIMATE SYSTEM. THE LARGEST HUMAN INFLUENCE HAS BEEN THE EMISSION OF GREENHOUSE GASES, SUCH AS CARBON DIOXIDE, METHANE AND NITROUS OXIDE.

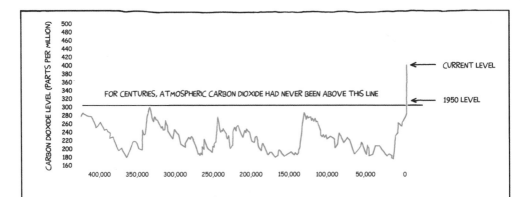

THIS GRAPH, BASED ON ATMOSPHERIC SAMPLES CONTAINED IN ICE CORES AND MORE RECENT DIRECT MEASUREMENTS, PROVIDES EVIDENCE THAT ATMOSPHERIC CARBON DIOXIDE HAS INCREASED SIGNIFICANTLY SINCE THE INDUSTRIAL REVOLUTION.

ACCORDING TO CLIMATE SCIENTISTS, IF THE WORLD HOPES TO STAY WITHIN THE RANGE OF CARBON EMISSIONS THOUGHT REASONABLE IN ORDER FOR ATMOSPHERIC TEMPERATURES TO REMAIN TOLERABLE IN THE 21ST CENTURY, THEN 80 PER CENT OF THE FOSSIL FUEL INDUSTRY'S RESERVES WOULD HAVE TO STAY IN THE GROUND.

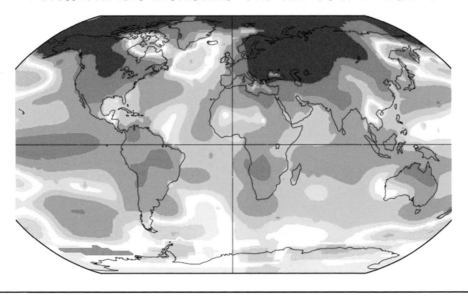

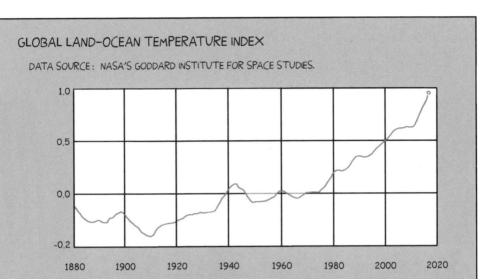

GLOBAL LAND–OCEAN TEMPERATURE INDEX

DATA SOURCE: NASA'S GODDARD INSTITUTE FOR SPACE STUDIES.

THIS GRAPH ILLUSTRATES THE CHANGES IN GLOBAL SURFACE TEMPERATURES RELATIVE TO 1951–1980 AVERAGE TEMPERATURES. SEVENTEEN OF THE 18 WARMEST YEARS IN THE 136–YEAR RECORD HAVE OCCURRED SINCE 2001, WITH THE EXCEPTION OF 1998. THE YEAR 2016 RANKS AS THE WARMEST ON RECORD.

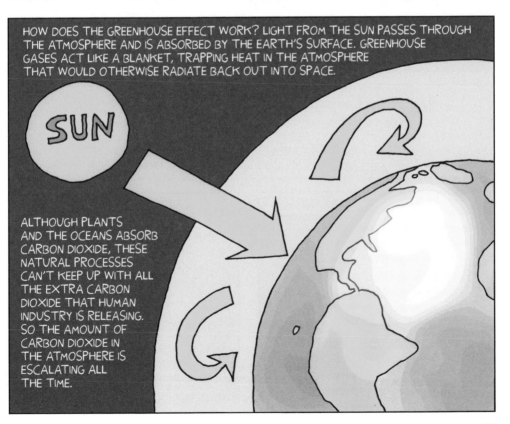

HOW DOES THE GREENHOUSE EFFECT WORK? LIGHT FROM THE SUN PASSES THROUGH THE ATMOSPHERE AND IS ABSORBED BY THE EARTH'S SURFACE. GREENHOUSE GASES ACT LIKE A BLANKET, TRAPPING HEAT IN THE ATMOSPHERE THAT WOULD OTHERWISE RADIATE BACK OUT INTO SPACE.

SUN

ALTHOUGH PLANTS AND THE OCEANS ABSORB CARBON DIOXIDE, THESE NATURAL PROCESSES CAN'T KEEP UP WITH ALL THE EXTRA CARBON DIOXIDE THAT HUMAN INDUSTRY IS RELEASING. SO THE AMOUNT OF CARBON DIOXIDE IN THE ATMOSPHERE IS ESCALATING ALL THE TIME.

ANY ACTION TO REDUCE CARBON EMISSIONS WAS SEEN AS AN INTOLERABLE THREAT TO THE OIL AND GAS INDUSTRY, AND ESPECIALLY TO THE KOCHS, WITH THEIR OWNERSHIP OF REFINERIES, PIPELINES, COAL SUBSIDIES, COAL-FIRED POWER PLANTS, PETROLEUM COKE MANUFACTURING AND LEASES ON OVER A MILLION ACRES OF UNTAPPED CANADIAN OIL SANDS. KOCH INDUSTRIES ALONE RELEASE OVER 300 MILLION TONS OF CARBON DIOXIDE A YEAR INTO THE ATMOSPHERE.

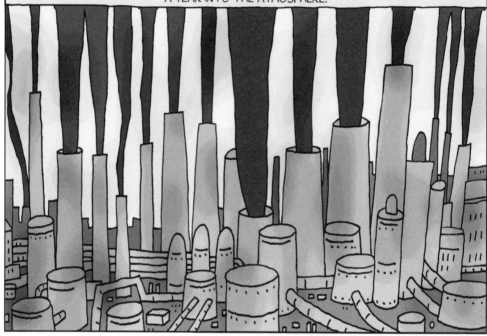

THE KOCHTOPUS AND THEIR ALLIES GOT TO WORK DISCREDITING THE SCIENCE AND ATTACKING CLIMATE SCIENTISTS. THINK TANKS LIKE THE CATO INSTITUTE PRODUCED A STREAM OF REPORTS CLAIMING THAT CLIMATE CHANGE WAS UNPROVEN. BOOKS AND PAPERS WERE WRITTEN BY AUTHORS WHO TESTIFIED IN CONGRESS AND APPEARED ON TALK SHOWS. FOX NEWS AND CONSERVATIVE RADIO HOSTS PORTRAYED CLIMATE SCIENTISTS AS SWINDLERS WHO WERE PUSHING A RADICAL ANTI-AMERICAN AGENDA.

SOCIALISM BY THE BACK DOOR.

IT'S NOT ABOUT SAVING THE PLANET.

RUSH LIMBAUGH

IT'S NOT ABOUT ANYTHING, FOLKS, OTHER THAN RAISING TAXES AND REDISTRIBUTING WEALTH.

ENORMOUS AMOUNTS OF MONEY WERE SPENT IN ORDER TO STOP OBAMA AND THE DEMOCRATS PASSING ANY LEGISLATION THAT WOULD AFFECT OIL INDUSTRY PROFITS. MONEY WAS ALSO SPENT AT STATE LEVEL ON ATTACKS AGAINST WIND POWER, SOLAR POWER AND CARBON POLLUTION REDUCTION PROGRAMMES.

MOST OF THIS MONEY WAS FUNNELLED THROUGH A TAX-EXEMPT NON-PROFIT CALLED DONORS TRUST. THIS HAD BEEN SET UP AS A WAY OF MAINTAINING ANONYMITY FOR ITS WEALTHY CONTRIBUTORS, SO IT LOOKED SUPERFICIALLY AS IF THE MONEY WASN'T COMING FROM THE PETROLEUM INDUSTRY. AS FUNDING FROM TRACEABLE BIG OIL SOURCES DECLINED, THE ANONYMOUS MONEY THAT DONORS TRUST RECEIVED INCREASED SUBSTANTIALLY.

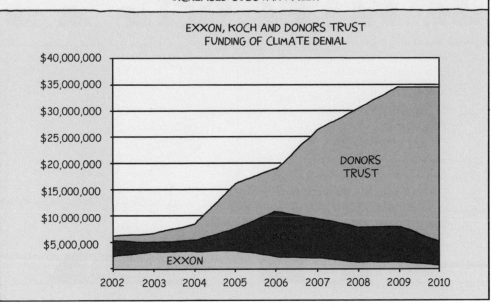

EXXON, KOCH AND DONORS TRUST FUNDING OF CLIMATE DENIAL

THIS FINANCIAL MUSCLE HELPED KILL OBAMA'S CAP AND TRADE BILL (THE AMERICAN CLEAN ENERGY AND SECURITY ACT, 2009) WHICH WOULD HAVE CREATED AN EMISSIONS–TRADING PLAN SIMILAR TO THE EUROPEAN UNION'S EMISSIONS TRADING SCHEME.

THE GOVERNMENT WOULD HAVE SET A LIMIT ON THE AMOUNT OF GREENHOUSE GASES THAT COULD BE EMITTED NATIONALLY (THE CAP). COMPANIES WOULD THEN HAVE BOUGHT PERMITS TO EMIT THESE GASES, CREATING A MARKET IN TRADEABLE PERMITS. THE NUMBER OF PERMITS WOULD BE REDUCED OVER TIME, ENCOURAGING COMPANIES TO INNOVATE.

MANY OF OBAMA'S EFFORTS TO FIGHT CLIMATE CHANGE WERE ROLLED BACK BY HIS SUCCESSOR, INCLUDING THE US BEING A SIGNATORY TO THE 2015 PARIS CLIMATE ACCORD.

THIS WAS A DEAL WHEREBY 179 COUNTRIES AND THE EU AGREED TO KEEP GLOBAL TEMPERATURE INCREASES TO BELOW 2 DEGREES CELSIUS AND 1.5 EGREES, IF POSSIBLE.

IN 2017 PRESIDENT TRUMP WITHDREW THE US FROM THE PARIS ACCORD.

WE DON'T WANT OTHER LEADERS AND OTHER COUNTRIES LAUGHING AT US ANY MORE.

I WAS ELECTED TO REPRESENT THE CITIZENS OF PITTSBURGH, NOT PARIS.

HE MADE NO MENTION OF THE VAST AMOUNT OF MONEY THE REPUBLICAN PARTY HAD RECEIVED FROM BIG OIL INTERESTS.

THE CITIZENS UNITED RULING

THE KOCHS HAD LONG WANTED ANY RESTRICTIONS ON ELECTION SPENDING TO BE ABOLISHED. IN 2010 THEY GOT THEIR WISH. IN A LANDMARK CASE, CITIZENS UNITED, A NON-PROFIT ORGANISATION FUNDED BY THE KOCHS AND OTHERS, SUED THE FEDERAL ELECTION COMMISSION WHICH SET CAMPAIGN FINANCE LAWS AND ELECTION RULES.

THE CASE MADE ITS WAY THROUGH THE LOWER COURTS UNTIL IT WAS GRANTED AN APPEAL BY THE SUPREME COURT. IN A 5-4 RULING, THE JUSTICES STRUCK DOWN AS UNCONSTITUTIONAL A FEDERAL LAW PROHIBITING CORPORATIONS AND UNIONS FROM SPENDING MONEY IN ELECTIONS. THEY ARGUED THAT LIMITS ON POLITICAL SPENDING WERE THE SAME AS BLOCKING FREE SPEECH. IN THEIR VIEW, CORPORATIONS SHOULD HAVE THE SAME RIGHTS AS PEOPLE.

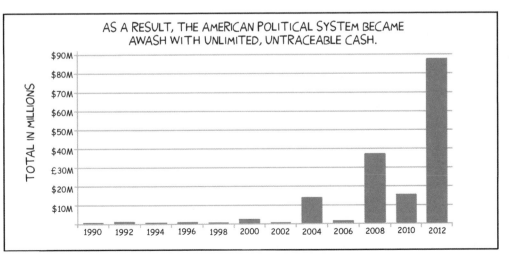

AS A RESULT, THE AMERICAN POLITICAL SYSTEM BECAME AWASH WITH UNLIMITED, UNTRACEABLE CASH.

KOCH INDUSTRY POLLUTION

THE LIST OF ENVIRONMENTAL POLLUTION INCIDENTS IN WHICH KOCH INDUSTRIES HAVE BEEN INVOLVED ARE ALMOST TOO NUMEROUS TO RELATE, BUT HERE ARE A FEW OF THE WORST EXAMPLES.

IN 2013, A LEAK IN A PIPELINE SPILLED 17,000 GALLONS OF CRUDE OIL NEAR AUSTIN, TEXAS. A ROAD WHICH HAD TO BE BUILT FOR THE CLEAN-UP CONTAMINATED LIVESTOCK PONDS.

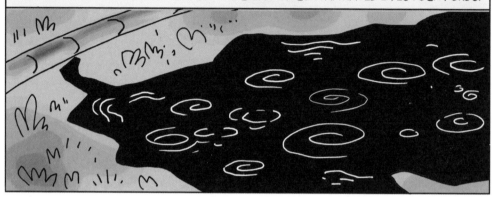

THAT SAME YEAR SUBSIDIARIES OF KOCH CARBON BEGAN ACCUMULATING ENORMOUS PILES OF PETROLEUM COKE, FIVE STOREYS HIGH, IN US CITIES LIKE DETROIT AND CHICAGO, WHERE TOXIC BLACK DUST BLEW OVER NEIGHBOURHOODS AND INTO PEOPLE'S HOMES.

PETROLEUM COKE (OR PETCOKE) IS A BYPRODUCT OF TAR SANDS REFINING. IT IS MORE CARBON-INTENSIVE THAN COAL AND IS TYPICALLY EXPORTED FROM THE USA AND BURNED IN COUNTRIES WHERE THERE IS LITTLE OR NO AIR OR CLIMATE REGULATION.

ONGOING LEGALLY PERMITTED RELEASES OF HAZARDOUS CHEMICALS, INCLUDING BENZENE, SULPHURIC ACID AND HYDROGEN CYANIDE FROM KOCH'S FLINT HILL OIL REFINERY IN CORPUS CHRISTI, TEXAS, ARE THOUGHT TO BE THE CAUSE OF HIGH RATES OF ILLNESS IN THE LOCAL COMMUNITY. RESIDENTS SAY THEY CAN'T DEFINITIVELY PROVE THAT THE REFINERY IS THE ORIGIN OF THE ILLNESSES, BUT MULTIPLE STUDIES BOLSTER THEIR OPINION THAT POPULATIONS LIVING NEAR REFINERIES HAVE ELEVATED RATES OF ASTHMA, LUNG DISEASE, BIRTH DEFECTS AND CANCER.

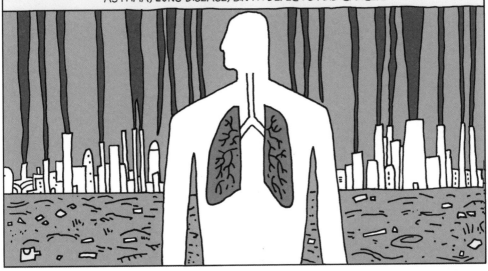

A 2011 COMPLAINT TO THE ENVIRONMENTAL PROTECTION AGENCY, FILED BY PUBLIC EMPLOYEES FOR ENVIRONMENTAL RESPONSIBILITY (PEER) AND OUACHITA RIVERKEEPERS, ALLEGED THAT MILLIONS OF GALLONS OF TOXIC PAPER MILL WASTE WAS BEING DISCHARGED INTO THE COFFEE CREEK RIVER IN CROSSETT, ARKANSAS, BY A KOCH-OWNED GEORGIA-PACIFIC FACILITY. POLLUTION INCLUDED AMMONIA, CHLORIDE AND METALS SUCH AS ZINC, COPPER AND MERCURY. THE COMPLAINT WAS DISMISSED BY THE EPA ON THE GROUNDS THAT COFFEE CREEK WAS SO ENVIRONMENTALLY DEGRADED THAT IT COULD NEVER BE RESTORED AS A BIOLOGICALLY VIABLE RIVER. PEER FIELD DIRECTOR BARRY SULKIN WAS QUOTED AS SAYING: 'NO WONDER THE KOCHS DISLIKE FEDERAL REGULATION. THEY HAVE COVERED COFFEE CREEK WITH SO MUCH FOAM IT SHOULD BE CALLED CAPPUCCINO CREEK.'

IN 2000, THE FLINT HILLS REFINERY IN CORPUS CHRISTI WAS CHARGED WITH COVERING UP THE ILLEGAL RELEASES OF 91 TONS OF THE CARCINOGEN BENZENE. INITIALLY FACING A 97-COUNT INDICTMENT AND POTENTIAL FINES OF $350 MILLION, KOCH INDUSTRIES CUT A DEAL WITH THE THEN ATTORNEY GENERAL, JOHN ASHCROFT, TO DROP ALL MAJOR CHARGES IN EXCHANGE FOR A GUILTY PLEA AND A $20-MILLION SETTLEMENT. A FORMER EMPLOYEE HAD BLOWN THE WHISTLE ON THE COMPANY FOR ALLEGEDLY FALSIFYING ITS EMISSION REPORTS.

ALSO IN 2000, THE EPA FINED KOCH INDUSTRIES $30 MILLION FOR ITS ROLE IN 300 OIL SPILLS THAT RESULTED IN MORE THAN THREE MILLION GALLONS OF CRUDE OIL LEAKING INTO PONDS, LAKES, STREAMS AND COASTAL WATERS.

IN 1999, A KOCH SUBSIDIARY HAD PLEADED GUILTY TO CHARGES THAT IT HAD ALLOWED AVIATION FUEL TO LEAK INTO WATERS NEAR THE MISSISSIPPI RIVER FROM ITS REFINERY IN ROSEMOUNT, MINNESOTA, AND THAT IT HAD ILLEGALLY DUMPED A MILLION GALLONS OF HIGH-AMMONIA WASTEWATER INTO THE GROUND AND INTO THE MISSISSIPPI.

IN 1993, KOCH INDUSTRIES TOOK OFFLINE A 70-MILE STRETCH OF DETERIORATED PIPELINE THAT RAN THROUGH KAUFMAN COUNTY, TEXAS, REPLACING IT WITH A NEW PIPELINE. BUT, AS DEMAND GREW, THE COMPANY REALISED THAT IT COULD MAKE A FURTHER $8 MILLION IN PROFITS ANNUALLY BY PATCHING UP THE OLD PIPELINE AND PUMPING BUTANE THROUGH IT.

THREE YEARS LATER, IN LIVELY, FIFTY MILES SOUTH OF DALLAS, TWO TEENAGERS, DANIELLE SMALLEY AND JASON STONE, NOTICED THE NAUSEATING SMELL OF GAS...

IN AND AROUND THE SMALLEY FAMILY TRAILER. WHERE DANIELLE LIVED WITH HER FATHER DANNY.

AFTER THEY COULD FIND NO SOURCE, THE TEENAGERS DECIDED TO DRIVE TO A NEIGHBOUR'S PLACE AND REPORT A GAS LEAK.

BUT THE PICKUP STALLED A FEW HUNDRED YARDS AWAY, AND WHEN DANIELLE TRIED TO RESTART THE TRUCK...

IT IGNITED A CLOUD OF BUTANE GAS, SETTING OFF AN EXPLOSION THAT SCORCHED MORE THAN A DOZEN ACRES OF LAND AND SENT FLAMES HUNDREDS OF FEET INTO THE AIR.

BOTH TEENAGERS WERE BURNED ALIVE. THEY RAN FROM THE TRUCK ON FIRE, FALLING TO THE GROUND IN A FOETAL POSITION. THEIR HAIR AND CLOTHES INCINERATED. DANIELLE'S FATHER WAS UNABLE TO TELL WHICH WAS HIS DAUGHTER'S BODY.

DURING THE ENSUING COURT CASE, TED LYON, THE LAWYER REPRESENTING DANNY SMALLEY AGAINST KOCH INDUSTRIES, PROJECTED A CLOCK ON A SCREEN IN ORDER TO DEMONSTRATE TO THE JURORS THE LONG 60 SECONDS IT TOOK FOR THE TEENAGERS TO DIE IN AGONY.

THERE IS NO MORE HORRIBLE DEATH THAN A BURN DEATH. THERE IS NO MORE HORRIBLE WAY TO LOSE SOMEONE THAN TO SEE THEM BURN TO DEATH IN FRONT OF YOUR EYES.

AS THE CASE WAS BEING PREPARED, TED LYON DISCOVERED THAT KOCH INDUSTRIES WAS HAVING DANNY SMALLEY FOLLOWED.

THE LAWYER HIRED HIS OWN PRIVATE DETECTIVE TO FOLLOW KOCH'S INVESTIGATOR...

WHO WAS THEN SUBPOENAED ONCE HIS IDENTITY HAD BEEN DISCOVERED.

YOU'VE BEEN SERVED.

LYON ALSO HIRED A SECURITY FIRM TO SWEEP FOR LISTENING DEVICES IN HIS OFFICE.

THERE WERE THINGS DURING THE CASE THAT NO ONE ELSE WOULD HAVE KNOWN ABOUT, BUT SOMEHOW THEY (KOCH INDUSTRIES) KNEW ABOUT IT.

TED LYON

THE SECURITY CONSULTANTS DISCOVERED THAT A TRANSMITTER HAD BEEN PLANTED SET TO BROADCAST ON AN FM FREQUENCY.

I'M NOT SAYING THAT THE KOCHS DID IT. I JUST THOUGHT IT WAS VERY INTERESTING THAT IT HAPPENED DURING THE TIME WE WERE LITIGATING THAT CASE.

THEY DID EVERYTHING THEY COULD TO INTIMIDATE US. IT WAS BATTLE AFTER BATTLE AFTER BATTLE.

IT WAS A WAR LYON WON. ON 22 OCTOBER 1999, THE JURY AWARDED DANNY SMALLEY $296 MILLION IN DAMAGES, THE LARGEST WRONGFUL DEATH AWARD IN US HISTORY UP TO THAT POINT.

MONEY TO THEM IS BLOOD. THAT'S ALL IT IS. THAT'S THEIR LIFE FORCE, IS MONEY. THE ONLY WAY I CAN HURT THEM IS TO TAKE THEM FOR EVERY PENNY I CAN GET.

DANNY SMALLEY

IN 2002, SMALLEY ESTABLISHED THE DANIELLE SMALLEY FOUNDATION IN HONOUR OF HIS DAUGHTER.

THE FOUNDATION DOES WORK EDUCATING FIRST RESPONDERS AND THE GENERAL PUBLIC ABOUT THE DANGERS OF OIL AND GAS LEAKS.

THE BIG KOCH OIL THEFT

IN 2001 ANOTHER LONG-STANDING SUIT AGAINST KOCH INDUSTRIES CAME TO AN END. BILL KOCH, STILL ANGRY OVER HOW, IN HIS BELIEF, HE AND HIS BROTHER FREDERICK HAD BEEN CHEATED IN THE SALE OF THEIR COMPANY STOCK ALMOST 20 YEARS EARLIER, HAD BROUGHT A SERIES OF LEGAL ACTIONS AGAINST KOCH INDUSTRIES.

ONE OF THESE LAWSUITS WAS OVER THE ALLEGED COMPANY PRACTICE OF STEALING OIL FROM FEDERAL AND NATIVE AMERICAN LANDS.

KOCH INDUSTRIES WAS THE INTERMEDIARY IN THESE TRANSACTIONS, BUYING OIL FROM WELL OWNERS AND SELLNG IT ON TO REFINERIES.

HERE'S HOW THE THEFT WORKED. A KOCH EMPLOYEE (A GAUGER) WOULD MEASURE THE VOLUME AND QUALITY OF THE OIL THE KOCHS WERE BUYING.

THEN THEY WOULD LEAVE A 'RUN TICKET' - A RECORD OF THE AMOUNT OF OIL REMOVED. THIS WORKED AS AN IOU TO THE WELL OWNER.

DEAR WELL OWNER,

WE OWE YOU PAYMENT FOR 15,000 BARRELS OF OIL.

YOUR PALS
KOCH INDUSTRIES

WHAT KOCH WAS DOING WAS TAKING ALL THESE MEASUREMENTS AND THEN FALSIFYING THEM ON THE RUN SHEETS.

IF THE DIPSTICK MEASURED FIVE FEET 10 INCHES AND ONE HALF-INCH, THEN THEY WOULD WRITE DOWN FIVE FEET NINE AND ONE HALF-INCHES.

THAT MAY NOT SEEM LIKE MUCH, BUT THE AMOUNTS ADDED UP.

WELL, THAT WAS THE BEAUTY OF THE SCHEME.

BECAUSE IF THEY'RE BUYING OIL FROM 50,000 DIFFERENT PEOPLE AND THEY'RE STEALING TWO BARRELS FROM EACH PERSON...

WHAT DOES THAT ADD UP TO? ONE YEAR, THEIR DATA SHOWED THEY STOLE A MILLION AND HALF BARRELS OF OIL.

JAMES SPALDING, KOCH INDUSTRY GAUGER, TOLD THE COURT...

I FEEL I'M UP HERE TELLING THE WORLD THAT I WAS A THIEF, AND AT THE TIME I THOUGHT I WAS DOING THE RIGHT THING.

ANOTHER FORMER KOCH OIL GAUGER, L.B. PERRY, SAID...

I HAD TO DO WHAT THEY TOLD ME TO DO OR I WOULDN'T HAVE A JOB.

THE JURY FOUND KOCH INDUSTRIES GUILTY OF NEARLY 20,000 FALSE CLAIMS. KOCH FACED A POTENTIAL PENALTY OF MORE THAN $200 MILLION.

THE ISSUE WAS RESOLVED IN 2001 WHEN BILL KOCH AND KOCH INDUSTRIES ANNOUNCED AN END TO ALL THEIR LEGAL DISPUTES. THE SETTLEMENT CALLED FOR KOCH INDUSTRIES TO PAY $25 MILLION IN PENALTIES TO THE US GOVERNMENT FOR IMPROPERLY TAKING OIL.

$7.4 MILLION OF THIS PAYOUT WENT TO BILL KOCH FOR BRINGING THE LAWSUIT. KOCH INDUSTRIES ALSO PAID BILL'S LEGAL FEES, ESTIMATED AT $25 MILLION.

THE AGREEMENT INCLUDED SIGNIFICANT FINANCIAL PENALTIES IF EITHER SIDE BREACHED THE PEACE ACCORD. THIS ENDED THE 20-YEAR KOCH FAMILY FEUD.

CRIMINAL JUSTICE REFORM

BOTH DAVID AND CHARLES KOCH HAVE LONG BEEN INTERESTED IN CRIMINAL JUSTICE REFORM. FOR A DECADE CHARLES HAS MADE CONTRIBUTIONS AMOUNTING TO SEVEN FIGURES TO THE NATIONAL ASSOCIATION OF CRIMINAL DEFENCE LAWYERS, MONEY THAT HAS BEEN USED TO PROVIDE LAWYERS FOR POOR DEFENDANTS. THE REFORMS FOR WHICH THEY HAVE ADVOCATED INCLUDE EASING THE EMPLOYMENT PROCESS FOR REHABILITATED PERSONS, AND THE DEFENCE OF PRIVATE PROPERTY FROM ASSET-FORFEITURE. THE KOCHS BELIEVE THAT THE SYSTEM HAS UNFAIRLY TARGETED LOW-INCOME AND MINORITY COMMUNITIES.

OVER THE PAST GENERATION, THE PRISON POPULATION OF THE UNITED STATES HAS BOOMED FROM 500,000 IN 1960 TO MORE THAN 2.3 MILLION TODAY. THAT'S MORE THAN ONE IN A HUNDRED ADULTS. IT IS THE HIGHEST RATE OF INCARCERATION IN THE WORLD. AMERICA NOW HOSTS 25 PER CENT OF THE WORLD'S PRISONERS, EVEN THOUGH AMERICANS MAKE UP LESS THAN FIVE PER CENT OF THE WORLD'S POPULATION.

THE KOCHS ARGUE THAT REFORM OF THE CRIMINAL JUSTICE SYSTEM WILL REDUCE THE PRISON POPULATION, SAVING TAXPAYERS BILLIONS OF DOLLARS.

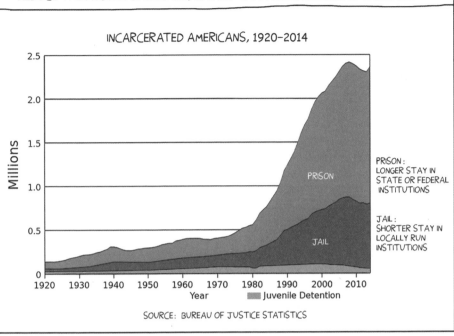

INCARCERATED AMERICANS, 1920–2014

PRISON: LONGER STAY IN STATE OR FEDERAL INSTITUTIONS

JAIL: SHORTER STAY IN LOCALLY RUN INSTITUTIONS

Juvenile Detention

SOURCE: BUREAU OF JUSTICE STATISTICS

THEIR INTENTION IS TO SHIFT THE CRIMINAL JUSTICE SYSTEM AWAY FROM PUNISHMENT AND TOWARDS REHABILITATION. THE KOCHS' INTEREST IN THIS SUBJECT HAS PUZZLED MANY OBSERVERS, AS REFORMS LIKE THESE ARE USUALLY CONSIDERED TO BE LIBERAL AIMS, NOT ASSOCIATED WITH THE POLITICAL RIGHT.

WHY WOULD TWO BILLIONAIRES WHO HAVE BENEFITED SO MUCH FROM POLLUTING THE AIR PEOPLE BREATHE AND THE WATER THEY DRINK...

BE SO CONCERNED ABOUT CRIMINAL JUSTICE REFORM?

AFTER ALL, THE KOCHS HAVE AIDED THE CAMPAIGN TO TAKE AFFORDABLE HEALTH-CARE FROM MILLIONS OF AMERICANS.

THEY HAVE ALSO FUNDED POLITICIANS WHO HAVE PASSED LAWS ATTACKING UNION POWER, MAKING IT EASIER FOR EMPLOYERS TO...

DRIVE DOWN WAGES AND DEGRADE WORKING CONDITIONS.

IN NO OTHER AREA HAVE THE KOCHS SHOWN ANY INTEREST IN ALLEVIATING THE INJUSTICES CAUSED BY WEALTH INEQUALITY. SO WHY THIS?

ARRRGH!

HOWEVER, THE KOCHS' INTEREST IN CRIMINAL JUSTICE REFORM MAKES PERFECT SENSE IF YOU LOOK AT IT FROM A LIBERTARIAN PERSPECTIVE.

GIVE ME FREEDOM.

LIBERTARIANISM

AS LONG-TIME LIBERTARIANS, THEY SEE MASS INCARCERATION AS A STATE OVERREACH PROBLEM.

HI.

BIG GOV

FROM THEIR POINT OF VIEW, CRIMINAL JUSTICE REFORM IS MORE ABOUT CURBING THE POWER OF GOVERNMENT THAN HELPING ORDINARY AMERICANS.

GOVERNMENT POWER IS EVIL EVEN IF IT HELPS PEOPLE.

THE POLITICAL RIGHT HAVE GIVEN ME THE FREEDOM TO STARVE TO DEATH WITHOUT HEALTH-CARE.

WILL WORK FOR FOOD

CHARLES KOCH HAS SAID THAT HE BECAME INTERESTED IN CRIMINAL JUSTICE REFORM AFTER A GRAND JURY 1995 INDICTMENT OF A KOCH REFINERY IN TEXAS FOR 97 FELONY VIOLATIONS OF ENVIRONMENTAL LAW. THE COMPANY SPENT SIX YEARS FIGHTING THE CHARGES, EVENTUALLY SETTLING WITH THE GOVERNMENT FOR $10 MILLION.

CRITICS OF THE KOCHS SAY THAT LIMITING THE LAW IS JUST ANOTHER WAY OF ADVANCING THE COMPANY'S INTERESTS. FOR THEM. PROMOTING CRIMINAL JUSTICE REFORM IS GOOD PUBLIC RELATIONS THAT DISTRACTS FROM THE ENVIRONMENTAL DAMAGE THEY DO.

IT PUTS A KIND FACE ON THE KOCHS' ATTEMPTS TO GUT MEDICAID...

WHEN THEY SAID THEY WERE GOING TO CUT MEDICAID, I THOUGHT THEY JUST MEANT FOR BLACK PEOPLE, NOT ME.

ABOLISH SOCIAL SECURITY...

I'M FREER EVERY DAY...THANKS TO THESE RICH LIBERTARIAN GUYS.

AND ERODE WORKERS' RIGHTS.

I'D LIKE A SAFE WORKING ENVIRONMENT AND FAIR PAY.

YOU'RE FIRED.

BUT ALSO ANYTHING THAT WEAKENS GOVERNMENT POWER IS GOOD FOR KOCH INDUSTRIES' BOTTOM LINE. PART OF THEIR AGENDA WOULD MAKE IT HARDER TO PROSECUTE VIOLATIONS OF ENVIRONMENTAL AND CORPORATE LAWS THAT PROTECT THE PUBLIC.

BIG GOV

BILL KOCH

AFTER BEING FIRED FROM KOCH INDUSTRIES, BILL KOCH FOUNDED OXBOW CARBON IN 1983. THIS IS A COMPANY THAT PRIMARILY BUYS AND RESELLS PETROLEUM COKE. PET COKE IS USED IN COAL-BURNING POWER GENERATORS, EITHER IN POWER PLANTS OR IN THE CEMENT, IRON OR STEEL BUSINESSES. THIS MAKES IT A DIRECT COMPETITOR OF KOCH INDUSTRIES, ALBEIT IN A SMALL WAY.

AN ENTHUSIASTIC SAILOR, BILL WON THE AMERICA'S CUP IN 1992 WITH THE YACHT *AMERICA 3*, BEATING AN ITALIAN TEAM BY 44 SECONDS. ALTHOUGH AN AMATEUR, BILL SAILED ON THE YACHT HIMSELF, SUPPORTED BY VETERAN SAILORS. THE WIN CONSUMED A YEAR AND A HALF OF BILL'S LIFE AND $68.5 MILLION OF HIS FORTUNE.

BILL USED THE SAME ALL-OR-NOTHING TACTICS TO WIN THE AMERICA'S CUP THAT HE USED IN BUSINESS.

THIS IS MORE THAN THE GENTLEMANLY SPORT IT USED TO BE. THIS IS WAR.

THESE TACTICS INCLUDED SPYING ON RIVAL TEAMS. THE *GUZZINI*, A 30-FOOT SPEEDBOAT, FULL OF ELECTRONIC SURVEILLANCE GEAR, CRUISED THE WATERS AROUND SAN DIEGO.

HELICOPTERS WERE USED TO KEEP TRACK OF AND PHOTOGRAPH COMPETITORS.

DIVERS WERE SENT TO STUDY THE KEELS OF RIVAL YACHTS, USING REBREATHERS SO THAT TELLTALE BUBBLES WOULDN'T GIVE THEM AWAY.

BILL'S TEAM WAS SAID TO HAVE SPENT $2 MILLION ON INTELLIGENCE AND COUNTER-ESPIONAGE ACTIVITIES.

AFTER 1992, AMERICA'S CUP OFFICIALS INSTITUTED A NEW REGULATION TO CURB FUTURE SPYING, WHICH WAS UNOFFICIALLY KNOWN AS THE BILL KOCH RULE.

A KEEN WINE COLLECTOR, BILL KOCH WAS DUPED A NUMBER OF TIMES INTO BUYING COUNTERFEIT WINE. IN RETALIATION, HE HAS WITH TYPICAL TENACITY TARGETED THOSE TRADING IN FAKE VINTAGE WINE, BRINGING SEVERAL HIGH-PROFILE LAWSUITS AGAINST CULPRITS.

ONE OF THESE TARGETS WAS SILICON VALLEY ENTREPRENEUR ERIC GREENBERG, WHO BILL KOCH ALLEGED KNOWINGLY SOLD HIM TWO DOZEN BOTTLES OF FAKE BORDEAUX. THE WINE'S VINTAGES RANGED FROM 1864 TO 1950. THE PRICE: $355,000.

ON LEARNING THAT THE WINE WAS COUNTERFEIT, GREENBERG OFFERED TO REIMBURSE BILL.

I'LL PAY IT BACK.

BUT BILL REFUSED THE OFFER. HE WANTED TO MAKE AN EXAMPLE OF GREENBERG.

I'LL SEE YOU IN COURT.

BILL WAS EVENTUALLY AWARDED $1.15 MILLION, INCLUDING $711,622 IN PUNITIVE DAMAGES.

I ABSOLUTELY CAN'T STAND TO BE CHEATED.

APART FROM BOATS, ART AND WINE, BILL KOCH IS ALSO A COLLECTOR OF AMERICAN WESTERN MEMORABILIA.

IN 2011, HE BOUGHT AT AUCTION A 130-YEAR-OLD PHOTO OF THE OUTLAW BILLY THE KID FOR $2.3 MILLION.

HE HAS BUILT A 50-BUILDING REPLICA OF A WESTERN TOWN AT HIS 4,500-ACRE BEAR RANCH PROPERTY IN PAONIA, COLORADO.

THE TOWN STRUCTURE LARGELY CAME FROM A DECOMMISSIONED MGM STUDIOS TOURIST ATTRACTION.

IT FEATURES FIVE SALOONS, A BANK, A CHURCH AND A BROTHEL (CONVERTED INTO GUEST ROOMS).

> IT ALL GETS BACK TO TRYING TO CREATE A PLACE WHERE I CAN ENJOY LIFE AND ENJOY MY FAMILY AND FRIENDS WITHOUT HAVING TO WORRY ABOUT MY ENEMIES. AND I'M DOING IT BECAUSE I CAN.

FREDERICK KOCH

AFTER SELLING HIS SHARES IN KOCH INDUSTRIES TO CHARLES AND DAVID, FREDERICK LIVED A QUIET BUT OPULENT LIFE AWAY FROM THE PUBLIC SPOTLIGHT. HE BUILT UP AN ENORMOUS COLLECTION OF RARE BOOKS, FINE ART AND OPERA MANUSCRIPTS.

IN THE 1980s HE FUNDED THE REFURBISHMENT OF SHAKESPEARE'S SWAN THEATRE IN STRATFORD-UPON-AVON. HE HAS DONATED TO PERMANENT COLLECTIONS AT THE FRICK COLLECTION, THE PIERPOINT MORGAN LIBRARY AND THE CARNEGIE MUSEUM OF ART.

IN 2010, THE *NEW YORKER* REPORTED THAT FREDRICK HAD MOVED TO MONACO, WHICH HAS NO TAX. HE OWNS PROPERTIES IN NEW YORK AND ACROSS EUROPE, INCLUDING AN AUSTRIAN HUNTING LODGE AND A FRENCH VILLA.

DAVID KOCH

IN FEBRUARY 1991, DAVID KOCH BOARDED A USAIR BOEING 737-300 FLIGHT IN COLUMBUS, OHIO, BOUND FOR LOS ANGELES. THE PLANE CRASHED ON LANDING AT LAX INTO A METROLINER TURBOPROP AIRCRAFT. THE ACCIDENT WAS CAUSED BY AN AIR TRAFFIC CONTROL ERROR AND NEGLIGENCE. THE METROLINER, A SKYWEST FLIGHT, HAD BEEN TOLD TO TAXI INTO TAKEOFF POSITION WHILE THE USAIR FLIGHT WAS LANDING ON THE SAME RUNWAY.

ALL 12 PEOPLE ON THE SMALLER PLANE WERE KILLED. TWENTY-THREE OF THE 89 PEOPLE ON THE BOEING DIED. THE BOEING SLID OFF THE RUNWAY, DRAGGING THE MANGLED REMAINS OF THE TURBOPROP WITH IT, THEN IT SLAMMED INTO A STAND OF MAINTENANCE BUILDINGS AT 60 MILES AN HOUR. BOTH AIRCRAFT WERE ENGULFED IN FLAMES.

STRUGGLING THROUGH THE SMOKE-FILLED BOEING, DAVID KOCH MANAGED TO FIND AN EXIT AT THE FRONT OF THE AIRCRAFT FROM WHERE HE JUMPED ONTO THE TARMAC. HE SPENT TWO DAYS IN INTENSIVE CARE SUFFERING FROM LUNG DAMAGE.

THIS MAY SOUND ODD. BUT I FELT THIS EXPERIENCE WAS VERY SPIRITUAL – THAT I WAS SAVED WHEN ALL THOSE OTHERS DIED.

I FELT THAT THE GOOD LORD SPARED MY LIFE FOR A PURPOSE. AND SINCE THEN I'VE BEEN BUSY DOING ALL THE GOOD WORKS I CAN THINK OF.

DAVID PAID FOR THE RENOVATION OF THE NEW YORK STATE THEATRE, (NOW THE DAVID H. KOCH THEATRE) AT A PRICE TAG OF $100 MILLION. HIS MONEY ALSO RENOVATED THE FOUNTAINS OUTSIDE THE METROPOLITAN MUSEUM OF ART AT A COST OF $10 MILLION.

HIS INTEREST IN THE ARTS LED HIM TO BECOME A TRUSTEE OF THE AMERICAN BALLET THEATRE. HE ALSO SAT ON THE BOARD OF THE TRUSTEES OF WGBH–TV, WHICH PRODUCES TWO-THIRDS OF THE PROGRAMMES BROADCAST BY THE PUBLIC BROADCASTING SERVICE (PBS).

IN 1992, DAVID KOCH WAS DIAGNOSED WITH PROSTATE CANCER. SINCE THEN HE IS SAID TO HAVE CONTRIBUTED AT LEAST $395 MILLION TO MEDICAL RESEARCH AND INSTITUTIONS. HE WAS ON THE BOARD OF DIRECTORS OF THE PROSTATE CANCER FOUNDATION, TO WHICH HE CONTRIBUTED $41 MILLION, INCLUDING $5 MILLION TO THE EMERGING FIELD OF NANOTECHNOLOGY.

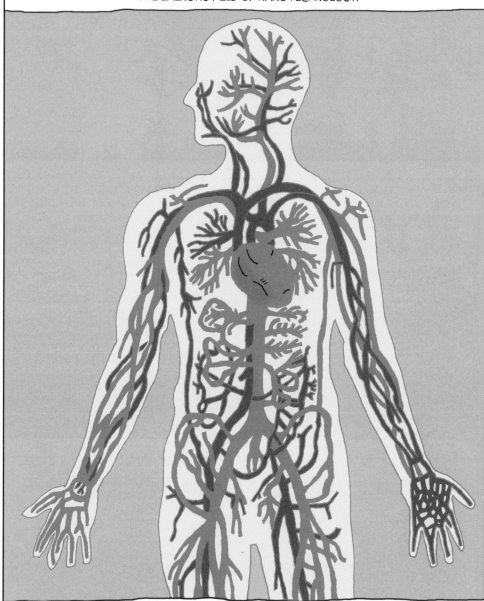

HE GAVE $20 MILLION TO THE JOHNS HOPKINS UNIVERSITY SCHOOL OF MEDICINE IN BALTIMORE. HE MADE A $100-MILLION DONATION TO ESTABLISH THE DAVID H. KOCH INSTITUTE FOR INTEGRATIVE CANCER RESEARCH AT THE MASSACHUSETTS INSTITUTE OF TECHNOLOGY, WHILE $66 MILLION WENT TO THE MEMORIAL SLOAN KETTERING HOSPITAL IN NEW YORK. THESE ARE JUST A FEW EXAMPLES OF HIS PHILANTHROPY.

DAVID KOCH'S FUNDING OF EDUCATION INCLUDED A $20-MILLION GIFT TO THE AMERICAN MUSEUM OF NATURAL HISTORY IN NEW YORK.

MONEY WHICH CREATED THE DAVID H. KOCH DINOSAUR WING.

HE ALSO DONATED $15 MILLION TO THE NATIONAL MUSEUM OF NATURAL HISTORY IN WASHINGTON...

TO BUILD THE DAVID H. KOCH HALL OF HUMAN ORIGINS.

THIS LAST EXHIBIT CAUSED CONTROVERSY BECAUSE IT DOWNPLAYED THE DANGERS OF CLIMATE CHANGE...

BY SUGGESTING THAT MODERN CIVILISATION IS CAPABLE OF ADAPTING TO CLIMATE CHANGE AS EARLY HUMANS DID IN THE REMOTE PAST.

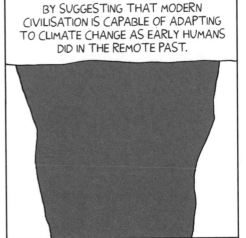

THE EXHIBITION CONFLATES TWO VERY DIFFERENT THINGS. THE NATURAL CLIMATE CHANGES THAT AFFECTED THE SMALL NUMBER OF HUMANS AND PRE-HUMANS IN THE DISTANT PAST, WHICH TOOK PLACE OVER HUNDREDS OF THOUSANDS OF YEARS, AND TODAY, WHEN SEVEN BILLION PEOPLE WILL HAVE TO DEAL WITH RAPID HUMAN-CAUSED CLIMATE CHANGE OVER A PERIOD OF DECADES.

UNLIKE MANY ON THE POLITICAL RIGHT, DAVID KOCH DOES NOT DISPUTE THE REALITY OF CLIMATE CHANGE. IN AN INTERVIEW FOR THE *NEW YORK MAGAZINE*, HE EXPOUNDED ON HOW HE BELIEVED CLIMATE CHANGE MIGHT BE GOOD FOR THE PLANET, SAYING, 'THE EARTH WILL BE ABLE TO SUPPORT MORE PEOPLE BECAUSE A FAR GREATER AREA WILL BE ABLE TO PRODUCE FOOD.'

HE DOESN'T APPEAR TO HAVE CONSIDERED HOW MUCH LAND MIGHT BE LOST.

CHARLES KOCH

CHARLES KOCH CONTINUED TO SUPPORT LIBERTARIAN AND FREE-ENTERPRISE POLICY ADVOCACY ORGANISATIONS. FOR HIM, THE ENEMY WAS STILL THE GOVERNMENT.

IN AN APRIL 2014 *WALL STREET JOURNAL* OPINION EDITORIAL, HE WROTE...

THE FUNDAMENTAL CONCEPTS OF DIGNITY, RESPECT, EQUALITY BEFORE THE LAW...

AND PERSONAL FREEDOMS ARE UNDER ATTACK BY THE NATION'S OWN GOVERNMENT.

HE HAD ONLY DISDAIN FOR BILLIONAIRES, SUCH AS WARREN BUFFET AND GEORGE SOROS, WHO WERE ON THE POLITICAL LEFT.

THEY SIMPLY HAVEN'T BEEN SUFFICIENTLY EXPOSED TO THE IDEA OF LIBERTY.

CHARLES IS AN OUTSPOKEN CRITIC OF CORPORATE WELFARE – A TERM OFTEN USED TO DESCRIBE A GOVERNMENT'S BESTOWING OF MONEY, GRANTS OR OTHER SPECIAL TREATMENT FOR CORPORATIONS.

THE FIRST THING WE'VE GOT TO GET RID OF IS BUSINESS WELFARE AND ENTITLEMENTS.

SINCE 2003 CHARLES AND DAVID HAVE ORGANISED SEMI-ANNUAL CONFERENCES TO PROMOTE THEIR POLITICS AND RAISE FUNDS.

THESE EVENTS ARE HIGHLY SECRETIVE. PARTICIPANTS ARE TOLD TO DESTROY ALL PAPERWORK.

ELABORATE SECURITY STEPS ARE TAKEN TO ENSURE THAT BOTH THE PARTICIPANTS' NAMES AND THE MEETINGS' AGENDAS ARE KEPT SECRET.

iPODS, PHONES, CAMERAS AND OTHER RECORDING DEVICES ARE CONFISCATED BEFORE THE SESSIONS.

HEY!

AUDIO-TECHNICIANS PLANT WHITE-NOISE-EMITTING LOUDSPEAKERS AROUND THE PERIMETER OF THE CONVENTION'S LOCATION, FACING OUTWARD, TO STOP EAVESDROPPING.

NEITHER THE AMOUNT OF MONEY RAISED NOR THE NAMES OF THE DONORS ARE PUBLICLY DISCLOSED. EACH ATTENDEE GIVES AT LEAST $100,000 ANNUALLY. THE MONEY IS USED TO FUND SCHOLARSHIPS, STARTUP COMPANY INVESTMENTS, INSTITUTIONS AND POLITICAL AND POLICY GROUPS.

HOWEVER, SOME OF THE CONFERENCE ATTENDEES' NAMES HAVE BEEN LEAKED. THEY INCLUDE...

ROBERT MERCER, EX-CEO OF THE HEDGE FUND RENAISSANCE TECHNOLOGIES.

NET WORTH $125 MILLION.

MERCER WAS INVOLVED IN THE CAMPAIGN TO PULL THE UK OUT OF THE EUROPEAN UNION IN THE REFERENDUM OF 2016.

HE WAS ALLEGED TO HAVE DONATED TO THE LEAVE CAMPAIGN THE SERVICES OF HIS POLITICAL CONSULTING FIRM CAMBRIDGE ANALYTICA, WHICH USED DATA MINED FROM THE SOCIAL MEDIA COMPANY FACEBOOK.

HE IS A MAJOR DONOR TO US RIGHT-WING CAUSES...

SUCH AS THE FAR-RIGHT OPINION AND COMMENTARY WEBSITE *BREITBART NEWS*.

PAUL SINGER OF THE HEDGE FUND, ELLIOT MANAGEMENT CORPORATION.

NET WORTH $2.8 BILLION.

ELLIOTT MANAGEMENT IS WHAT CRITICS OF SUCH FINANCIAL COMPANIES CALL A 'VULTURE FUND'.

A VULTURE FUND IS A COMPANY THAT BUYS DISTRESSED DEBT IN ECONOMICALLY FAILING COUNTRIES AT A DISCOUNT...

AFTER WHICH IT TAKES AGGRESSIVE LEGAL ACTION TO FORCE IMPOVERISHED COUNTRIES TO PAY UP.

KEN LANGONE, CO-FOUNDER OF HOME DEPOT, THE AMERICAN HOME IMPROVEMENT SUPPLY CHAIN.

NET WORTH, $3.5 BILLION.

RICHARD STRONG, FOUNDER OF THE MUTUAL FUND, STRONG CAPITAL MANAGEMENT.

STRONG WAS BANNED FOR LIFE FROM THE FINANCIAL INDUSTRY AFTER AN INVESTIGATION INTO IMPROPER TRADING.

HE PERSONALLY PAID A $66 MILLION FINE. HIS COMPANY PAID A FURTHER $115 MILLION.

NET WORTH AFTER FINE, $800 MILLION.

RICHARD DeVOS, CO-FOUNDER OF AMWAY.

THE DeVOS FAMILY. NET WORTH, $5.3 BILLION.

AMWAY IS A COMPANY THAT SPECIALISES IN THE USES OF MULTI-LEVEL MARKETING TO SELL BEAUTY AND HOME CARE PRODUCTS.

MAKE MONEY FROM HOME.

IN 1982 DeVOS PLEADED GUILTY TO DEFRAUDING THE CANADIAN GOVERNMENT OF $22 MILLION IN CUSTOMS DUTIES.

IT WAS A MISUNDERSTANDING.

IN 2010, AMWAY AGREED TO PAY $56 MILLION TO SETTLE A CLASS ACTION LAWSUIT THAT ALLEGED IT WAS A PYRAMID SCHEME.

WE'VE MADE CHANGES TO OUR BUSINESS PRACTICES SINCE THEN.

RICHARD DeVOS'S DAUGHTER-IN-LAW, BETSY DeVOS, IS ALSO A MAJOR KOCH DONOR.

AN EX-CHAIR OF THE MICHIGAN REPUBLICAN PARTY, SHE WAS APPOINTED TRUMP'S SECRETARY OF EDUCATION IN 2017.

I'M IN CHARGE.

THERE ARE ONLY A FEW WOMEN ON THE KOCH DONOR LIST. THE MAJORITY OF THE DONORS ARE MALE AND WHITE.

SOME HAVE MADE THEIR OWN MONEY, BUT MANY HAVE INHERITED VAST FORTUNES WHICH THEY ARE INTENT ON PRESERVING.

MUCH LIKE THE KOCHS THEMSELVES.

SPEAKERS AT THE KOCH CONFERENCES HAVE INCLUDED SOME OF THE MOST INFLUENTIAL FIGURES ON THE RIGHT.

AND OUR NEXT SPEAKER IS...

EX-FOX NEWS PRESENTER GLENN BECK.

TALK SHOW HOST RUSH LIMBAUGH.

SUPREME COURT JUSTICE ANTONIN SCALIA.

SUPREME COURT JUSTICE CLARENCE THOMAS.

PULITZER PRIZE-WINNING *WASHINGTON POST* COLUMNIST CHARLES KRAUTHAMMER.

UNITED STATES SENATOR FOR SOUTH CAROLINA, JIM DeMINT.

THE 48TH VICE PRESIDENT OF THE UNITED STATES, MIKE PENCE.

THE 54TH SPEAKER OF THE UNITED STATES HOUSE OF REPRESENTATIVES, PAUL RYAN.

SINCE THE 1970s THE KOCH BROTHERS HAVE SPENT MILLIONS BUILDING THEIR SPRAWLING NETWORK OF THINK TANKS...

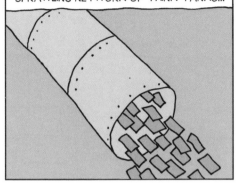

MAGAZINES, ADVOCACY GROUPS, SEMINARS AND EDUCATIONAL COURSES, DEVOTED TO LIBERTARIAN CAUSES.

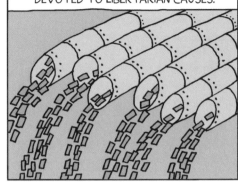

YET, DESPITE ALL THE MONEY SPENT, THEY HAVEN'T ALWAYS GOT THE RESULTS THEY WANTED.

THE KOCHS DID NOT SUPPORT DONALD TRUMP IN THE 2016 PRESIDENTIAL ELECTION.

KOCH-FRIENDLY CANDIDATES SUCH AS SCOTT WALKER, JEB BUSH AND MARCO RUBIO WERE EASILY SWEPT ASIDE BY THE REAL-ESTATE DEVELOPER.

TRUMP WON ON A PLATFORM OF ANTI-IMMIGRATION AND ANTI-FREE TRADE THAT WAS ANATHEMA TO THE KOCHS.

ASKED PRIOR TO THE ELECTION HIS THOUGHTS ON DEMOCRATIC PARTY CANDIDATE HILLARY CLINTON AND REPUBLICAN CANDIDATE DONALD TRUMP, CHARLES SAID...

IF I HAD TO VOTE FOR CANCER OR HEART ATTACK, WHY WOULD I VOTE FOR EITHER?

IN JUNE 2018, DAVID KOCH ANNOUNCED THAT HE WAS STEPPING DOWN FROM HIS POSITION AS EXECUTIVE VICE-PRESIDENT OF KOCH INDUSTRIES.

ILL HEALTH HAD OBLIGED THE 78-YEAR-OLD TO RETIRE FROM ALL INVOLVEMENT WITH THE COMPANY AND THE KOCH NETWORK.

THIS LEFT CHARLES KOCH, THEN 84, IN SOLE CHARGE OF THE FAMILY FIRM.

SOME MIGHT SAY THIS ONLY REVEALED WHAT HAD BEEN TRUE FROM THE BEGINNING: THAT CHARLES WAS, AND HAD ALWAYS BEEN, THE KING.

CHARLES, AFTER INHERITING BILLIONS, HAD TAKEN HIS FATHER'S COMPANY AND TURNED IT INTO A COLOSSAL MONEY-MAKING-MACHINE, VAST SUMS OF WHICH HE AND HIS BROTHER THEN USED TO RESHAPE AMERICAN POLITICS FOR THEIR OWN PURPOSES.

BUT IN THE END, INSTEAD OF USHERING IN THE LIBERTARIAN, SMALL GOVERNMENT, FREE-MARKET ERA THEY HAD LONG DREAMED OF, THEY HAVE ONLY HELPED WEAKEN THE DEMOCRATIC SAFEGUARDS THAT HAD PREVIOUSLY KEPT AT BAY WOULD-BE DEMAGOGUES LIKE DONALD TRUMP, WITH A FLOOD OF MONEY THAT HAS CORRUPTED THE ENTIRE POLITICAL SYSTEM.

THE REPUBLICAN PARTY HAS BEEN TRANSFORMED BY THIS PROCESS INTO AN ANTI-DEMOCRATIC AUTHORITARIAN PARTY, WILLING TO SUPPRESS VOTES AND TURN A BLIND EYE TO FOREIGN INTERFERENCE IN US ELECTIONS.

THE KOCHS ARE NOT JUST POLLUTERS WHO HAVE PUSHED THE WORLD CLOSE TO ENVIRONMENTAL AND CLIMATE DISASTER, BUT BY DEFAULT THEY HAVE ALSO AIDED WHITE NATIONALISM, RACISM, ATTACKS ON FREE SPEECH, WIDESPREAD POLITICAL CORRUPTION AND THE UNDERMINING OF US DEMOCRACY ITSELF.

THE KOCHS AND THE MEMBERS OF THE KOCH NETWORK, SEALED OFF AS THEY ARE FROM THE PROBLEMS OF THE GENERAL PUBLIC BY THEIR GREAT WEALTH, ARE UNLIKELY TO SUFFER THE CONSEQUENCES OF THEIR DISASTROUS INTERFERENCE.

THE SUPER-RICH DON'T HAVE TO STRUGGLE TO GET AFFORDABLE HOUSING, HEALTH-CARE, QUALITY EDUCATION, A LIVING WAGE, A SAFE WORKING ENVIRONMENT AND GOOD PUBLIC TRANSPORT INFRASTRUCTURE. ALL THINGS THE KOCH NETWORK HAVE WORKED HARD TO DEGRADE. INSTEAD IT WILL BE MILLIONS OF ORDINARY AMERICANS WHO WILL HAVE TO PAY THE PRICE – AND NOT JUST FOR A FEW YEARS, BUT FOR GENERATIONS TO COME.

END.

JEFF BEZOS AND AMAZON

JEFF BEZOS WAS BORN JEFFREY PRESTON JORGENSEN IN ALBUQUERQUE, NEW MEXICO, 1964.

HIS PARENTS WERE JACKIE GISE (AGE 17) AND TED JORGENSEN (AGE 18).

THEIR MARRIAGE DIDN'T LAST LONG. TED WAS AN INDIFFERENT HUSBAND AND FATHER WHO WAS PRONE TO STAYING OUT LATE TO DRINK WITH HIS BUDDIES.

THE COUPLE WERE ALWAYS BROKE. TED WAS A MEMBER OF A UNICYCLE TROUPE. THIS EMPLOYMENT DIDN'T EARN HIM MUCH MONEY.

THE TROUPE TOURED COUNTY FAIRS, SPORTING EVENTS AND CIRCUSES.

EVENTUALLY JACKIE TOOK THE BABY AND MOVED BACK WITH HER PARENTS. JEFF WAS A MERE 17 MONTHS OLD WHEN HIS MOTHER FILED FOR DIVORCE.

IN 1968 JACKIE REMARRIED AND MOVED WITH HER NEW HUSBAND, MIGUEL ANGEL BEZOS PEREZ, TO HOUSTON, TEXAS.

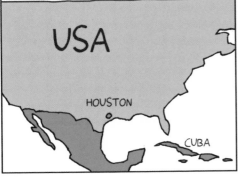

THE BOY WAS RENAMED JEFFREY PRESTON BEZOS. TED AGREED TO GIVE UP ALL RIGHTS TO HIS SON AND PROMISED TO STAY AWAY.

AFTER A FEW YEARS, NOT ONLY DID TED LOSE TRACK OF THE BEZOS FAMILY, BUT HE FORGOT THEIR LAST NAME.

BESTO, BANKO, BEESTA? WHAT WAS IT?

HE WOULD NOT KNOW THE WHEREABOUTS OF HIS SON FOR DECADES.

JEFF'S ADOPTIVE FATHER, MIGUEL, WAS A CUBAN IMMIGRANT. HE'D ARRIVED IN MIAMI IN 1962, AGED 16, KNOWING ONLY ONE WORD OF ENGLISH.

HAMBURGER.

HIS PARENTS HAD GOT HIM INTO THE CATHOLIC CHURCH'S OPERATION PEDRO PAN, A RESCUE PROGRAMME PARTLY FUNDED BY THE US GOVERNMENT, THAT REMOVED THOUSANDS OF TEENAGERS FROM CASTRO'S CUBA IN THE EARLY 1960s.

AFTER GRADUATING FROM THE UNIVERSITY OF NEW MEXCO, MARRYING JACKIE, ADOPTING BABY JEFF...

AND MOVING TO HOUSTON, MIGUEL (NOW CALLING HIMSELF MIKE) BEGAN WORK AS AN ENGINEER FOR EXXON.

JEFF WAS SOON JOINED BY SIBLINGS CHRISTINA AND THEN MARK.

FROM THE BEGINNING JEFF WAS BRIGHT AND DETERMINED. AT AGE EIGHT HE SCORED HIGH ON THE STANDARD EDUCATION TEST.

HE WAS ONE OF THE FIRST STUDENTS ENROLLED IN THE PUBLIC SCHOOL PROGRAMME FOR GIFTED CHILDREN, CALLED VANGUARD.

TECHNOLOGY AND SPACE WERE EARLY INTERESTS. AS A CHILD, JEFF SAW THE APOLLO 11 MOON LANDING AND WOULD WATCH RERUNS OF STAR TREK ON HIS PARENTS' TV.

ANOTHER INFLUENCE ON YOUNG JEFF WAS JACKIE BEZOS'S FATHER, LAWRENCE PRESTON GISE.

PRESTON 'POP' GISE WAS THE REGIONAL DIRECTOR OF THE US ATOMIC ENERGY COMMISSION.

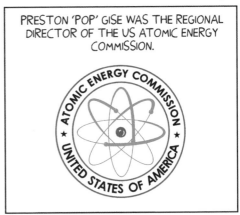

BUT IN 1968, AGED 53, HE RESIGNED FROM THE COMMISSION OVER A BUREAUCRATIC SQUABBLE WITH HIS SUPERIORS IN WASHINGTON.

I QUIT.

EXIT

HE AND HIS WIFE MATTIE RETIRED TO THEIR RANCH IN COTULLA, TEXAS.

THROUGHOUT HIS CHILDHOOD JEFF BEZOS SPENT EVERY SUMMER WITH HIS GRANDPARENTS ON A RANCH THAT WAS A HUNDRED MILES FROM THE NEAREST STORE OR HOSPITAL.

HOUSTON

COTULLA

JACKIE BEZOS SAID OF HER FATHER...

THERE WAS VERY LITTLE HE COULDN'T DO HIMSELF. HE THOUGHT EVERYTHING WAS SOMETHING YOU COULD TACKLE IN A GARAGE.

JEFF'S GRANDFATHER INSPIRED IN THE BOY A LOVE OF PRACTICAL HANDS-ON PROBLEM-SOLVING.

TOGETHER THEY BUILT AN AUTOMATIC GATE OPENER, REPAIRED WINDMILLS, LAID PIPES AND CASTRATED BULLS.

POP GISE TAUGHT JEFF CHECKERS AND THEN PROCEEDED TO REGULARLY BEAT HIM.

CAN'T YOU LET JEFF WIN ONE GAME?

HE'LL BEAT ME WHEN HE'S READY TO.

JEFF JOINED THE THE LOCAL COTULLA LIBRARY AND WORKED HIS WAY THROUGH ITS SCIENCE FICTION COLLECTION.

HIS IMAGINATION WAS FIRED BY JULES VERNE, ISAAC ASIMOV AND ROBERT HEINLEIN.

IN 1977, WHEN JEFF WAS 13, MIKE BEZOS'S JOB WITH EXXON OBLIGED HIM TO MOVE HIS FAMILY TO PENSACOLA, FLORIDA.

PENSACOLA

MIAMI

THE ALWAYS DETERMINED JACKIE BEZOS IMMEDIATELY GOT HER SON INTO THE LOCAL GIFTED PROGRAMME, DESPITE THERE USUALLY BEING A ONE-YEAR WAITING LIST.

GIFTED
THIS WAY

AFTER TWO YEARS THEY MOVED AGAIN, THIS TIME TO MIAMI, WHERE 15 YEARS EARLIER MIKE HAD ARRIVED AS A PENNILESS IMMIGRANT.

NOW HE WAS AN EXXON EXECUTIVE WITH A FOUR-BEDROOM HOUSE AND A BACKYARD POOL IN THE AFFLUENT SUBURB OF PALMETTO BAY.

JEFF ENROLLED IN THE MIAMI PALMETTO SENIOR HIGH SCHOOL WHERE HE JOINED THE SCIENCE AND CHESS CLUBS.

JEFF'S CHILDHOOD FRIEND JOSHUA WEINSTEIN SAID OF HIM...

HE WAS EXCRUCIATINGLY FOCUSED. NOT LIKE MAD SCIENTIST FOCUSED, BUT HE WAS CAPABLE OF REALLY FOCUSING, IN A CRAZY WAY, ON CERTAIN THINGS. HE WAS EXTREMELY DISCIPLINED, WHICH IS WHY HE IS ABLE TO DO ALL THESE THINGS.

WHEN HE WAS 16, JEFF TOOK A SUMMER JOB AT MCDONALD'S, WHERE HE LEARNED MORE THAN HOW TO FLIP BURGERS.

HAMBURGER.

THE MOST CHALLENGING THING WAS TO KEEP EVERYTHING GOING AT THE RIGHT PACE DURING A RUSH.

THE MANAGER AT MY MCDONALD'S WAS EXCELLENT. HE HAD A LOT OF TEENAGERS WORKING FOR HIM AND HE KEPT US FOCUSED EVEN WHILE WE HAD FUN.

YOUNG BEZOS WAS FIERCELY COMPETITIVE. HE WON MULTIPLE AWARDS, INCLUDING BEST SCIENCE STUDENT FOR THREE YEARS AND BEST MATHS STUDENT FOR TWO.

HE WON A STATE-WIDE SCIENCE FAIR FOR AN ENTRY CONCERNING THE EFFECTS OF ZERO-GRAVITY ON THE HOUSEFLY.

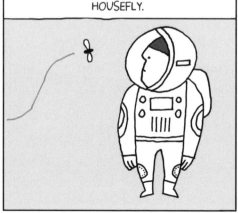

HE GAVE THE VALEDICTORY ADDRESS AT HIS HIGH-SCHOOL GRADUATING CEREMONY.

HE WON THE *MIAMI HERALD* SILVER KNIGHT AWARD, GIVEN IN RECOGNITION TO OUTSTANDING INDIVIDUALS AND LEADERS...

WHO HAD MAINTAINED GOOD GRADES AND APPLIED THEIR KNOWLEDGE AND TALENTS TO CONTRIBUTE TO THEIR SCHOOLS AND COMMUNITIES.

WELL DONE, BUDDY.

THIS ACADEMIC EXCELLENCE CONTINUED WHEN BEZOS WENT TO PRINCETON UNIVERSITY...

FROM WHERE HE GRADUATED IN 1987 WITH A 4.2 GRADE POINT AVERAGE AND A BACHELOR OF SCIENCE DEGREE IN ELECTRICAL ENGINEERING AND COMPUTER SCIENCE.

THEN CAME A NUMBER OF JOBS. FIRST AT FITEL, A FINANCIAL TELECOMMUNICATIONS START-UP, WHERE HE BECAME HEAD OF DEVELOPMENT AND DIRECTOR OF CUSTOMER SERVICE.

FROM THERE HE MADE THE JUMP INTO THE BANKING INDUSTRY IN 1988 AS A PRODUCT MANAGER AT BANKERS TRUST.

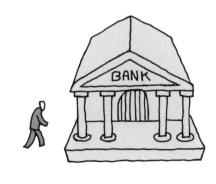

IN 1990 HE JOINED D.E. SHAW AND CO., A NEWLY FOUNDED HEDGE FUND INVESTMENT FIRM.

IT WAS HERE THAT HE MET HIS FUTURE WIFE, MACKENZIE TUTTLE, WHO HAD JOINED THE COMPANY AS AN ADMINISTRATIVE ASSISTANT...

AND LATER WENT TO WORK THERE AS BEZOS'S ASSISTANT.

MY OFFICE WAS NEXT DOOR TO HIS, AND ALL DAY LONG I LISTENED TO THAT FABULOUS LAUGH. HOW COULD YOU NOT FALL IN LOVE WITH THAT LAUGH?

HA HA HA HA HA!

THEY WERE MARRIED IN 1993.

D.E. SHAW WASN'T JUST A HEDGE FUND. IT HAD BEEN CREATED BY ITS CEO, DAVID SHAW, AS A LAB FILLED WITH INNOVATORS AND TALENTED ENGINEERS.

SHAW RECRUITED NOT FINANCIERS, BUT SCIENTISTS AND MATHEMATICIANS – SMART PEOPLE FROM UNUSUAL BACKGROUNDS WHO HAD BIG IDEAS. AND THE DRIVE TO DEVELOP THEM.

IN THE 1990s, WHEN THE INTERNET WAS IN ITS INFANCY, SHAW FELT THAT HIS COMPANY WAS IN A GOOD POSITION TO EXPLOIT THE EMERGING TECHNOLOGY. HE CHOSE JEFF BEZOS TO SPEARHEAD THIS EFFORT.

INTERNET UNDER CONSTRUCTION

TIME REMAINING...   COULD BE A WHILE

D.E. SHAW WAS ONE OF THE FIRST WALL STREET FIRMS TO REGISTER ITS INTERNET ADDRESS (OR UNIFORM RESOURCE LOCATION – URL) IN 1992. BY COMPARISON, GOLDMAN SACHS DIDN'T REGISTER ITS URL UNTIL 1995.

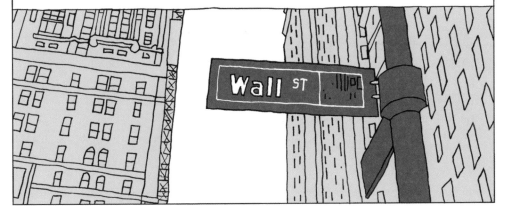

IN EARLY 1994 SEVERAL BUSINESS CONCEPTS EMERGED OUT OF THE WEEKLY DISCUSSIONS SHAW HAD WITH BEZOS. THESE IDEAS INCLUDED A FREE-TO-CONSUMER, BUT ADVERTISER-SUPPORTED, EMAIL SERVICE.

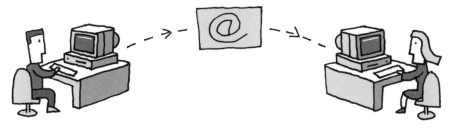

D.E. SHAW DEVELOPED THAT IDEA INTO A COMPANY CALLED JUNO, WHICH WENT PUBLIC IN 1999 AND SOON AFTER MERGED WITH ITS RIVAL, NETZERO.

ALSO DEVELOPED WAS A NEW KIND OF FINANCIAL SERVICE THAT ALLOWED INTERNET USERS TO TRADE STOCKS AND BONDS ONLINE. THIS BECAME A SHAW SUBSIDIARY CALLED FARSIGHT FINANCIAL SERVICES, WHICH WAS LATER SOLD TO MERRILL LYNCH.

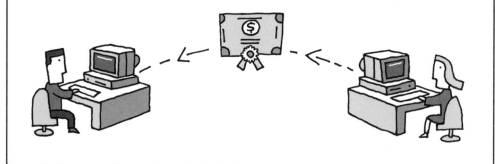

ANOTHER IDEA THEY HAD WAS THE EVERYTHING STORE – AN INTERNET COMPANY THAT WOULD SERVE AS THE INTERMEDIARY BETWEEN CUSTOMERS AND MANUFACTURERS, WHICH WOULD SELL ALMOST EVERY TYPE OF PRODUCT GLOBALLY.

CUSTOMERS WOULD BE ABLE TO LEAVE WRITTEN REVIEWS OF THE PRODUCTS.

FEEDBACK

◯ AWESOME

THIS SUCKS

BEZOS RESEARCHED THE IDEA AND SOON REALISED THAT AN ONLINE STORE SELLING EVERYTHING WOULD BE IMPRACTICAL AT FIRST.

HE WOULD HAVE TO START SMALL AND ADD GOODS TO THE STORE OVER TIME. IT SEEMED TO HIM THAT BOOKS WERE THE OBVIOUS PRODUCT TO BEGIN WITH.

BEZOS AND CHARLES ARDAI, D.E. SHAW'S CHIEF RECRUITER, INVESTIGATED SOME OF THE ONLINE BOOKSTORES THAT ALREADY EXISTED.

AS A TEST, ARDAI BOUGHT A COPY OF *ISAAC ASIMOV'S CYBERDREAMS* EDITED BY GARDNER DOZOIS FROM THE WEBSITE OF THE FUTURE FANTASY BOOKSTORE IN CALIFORNIA.

THE BOOK COST $6.04, TOOK TWO WEEKS TO ARRIVE AND WAS DAMAGED IN TRANSIT.

IT'S RIPPED.

BEZOS FELT THERE WAS A HUGE OPPORTUNITY THERE IF HE COULD WORK OUT HOW TO SELL BOOKS CHEAPLY AND QUICKLY ONLINE.

HE ALSO REALISED THAT THE NEW COMPANY WOULD NEVER REALLY BE HIS IF HE DEVELOPED THE IDEA AS PART OF D.E. SHAW.

BEZOS THEN USED WHAT HE CALLED 'THE REGRET-MINIMISATION FRAMEWORK' IN ORDER TO DECIDE WHETHER TO LEAVE D.E. SHAW.

WHEN YOU ARE IN THE THICK OF THINGS YOU CAN GET CONFUSED BY SMALL STUFF.

I KNEW WHEN I WAS 80 THAT I WOULD NEVER, FOR EXAMPLE, THINK ABOUT WHY I WALKED AWAY FROM MY 1994 WALL STREET BONUS RIGHT IN THE MIDDLE OF THE YEAR AT THE WORST POSSIBLE TIME.

THAT KIND OF THING JUST ISN'T SOMETHING YOU WORRY ABOUT WHEN YOU'RE 80 YEARS OLD. AT THE SAME TIME, I KNEW THAT I MIGHT SINCERELY REGRET NOT HAVING PARTICIPATED IN THIS THING CALLED THE INTERNET THAT I THOUGHT WAS GOING TO BE A REVOLUTIONISING EVENT.

WHEN I THOUGHT ABOUT IT THAT WAY, IT WAS INCREDIBLY EASY TO MAKE THE DECISION.

IN MAY 1994, BEZOS HELD A PARTY AT HIS, UPPER WEST SIDE APARTMENT IN NEW YORK, TO WATCH THE FINAL EPISODE OF *STAR TREK: THE NEXT GENERATION*.

SHORTLY AFTER THIS HE TOOK A TRIP TO SANTA CRUZ, CALIFORNIA TO MEET TWO EXPERIENCED PROGRAMMERS AND LOOK AT POTENTIAL OFFICE SPACE. WHEN HE RETURNED TO NEW YORK HE TOLD THE STAFF OF D.E. SHAW THAT HE WAS LEAVING.

THE FUTURE

BEZOS FIRST CONSIDERED CALLING HIS NEW COMPANY MAKEITSO.COM, A REFERENCE TO *STAR TREK*, BUT SETTLED ON CADABRA. THIS NAME HAD A PROBLEM THOUGH. PEOPLE TENDED TO HEAR CADAVER.

DID YOU SAY CADAVER?

POSSIBLE REPLACEMENT NAMES DISCUSSED WERE AWAKE.COM, BROWSE.COM, BOOKMAIL.COM AND RELENTLESS.COM.

RELENTLESS SOUNDS A BIT SINISTER, JEFF.

WELL, I LIKE IT.

IN THE END, WHATEVER BEZOS'S COMPANY WAS GOING TO BE CALLED, IT WOULDN'T BE STARTED IN CALIFORNIA. BEZOS HAD LEARNED OF A SUPREME COURT RULING THAT MERCHANTS DID NOT HAVE TO COLLECT SALES TAX IN STATES WHERE THEY WERE NOT PHYSICALLY PRESENT.

IT MADE SENSE TO RELOCATE TO A LESS POPULOUS STATE WHERE SALES TAX WAS LOW. THIS MEANT AVOIDING NEW YORK OR CALIFORNIA WHERE THE POPULATION WAS HIGH. FOR THIS REASON BEZOS TURNED HIS ATTENTION TO SEATTLE IN WASHINGTON STATE. THE TECH GIANT MICROSOFT WAS ALREADY BASED THERE AND THE CITY WAS DEVELOPING A FASHIONABLE ART AND GRUNGE ROCK SCENE.

SEATTLE WAS ALSO ATTRACTIVE BECAUSE INGRAMS, ONE OF THE TWO BIG US BOOK DISTRIBUTORS, HAD A WAREHOUSE A MERE SIX HOURS AWAY IN ROSEBURG, OREGON.

BEZOS BOUGHT A HOUSE IN BELLEVUE JUST ACROSS LAKE WASHINGTON FROM SEATTLE.

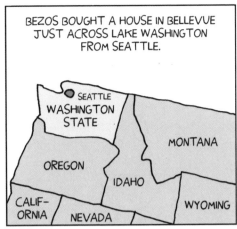

HE STARTED THE NEW COMPANY IN HIS GARAGE. HE BUILT TWO DESKS OUT OF $60 WOOD DOORS BOUGHT AT HOME DEPOT.

THEN HE DROVE TO PORTLAND, OREGON TO TAKE A FOUR-DAY COURSE ON BOOKSELLING.

AT FIRST BEZOS PUT $10,000 OF HIS OWN MONEY INTO THE START-UP.

THEN HE MANAGED, OVER A 16-MONTH PERIOD, TO RAISE $84,000 IN INTEREST-FREE LOANS.

THE COMPANY'S FIRST EMPLOYEE WAS SHEL KAPHAN, WHO WAS ONE OF THE PROGRAMMERS BEZOS HAD MET ON HIS BRIEF VISIT TO CALIFORNIA.

KAPHAN WAS RESPONSIBLE FOR BUILDING THE TECHNOLOGICAL INFRASTRUCTURE IN THE EARLY YEARS OF AMAZON, AND PLAYED A CRITICAL ROLE IN ITS GROWTH.

KAPHAN'S CONTRACT REQUIRED HIM TO BUY $5,000 OF STOCKS ON JOINING THE COMPANY. BUT HE PASSED ON THE OPPORTUNITY OF BUYING ANY FURTHER STOCKS.

NO, THANKS.

THE WHOLE THING SEEMED PRETTY IFFY AT THAT STAGE. THERE WASN'T REALLY ANYTHING EXCEPT A GUY WITH A BARKING LAUGH BUILDING DESKS OUT OF DOORS IN HIS CONVERTED GARAGE.

BEZOS'S PARENTS, JACKIE AND MIKE, AT FIRST INVESTED $10,000 AND ULTIMATELY AS MUCH AS $250,000 IN THE START-UP.

WE SAW THE BUSINESS PLAN BUT ALL OF THAT WENT OVER OUR HEADS TO A LARGE EXTENT.

AS CORNY AS IT SOUNDS, WE WERE BETTING ON JEFF.

THE NEXT EMPLOYEE HIRED WAS BRITISH BORN PAUL DAVID. TOGETHER HE AND KAPHAN BUILT A PRIMITIVE BETA WEBSITE.

BEZOS STILL NEEDED A NEW NAME FOR THE COMPANY. HE LOOKED THROUGH THE 'A' SECTION OF A DICTIONARY AND STOPPED WHEN HE GOT TO THE WORD AMAZON.

THAT'S IT!

HE INFORMED HIS STAFF OF THE NEW NAME.

THIS IS NOT ONLY THE LARGEST RIVER IN THE WORLD.

IT'S MANY TIMES LARGER THAN THE NEXT BIGGEST RIVER. IT BLOWS ALL OTHER RIVERS AWAY.

BEZOS REGISTERED THE NEW NAME ON 1 NOVEMBER 1994.

AMAZON.COM

IN THE SPRING OF 1995 AMAZON MOVED FROM THE GARAGE TO A NEW OFFICE SPACE ABOVE A TILE RETAIL STORE IN SEATTLE.

COLOR TILE

BEZOS AND KAPHAN SENT OUT LINKS TO THE BETA WEBSITE TO FRIENDS AND FAMILY.

THE FIRST PERSON TO BUY A BOOK FROM AMAZON WAS KAPHAN'S FORMER CO-WORKER, JOHN WAINWRIGHT, ON 3 APRIL 1995.

HE BOUGHT A SCIENCE BOOK, *FLUID CONCEPTS AND CREATIVE ANALOGIES: COMPUTER MODELS OF THE FUNDAMENTAL MECHANISM OF THOUGHT* BY DOUGLAS R. HOFSTADTER.

HE (SHEL KAPHAN), SENT ME AN EMAIL AND SAID, 'CREATE AN ACCOUNT AND ORDER SOME BOOKS.'

I THOUGHT I WAS GOING TO GET SOME FREE BOOKS, BUT THEY TOOK MY CREDIT CARD AND CHARGED IT. THAT PURCHASE IS STILL PART OF MY AMAZON HISTORY.

IN AMAZON'S FIRST WEEKS A BELL WOULD RING EACH TIME SOMEONE MADE AN ORDER.

WE GOT ONE.

DING!

THE TEAM WOULD GATHER ROUND TO SEE WHETHER IT WAS ANYONE THEY KNEW.

WHO IS IT?

WE DON'T KNOW.

WITHIN A MONTH OF THE LAUNCH THE BELL WAS RINGING SO OFTEN IT HAD TO BE TURNED OFF.

ARRGH!

DING! DING! DING! DING! DING! DING! DING!

BACK THEN, WHEN A CUSTOMER BOUGHT A BOOK, AMAZON WOULD ORDER IT FROM THE DISTRIBUTOR AND IT WOULD ARRIVE AT THEIR OFFICE IN A FEW DAYS.

I ORDERED A BOOK OFF AMAZON.

CUSTOMER

THEN IT WOULD BE STORED IN THE BASEMENT UNTIL IT COULD BE SHIPPED OFF TO THE CUSTOMER.

I'M WAITING FOR IT TO ARRIVE.

MOST BOOKS WOULD TAKE A WEEK TO DELIVER. RARE ITEMS MIGHT TAKE MORE THAN A MONTH.

I'M STILL WAITING.

KAPHAN ADDED A CUSTOMER REVIEW SECTION THAT HE CODED OVER A WEEKEND.

MOST OF THE EARLY REVIEWS WERE WRITTEN BY AMAZON EMPLOYEES AND FRIENDS.

SOME OF THESE REVIEWS WERE NEGATIVE. BEZOS RECEIVED AN ANGRY LETTER FROM A BOOK PUBLISHING EXECUTIVE.

LETTER FOR YOU, JEFF.

?

YOUR JOB SHOULD BE TO SELL BOOKS, NOT TRASH THEM.

WE SAW IT VERY DIFFERENTLY. WHEN I READ THAT LETTER, I THOUGHT WE DON'T MAKE MONEY WHEN WE SELL THINGS. WE MAKE MONEY WHEN WE HELP CUSTOMERS MAKE PURCHASES.

AMAZON STILL HADN'T HIRED ANYONE TO PACK BOOKS. THE STAFF, INCLUDING BEZOS HIMSELF, HAD TO TROOP DOWN TO THE BASEMENT AT NIGHT...

WHERE THEY WOULD PUT TOGETHER THE CUSTOMER ORDERS READY TO BE SENT OUT THE NEXT DAY BY U.P.S. OR THE POST OFFICE.

IN ITS FIRST TWO MONTHS OF BUSINESS AMAZON SOLD TO ALL 50 STATES AND TO OVER 45 COUNTRIES.

IN MARCH 1996 THE COMPANY MOVED PREMISES TO A LARGER BUILDING WITH MORE WAREHOUSE SPACE A FEW BLOCKS AWAY.

AMAZON NEEDED MORE STAFF. BEZOS INTERVIEWED ALL APPLICANTS HIMSELF, A PRACTICE THAT CONTINUED FOR YEARS.

EVERY TIME WE HIRE SOMEONE, HE OR SHE SHOULD RAISE THE BAR FOR THE NEXT HIRE SO THAT THE OVERALL TALENT POOL IS ALWAYS IMPROVING.

BEZOS WOULD ASK ALL SORTS OF ODD QUESTIONS IN ORDER TO TEST THE CANDIDATE'S THINKING.

WHY ARE ALL MANHOLE COVERS ROUND?

WHAT BEZOS DIDN'T WANT TO HEAR WAS THE CANDIDATE SAYING...

I'D LIKE A GOOD WORK AND LIFE BALANCE.

HE WANTED HIS EMPLOYEES TO BE TOTALLY COMMITTED TO AMAZON, AND WORK 60 HOURS A WEEK, AS HE DID.

THANK YOU FOR COMING AND GOODBYE.

IN MAY 1996 BEZOS WAS FEATURED IN THE WALL STREET JOURNAL.

HOW A WALL ST. WHIZ FOUND A NICHE SELLING BOOKS ON THE INTERNET

INVESTMENT FLOODED IN.

AMAZON THEN LAUNCHED WHAT IT CALLED 'AFFILIATE MARKETING', WHICH ALLOWED OTHER WEBSITES TO COLLECT A FEE WHEN THEY SENT CUSTOMERS TO AMAZON. THIS WASN'T A NEW INNOVATION, BUT ITS USE EXTENDED THE COMPANY'S REACH ACROSS THE INTERNET AND HELPED IT OUTPACE ITS COMPETITION.

THEN CAME A TIME OF RAPID EXPANSION. AMAZON'S MOTTO BECAME 'GET BIG FAST'. THE COMPANY THAT GOT THE LEAD NOW, BEZOS EXPLAINED TO HIS STAFF, WOULD LIKELY KEEP IT.

THIS MEANT EVERYONE WORKING HARDER. FOR MANY LIFE BECAME A BLUR.

IS THAT MIDDAY OR MIDNIGHT?

I'M NOT SURE.

IT WAS ASSUMED STAFF WOULDN'T BE TAKING WEEKEND DAYS OFF.

NOBODY SAID YOU COULDN'T, BUT NOBODY THOUGHT YOU WOULD.

SUSAN BENSON
EDITORIAL STAFF
1996–2001

A TYPICAL DAY FOR AN EMPLOYEE LIKE 23-YEAR-OLD CHRISTOPHER SMITH WOULD SEE HIM BIKE TO WORK AT 4.30AM.

HE'D LET IN THE COURIER FROM THE BOOK DISTRIBUTOR AT 6.30.

THEN HE WOULD PACK ORDERS AND ANSWER CUSTOMER EMAILS ALL DAY.

IN THE EVENING HE'D HAVE A FEW BEERS IN THE WAREHOUSE AND BIKE HOME AFTER MIDNIGHT.

OVER ONE EIGHT-MONTH PERIOD, SMITH WORKED SO MANY HOURS THAT HE FORGOT ALL ABOUT HIS PEUGEOT STATION WAGON, WHICH HAD BEEN PARKED IN THE CAPITOL HILL DISTRICT OF SEATTLE.

THE PILE OF MAIL AT HOME HE HAD NEGLECTED TO OPEN REVEALED TO HIM THAT THE CAR HAD FIRST ACCUMULATED SEVERAL PARKING TICKETS...

BEFORE BEING TOWED AWAY...

AND SOLD AT AUCTION.

AMAZON CONTINUED TO EXPAND AS MORE INVESTMENT POURED IN. THE COMPANY RELOCATED AGAIN, THIS TIME ACQUIRING A SEPARATE WAREHOUSE.

IT'S BIG.

BEZOS WENT SHOPPING FOR EXPERIENCED EXECUTIVES, RECRUITING FROM BARNES & NOBLE, SYMANTEC AND MICROSOFT AMONGST OTHERS.

AMAZON ISSUED ITS INITIAL PUBLIC OFFERING (IPO) OF STOCK ON 15 MAY 1997.

WANT TO BUY A PIECE OF ME?

AN IPO IS WHEN A PRIVATE COMPANY OR CORPORATION RAISES INVESTMENT CAPITAL BY OFFERING STOCK TO THE PUBLIC FOR THE FIRST TIME.

AMAZON. NEVER HEARD OF THEM.

THEY'RE ONLY $18.

AMAZON RAISED $54 MILLION. THE COMPANY ENDED THAT YEAR HAVING 900-PER-CENT GROWTH IN ANNUAL REVENUE.

BEZOS'S PARENTS' INVESTMENT IN THEIR SON HAD PAID OFF. THEY WERE NOW MULTIMILLIONAIRES.

ONE PERSON WHO WASN'T HAPPY WAS SHEL KAPHAN. BEZOS HAD BROUGHT IN NEW TECHNICAL MANAGEMENT WHO HAD LARGELY SIDELINED KAPHAN.

HE'D BEEN PROMOTED TO CHIEF TECHNOLOGY OFFICER, BUT THE ROLE WAS ADVISORY. HE HAD NO STAFF AND NO REAL INFLUENCE ANY MORE.

JEFF, CAN WE...?

NO.

WHEN HE REPLACED ME IN MY ORIGINAL JOB AND I WAS MOVED INTO THE CTO SLOT, I WAS NOMINALLY IN CHARGE OF ARCHITECTURE.

BUT IN FACT THAT JUST MEANT RUBBER-STAMPING PROJECTS THAT WERE 95-PER-CENT COMPLETE.

THAT WAS ALL AFTER HAVING TOLD ME THAT MY JOB WAS MINE AS LONG AS I WANTED IT. AND I DIDN'T HAVE RESOURCES OTHER THAN MYSELF TO WORK ON ANYTHING I WAS INTERESTED IN EITHER.

SO I WOULD SAY WE WERE NOT REALLY ON PARTICULARLY FRIENDLY TERMS AT THAT POINT.

KAPHAN FELT THAT THE WAY HE WAS TREATED AT AMAZON WAS...

ONE OF THE BIGGEST DISAPPOINTMENTS OF MY LIFE.

KAPHAN LEFT AMAZON IN LATE 1999. BEZOS MADE LITTLE EFFORT TO PERSUADE HIM TO STAY.

NEW PEOPLE BEZOS HIRED INCLUDED JIMMY WRIGHT, AN EX-WALMART VICE-PRESIDENT OF DISTRIBUTION.

BEZOS WANTED A DISTRIBUTION SYSTEM TEN TIMES LARGER THAN IT CURRENTLY WAS.

WHAT PRODUCT WILL YOU BE SHIPPING?

I DON'T KNOW. JUST DESIGN SOMETHING THAT CAN HANDLE ANYTHING.

WRIGHT SPENT $300 MILLION BUILDING A NEW WAREHOUSE AND RETROFITTING TWO OTHERS AMAZON HAD BOUGHT.

THEY WERE AUTOMATIC, WITH BLINKING LIGHTS ON AISLES AND SHELVES THAT DREW HUMAN WORKERS TO THE CORRECT PRODUCTS.

ENORMOUS MACHINES CALLED CRISPLANTS TOOK ORDERS TO BE PACKAGED AND SHIPPED. AMAZON NEEDED THIS AS THEY HAD BEGUN TO EXPAND INTO CDs, DVDs, ELECTRONICS, TOOLS AND TOYS.

1995 TO 2000 WERE THE YEARS OF THE DOT-COM BUBBLE. VENTURE CAPITALISTS KEEN TO FIND THE NEXT BIG SCORE FREELY INVESTED IN ANY COMPANY THAT HAD A .COM AFTER ITS NAME IN THE HOPE THAT THOSE BUSINESSES WOULD BECOME PROFITABLE. MANY INVESTORS ABANDONED A CAUTIOUS APPROACH FOR FEAR OF MISSING OUT ON THE GROWING USE OF THE INTERNET.

NASDAQ COMPOSITE.

RIGHT AT THE MARKET'S PEAK IN 2000, SEVERAL OF THE LEADING HIGH-TECH COMPANIES, SUCH AS DELL AND CISCO, PLACED HUGE ORDERS ON THEIR STOCKS, SPARKING PANIC-SELLING AMONG INVESTORS.

WITHIN A FEW WEEKS THE US STOCK MARKET HAD LOST TEN PER CENT OF ITS VALUE. DOT-COM COMPANIES THAT WERE PREVIOUSLY VALUED AT HUNDREDS OF MILLIONS OF DOLLARS BECAME WORTHLESS.

AMAZON SURVIVED THE DOT-COM BUST, BUT NOT WITHOUT SOME PAIN. IT EXPANDED RAPIDLY DURING THOSE YEARS.

FUELLED BY THREE BOND OFFERINGS THAT RAISED A COLOSSAL $2.2 BILLION.

IT SPENT MUCH OF THIS MONEY ON ACQUISITIONS. IT BOUGHT THE BRITISH WEB BOOKSTORE BOOKPAGES.COM...

THE GERMAN WEB BOOKSTORE TELEBUCH, THE ONLINE MARKETPLACE EXCHANGE.COM, THE SOCIAL NETWORKING SERVICE PLANETALL, AND MANY OTHERS.

IT ALSO INVESTED IN A VARIETY OF START-UPS. ALMOST NONE OF WHICH SURVIVED THE EVENTUAL CRASH, CAUSING AMAZON TO LOSE HUNDREDS OF MILLIONS.

THE PACE OF EXPANSION HAD TO STOP. THE COMPANY HAD GONE FROM 1,000 EMPLOYEES IN 1998 TO 7,600 IN 2000.

HUP!

REVENUE FOR THE FOURTH QUARTER OF 1999 WAS $650 MILLION, MORE THAN DOUBLE THE PREVIOUS YEAR'S HOLIDAY SEASON. DESPITE THIS TURNOVER, INVESTORS WERE NERVOUS AND THE MEDIA WERE CRITICAL. IN ITS SEVEN YEARS OF EXISTENCE AMAZON HAD NEVER MADE A PROFIT.

IT MAY SEEM STRANGE THAT A COMPANY COULD SURVIVE FOR YEARS WITHOUT MAKING A PROFIT, BUT IN THE WORLD OF BIG BUSINESS IT'S NOT THAT UNUSUAL.

IF EARNINGS ARE LARGE ENOUGH, AS LONG AS IT CAN PAY ITS BILLS, A COMPANY CAN CHOOSE TO PLOUGH MOST OF ITS REVENUES BACK INTO THE BUSINESS TO PROPEL GROWTH.

THIS IS WHAT BEZOS DID. HIS ARGUMENT WAS THAT WITHOUT CONSTANT INVESTMENT AMAZON WOULD BE OVERTAKEN BY COMPETITORS. FOR HIM, MARKET SHARE WAS EVERYTHING.

THAT CHANGED IN 2000. AMAZON CHIEF ACCOUNTANT KELYN BRANNON AND CHIEF FINANCIAL OFFICER JOY COVEY PULLED BEZOS ASIDE ONE DAY.

CAN WE TALK?

THEY SHOWED BEZOS FIGURES WHICH PROVED THAT AT THE CURRENT RATE OF GROWTH AMAZON WOULDN'T BE PROFITABLE FOR DECADES.

THIS SEEMS TO HAVE BEEN A TURNING POINT FOR THE CEO. HE REFOCUSED THE COMPANY AND WITHIN TWO YEARS (JANUARY 2002) AMAZON REPORTED ITS FIRST PROFITABLE QUARTER – A MODEST NET INCOME OF $5 MILLION.

THE STOCK PRICE, WHICH HAD BEEN LANGUISHING IN SINGLE FIGURES, JUMPED 25 PER CENT.

POP!

PROFITS COULD HAVE BEEN LARGER IF BEZOS HAD RAISED AMAZON'S PRICES EVEN A LITTLE.

THERE HE IS. LET'S DISCUSS IT WITH HIM.

BUT HIS MAIN CONCERN, IN THE FACE OF OPPOSITION FROM MANY OF HIS EXECUTIVES, WAS KEEPING PRICES LOW.

JEFF, CAN WE...

NO.

THERE ARE TWO KINDS OF COMPANIES. THOSE THAT WORK TO TRY TO CHARGE MORE AND THOSE THAT WORK TO CHARGE LESS. WE WILL BE THE SECOND.

YES, BOSS.

BEZOS'S SECOND AIM WAS TO MAKE THE CUSTOMER EXPERIENCE AS EASY AS POSSIBLE.

GET IT DONE.

ONE-CLICK BUYING WAS DEVELOPED, WHICH ALLOWED CUSTOMERS TO PURCHASE ITEMS WITHOUT HAVING TO USE THE SHOPPING CART. AMAZON WAS GRANTED A PATENT FOR THIS INNOVATION.

THE COMPANY SUED BARNES & NOBLE FOR INFRINGING ON THIS PATENT, FORCING ITS COMPETITOR TO ADD AN EXTRA STEP TO ITS CHECKOUT PROCESS.

THIEF!

WHO, ME?

IN 2000, AMAZON LICENSED APPLE TO USE ONE-CLICK ORDERING ON ITS OWN ONLINE STORES.

HERE'S SOME CASH FOR YOU, JEFF.

THE GROWING NUMBER OF WAREHOUSES BECAME EVER MORE EFFICIENT. COST PER UNIT (THE OVERALL EXPENSE OF FULFILLING THE ORDER OF AN ITEM) FELL, WHILE CLICK-TO-SHIP TIMES (THE SPEED MERCHANDISE ORDERED ON THE WEBSITE WAS LOADED ONTO TO A TRUCK) DECREASED TO FOUR HOURS, EASILY BEATING THEIR ONLINE COMPETITORS, WHOSE AVERAGE CLICK-TO-SHIP TIME WAS 12 HOURS.

WE CALL OUR WAREHOUSES FULFILMENT CENTRES.

IN 2006, AMAZON BEGAN OFFERING INFORMATION TECHNOLOGY SERVICES TO THE MARKET ON A PAID SUBSCRIPTION BASIS. THE TECHNOLOGY ALLOWED SUBSCRIBERS TO HAVE A CLUSTER OF COMPUTERS AVAILABLE AT ALL TIMES THROUGH THE INTERNET. CUSTOMERS ONLY PAID FOR WHAT THEY USED, AND COULD INCREASE OR DECREASE THEIR CONSUMPTION AS THEY NEEDED.

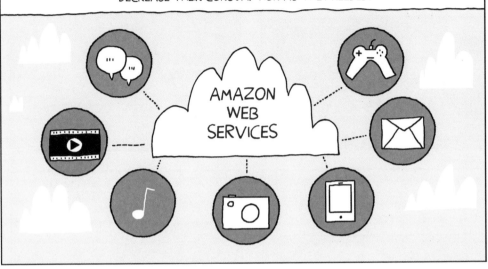

THE BEST ANALOGY THAT I KNOW IS THE ELECTRIC GRID. YOU GO BACK IN TIME A HUNDRED YEARS, IF YOU WANTED TO HAVE ELECTRICITY, YOU HAD TO BUILD YOUR OWN LITTLE ELECTRIC POWER PLANT. A LOT OF FACTORIES DID THIS. AS SOON AS THE ELECTRIC GRID CAME ONLINE THEY DUMPED THEIR ELECTRIC POWER GENERATOR AND THEY STARTED BUYING POWER OFF THE GRID. IT JUST MAKES MORE SENSE.

THE EMERGENCE OF WEB SERVICES LIKE AMAZON'S WAS A POSITIVE DEVELOPMENT IN MANY WAYS. THOUSANDS OF NEW INTERNET BUSINESSES TOOK ADVANTAGE OF THESE SERVICES WHICH OTHERWISE WOULD HAVE HAD THE ENORMOUS EXPENSE OF BUILDING THEIR OWN INFRASTRUCTURE. AMAZON TOOK THE LEAD IN THIS AREA, MANAGING TO OUTPACE SEASONED HARDWARE COMPANIES LIKE SUN MICROSYSTEMS AND HEWLETT-PACKARD.

NOTABLE CUSTOMERS OF AMAZON WEB SERVICES (AWS) INCLUDE NASA, THE OBAMA PRESIDENTIAL CAMPAIGN OF 2012 AND NETFLIX (WHO USE AWS TO STREAM MOVIES TO THEIR SUBSCRIBERS).

AWS HAS BEEN HUGELY LUCRATIVE FOR AMAZON. IN THE FIRST QUARTER OF 2016 ALONE, IT MADE A NET INCOME OF $604 MILLION.

BEZOS HAD ALWAYS CONCEIVED AMAZON AS A TECH COMPANY RATHER THAN AN ONLINE RETAIL STORE. WITH AWS HE HAD FINALLY ACHIEVED THIS AIM.

AMAZON WAS TO GO EVEN FURTHER DOWN THE TECH ROUTE WITH ITS NEXT MAJOR DEVELOPMENT.

I WONDER WHAT MY NEXT MOVE WILL BE?

BEZOS HAD LEARNED THAT COMPANIES CAN FAIL IF THEY ARE RELUCTANT TO EMBRACE MARKETS THAT WOULD UNDERMINE THEIR EXISTING BUSINESS. AN EXAMPLE OF THIS WOULD BE KODAK, WHICH INVENTED DIGITAL PHOTOGRAPHY, BUT THEN FAILED TO INVEST IN THE TECHNOLOGY, ALLOWING OTHERS TO TAKE THE LEAD.

WE DON'T NEED THIS NEW BUSINESS. WE'RE DOING FINE WITHOUT IT.

KODAK

A FEW YEARS LATER.

I GUESS WE WERE WRONG.

KODAK

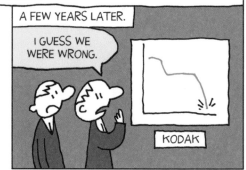

BY 2004 APPLE DOMINATED THE SALES OF DIGITAL MUSIC WITH ITS PORTABLE MUSIC PLAYER THE iPOD.

BEZOS BELIEVED THAT AMAZON COULD SIMILARLY COMMAND THE DIGITAL BOOK MARKET IF THE COMPANY DEVELOPED A HAND-HELD ELECTRONIC READING DEVICE.

AH, STEVE.

THE PERSON HE CHOSE TO SPEARHEAD THIS EFFORT WAS AN EXECUTIVE NAMED STEVE KESSEL.

BEZOS IMPRESSED ON KESSEL THAT IF AMAZON DIDN'T LEAD THE WORLD INTO THE AGE OF DIGITAL BOOKS, THEN APPLE OR GOOGLE WOULD.

YOUR JOB IS TO KILL YOUR OWN BUSINESS. I WANT YOU TO PROCEED AS IF YOUR GOAL IS TO PUT EVERYONE SELLING PHYSICAL BOOKS OUT OF A JOB.

AND WHAT'S THE DEADLINE FOR THIS PROJECT?

YOU'RE BASICALLY ALREADY LATE.

THERE HAD BEEN E-READERS BEFORE, SUCH AS THE POCKETBOOK AND THE SONY LIBRIE, BUT NONE HAD BEEN SUCCESSFUL. PREVIOUS ATTEMPTS WERE EXPENSIVE AND LIMITED IN THEIR SELECTION OF BOOKS. AMAZON'S NEW DEVICE WOULD HAVE TO BE LIGHT, SIMPLE TO USE AND ABLE TO ACCESS A VAST LIBRARY OF DIGITISED BOOKS THAT THE USER COULD BUY AND DOWNLOAD. THE COMPANY PUT ENORMOUS PRESSURE ON PUBLISHERS TO DIGITISE THEIR BOOKS READY FOR THE E-READER'S EVENTUAL RELEASE.

SOME AMAZON EXECUTIVES WERE UNHAPPY WITH THIS APPROACH.

I DIDN'T LIKE TO BULLY PEOPLE. EVERY REASONABLE BUSINESS DEVELOPMENT DEAL SHOULD INVOLVE SOME SORT OF COMPROMISE.

JEFF STEELE. AMAZON EXECUTIVE..

STEELE FELL OUT WITH KESSEL OVER THE TERMS OF CONTRACT WITH OXFORD UNIVERSITY PRESS, WHICH SUPPLIED THE DICTIONARY THAT WOULD BE EMBEDDED IN THE E-READER.

I JUST GOT UNCOMFORTABLE.

AS THE DEAL HAD ALREADY BEEN NEGOTIATED, STEELE BELIEVED IT WAS UNETHICAL TO ATTEMPT TO CHANGE IT.

IT'S JUST PLAIN WRONG.

HE GOT INTO A HEATED ARGUMENT WITH LAURA PORCO, ANOTHER MEMBER OF THE E-READER TEAM...

AFTER WHICH HE WAS FIRED.

GO.

LAURA PORCO THEN TOOK OVER THE E-READER EFFORT. PORCO, WHO HAD PREVIOUSLY BEEN THE MERCHANDISING DIRECTOR IN THE PHYSICAL BOOKS GROUP, HAD A FEARSOME REPUTATION.

SHE'D RUTHLESSLY SQUEEZED PROFITS FROM AMAZON'S SUPPLIERS WHEREVER SHE COULD.

LAURA CAN BE ONE OF THE KINDEST PEOPLE, BUT WHEN IT COMES TO AMAZON SHE WANTS TO DRINK BLOOD.

CHRISTOPHER SMITH, AMAZON SENIOR BOOK BUYER.

BEZOS'S GOAL WAS TO HAVE ONE HUNDRED THOUSAND DIGITAL TITLES AVAILABLE FOR DOWNLOAD WHEN THE E-READER WAS LAUNCHED.

TO ACHIEVE THIS AIM, THREATS WERE USED AGAINST PUBLISHERS WHO DIDN'T DIGITISE THEIR CATALOGUES FAST ENOUGH.

PUBLISHERS WERE TOLD THAT THEY WERE LESS LIKELY TO FEATURE PROMINENTLY IN AMAZON'S SEARCH RESULTS AND RECOMMENDATIONS.

BY LATE 2007 AMAZON HAD NINETY THOUSAND BOOKS IN THE E-BOOK LIBRARY. THIS WAS CLOSE ENOUGH TO BEZOS'S MAGIC NUMBER FOR THE COMPANY TO DECIDE TO LAUNCH THEIR MUCH DELAYED E-READER.

19 NOVEMBER 2007, AT THE W HOTEL, LOWER MANHATTAN.

HERE IT IS, EVERYONE. I GIVE YOU...

THE KINDLE.

THE KINDLE ITSELF WOULD RETAIL AT $399, BUT WHAT CAME AS A SHOCK TO PUBLISHERS WAS THE COST OF A DOWNLOADED BOOK – A FLAT PRICE OF $9.99.

HOW MUCH DID HE SAY A BOOK WAS?

THEY MADE NO MENTION OF THIS IN THE RUN-UP TO THE THE LAUNCH.

BRAD STONE, IN HIS BOOK ON AMAZON, *THE EVERYTHING STORE*, QUOTES ONE PUBLISHING EXECUTIVE AS SAYING...

IT LEFT AN INCREDIBLY BAD TASTE IN OUR MOUTHS...

THAT THEY WOULD SLIP THAT ONE BY US AFTER HAMMERING US FOR MONTHS WITH THEIR GODDAMN LISTS.

I DON'T THINK THEY WERE DOING THE WRONG THING, BUT I THINK THE WAY THEY HANDLED IT WAS WRONG.

IT WAS JUST ONE MORE NAIL IN THE COFFIN THAT NO ONE KNEW WAS BEING CLOSED OVER US.

THE SUCCESS OF THE KINDLE TIPPED THE BALANCE AWAY FROM PHYSICAL BOOKS TOWARDS DIGITAL.

IT'S SO CONVENIENT.

THIS GAVE AMAZON THE LEVERAGE TO SQUEEZE EVEN MORE CONCESSIONS FROM SUPPLIERS.

THE COMPANY ALREADY HAD HUGE ADVANTAGES. THEY COULD TAKE ONLINE ORDERS AND SHIP GOODS FASTER THAN ANY COMPETITOR.

PARCEL FOR YOU.

ALREADY? I'VE ONLY JUST ORDERED IT.

AMAZON REPORTED $14.8 BILLION IN SALES IN 2007. MORE THAN TWICE THE SALES OF ITS TWO NEAREST COMPETITORS ADDED TOGETHER.

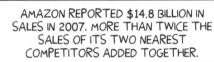

BARNES & NOBLE PULLED IN $5.4 BILLION THAT YEAR AND EBAY A MERE $7.7 BILLION.

WE JUST CAN'T KEEP UP.

B+N

EBAY

IN THIS NEW AGE, NOT ALL TRADITIONAL BOOKSTORES WOULD MAKE IT.

BORDERS
1971-2011

MEANWHILE PUBLISHERS ATTEMPTED TO PUSH BACK AGAINST AMAZON'S $9.99 E-BOOK PRICE. THEY WANTED TO SET THEIR OWN PRICES ON THE KINDLE.

THERE WAS A SUCCESSION OF MEETINGS BETWEEN EXECUTIVES OF PENGUIN, SIMON & SCHUSTER, HACHETTE, MACMILLAN, HARPERCOLLINS AND RANDOM HOUSE...

IN VARIOUS UPSCALE MANHATTAN RESTAURANTS.

THESE MEETINGS LATER BECAME THE FOCUS OF A DEPARTMENT OF JUSTICE PRICE-FIXING ENQUIRY.

THE DOJ BELIEVED THAT THE SIX PUBLISHERS, TOGETHER WITH APPLE, HAD COLLUDED TO FIX THE PRICE OF E-BOOKS ON THE iPAD (WHICH WAS ABOUT TO BE LAUNCHED) AND IN THIS WAY FORCE AMAZON TO RAISE PRICES ON THE KINDLE.

ALL SIX PUBLISHERS EVENTUALLY SETTLED THE DOJ's LAWSUIT. APPLE LOST THE ENSUING TRIAL AND WERE OBLIGED TO PAY A FINE OF $450 MILLION.

ULTIMATELY THE LARGER PUBLISHERS DID WREST SOME CONTROL OF E-BOOK PRICING FROM AMAZON. HACHETTE GOT INTO A LONG AND BITTER DISPUTE WITH THE ONLINE RETAILER OVER THIS ISSUE...

DURING WHICH AMAZON STOPPED CUSTOMERS FROM BEING ABLE TO PRE-ORDER THE PUBLISHER'S TITLES...

AND DELAYED SHIPMENTS OF SOME OF HACHETTE'S BOOKS.

A DEAL BETWEEN THE TWO COMPANIES WAS EVENTUALLY FINALISED THAT ALLOWED HACHETTE TO SET THE PRICE OF ITS OWN E-BOOKS.

IN RETURN AMAZON GOT A SPECIFIC CUT OF THE SALE PRICE AND RETAINED A LIMITED RIGHT TO DISCOUNT.

IN THE END THESE DISPUTES MATTERED LITTLE. BY 2009 AMAZON HAD EXPANDED FAR BEYOND ITS CORE BUSINESS OF SELLING BOOKS. BEZOS'S DREAM OF CREATING AN EVERYTHING STORE WAS IN SIGHT.

THE COMPANY HAD MOVED INTO TOYS, MUSIC, HARDWARE, GROCERIES (AMAZONFRESH WAS LAUNCHED IN 2007)...

AND SHOES (THE ONLINE FOOTWEAR MERCHANT, ZAPPOS, HAD BEEN BOUGHT BY AMAZON FOR $1.2 BILLION).

BY THE LATE 2000s THE COMPANY WAS KEEN TO MOVE INTO THE LUCRATIVE MARKET OF BABY PRODUCTS. HERE AMAZON'S MAIN COMPETITOR WAS QUIDSI, WHO SOLD THROUGH THEIR WEBSITE DIAPERS.COM.

QUIDSI WERE AS EFFICIENT IN DELIVERY AS AMAZON. THEY MADE IT EASY FOR TIME-PRESSED PARENTS TO REPEAT-ORDER GOODS. QUIDSI'S WAREHOUSES WERE OUTSIDE MAJOR POPULATION CENTRES TO TAKE ADVANTAGE OF CHEAP GROUND-SHIPPING RATES.

THEY WERE ABLE TO PROMISE FREE OVERNIGHT DELIVERY IN TWO-THIRDS OF THE US. QUIDSI SOLD EVERYTHING PARENTS MIGHT NEED, INCLUDING BABY WIPES, INFANT FORMULA, CLOTHES AND STROLLERS.

JEFF BLACKBURN, AMAZON'S THEN MERGERS AND ACQUISITIONS CHIEF, LET IT BE KNOWN THAT THE COMPANY WERE VERY SERIOUS ABOUT THE BABY PRODUCTS MARKET.

HE TOLD QUIDSI'S FOUNDERS, MARC LORE AND VINIT BHARARA...

YOU SHOULD CONSIDER SELLING TO AMAZON.

NO.

WELL, CALL ME IF YOU CHANGE YOUR MIND.

SOON AFTER THIS QUIDSI NOTICED THAT AMAZON BEGAN DROPPING THEIR PRICES ON BABY PRODUCTS BY UP TO 30 PER CENT.

QUIDSI EXPERIMENTALLY LOWERED THEIR OWN PRICES AND THEN WATCHED AS THE PRICES ON AMAZON'S WEBSITE FELL EVEN FURTHER IN RESPONSE. AMAZON WAS TARGETING DIAPERS.COM.

SALE

THE SQUEEZE WAS ON. QUIDSI HAD GROWN FROM NOTHING TO $300 MILLION IN AN HANDFUL OF YEARS, BUT, UNDER AMAZON'S ASSAULT, GROWTH BEGAN TO SLOW. THIS WAS A PROBLEM BECAUSE INVESTORS WERE RELUCTANT TO FURNISH QUIDSI WITH MORE CAPITAL AND THE COMPANY WAS NOT YET MATURE ENOUGH FOR AN INITIAL PUBLIC OFFERING (IPO).

IN SEPTEMBER 2010 AMAZON LAUNCHED A NEW SERVICE CALLED AMAZON MOM. PARENTS COULD GET UP TO A YEAR'S WORTH OF TWO-DAY AMAZON PRIME SHIPPING (A SERVICE THAT USUALLY COST $79 TO JOIN) AND GET AN ADDITIONAL 30 PER CENT OFF THE ALREADY DISCOUNTED REGULAR DIAPERS.

DIAPERS.COM WERE LISTING A CASE OF PAMPERS AT $45. AMAZON MOM SUBSCRIBERS COULD BUY A CASE FOR LESS THAN $30.

THAT'S A GOOD DEAL.

YEAH!

QUIDSI EXECUTIVES CALCULATED THAT AMAZON WOULD LOSE $100 MILLION OVER THE FIRST THREE MONTHS ON DIAPERS ALONE.

THAT'S CRAZY.

MAYBE?

BUT THESE TACTICS WORKED. QUIDSI WAS UNABLE TO COMPETE. LORE AND BHARARA WERE FORCED TO GO OUT AND LOOK FOR A BUYER FOR THEIR COMPANY. THERE WAS A BRIEF FLIRTATION WITH THE US RETAIL GIANT WALMART...

BUT IN THE END QUIDSI WAS SOLD TO AMAZON IN NOVEMBER 2010 FOR $545 MILLION. BEZOS HAD ABSORBED ANOTHER BUSINESS.

HA HA HA HA HA HA HA!

THE COMPANY CONTINUED TO EXPAND. IN 2011 AMAZON BOUGHT THE WEB-BASED DVD RENTAL COMPANY LOVEFILM, FOR CLOSE TO $317 MILLION.

LOVEFILM PROVIDED DVD-BY-MAIL AND STREAMED VIDEO ON DEMAND TO ITS TWO MILLION SUBSCRIBERS.

THIS LATTER SERVICE BECAME THE BACKBONE OF AMAZON'S OWN ONLINE TV-SHOW-AND-MOVIE-STREAMING BUSINESS.

AMAZON DISCONTINUED THE DVD-BY-MAIL SERVICE IN 2017, CITING LACK OF DEMAND.

SINCE THEN, THROUGH ITS SUBSIDIARY, AMAZON STUDIOS, AMAZON HAS SPENT MILLIONS DEVELOPING ITS OWN TV SHOWS AND MOVIES. IN 2017 IT BOUGHT THE GLOBAL TV RIGHTS TO *THE LORD OF THE RINGS* FOR $1 BILLION.

BY 2018 AMAZON HAD OPENED WAREHOUSES (FULFILMENT CENTRES) IN AUSTRALIA, CANADA, CHINA, THE CZECH REPUBLIC, BRAZIL, FRANCE, GERMANY, INDIA, ITALY, JAPAN, KUWAIT, MEXICO, POLAND, SAUDI ARABIA, SLOVAKIA, SPAIN, SINGAPORE, THE UNITED ARAB EMIRATES AND THE UNITED KINGDOM. BEZOS'S LITTLE COMPANY, WHICH HAD STARTED OUT IN HIS GARAGE, HAD BECOME A WORLDWIDE PRESENCE THAT EMPLOYED 566,000 PEOPLE.

THIS COLOSSAL GROWTH HAD BEEN DRIVEN BY BEZOS'S OBSESSION WITH DELIVERING LOW PRICES, FAST DELIVERY AND A FRICTIONLESS EXPERIENCE FOR THE CUSTOMER (MEANING THAT THE CUSTOMER COULD ORDER AN ITEM WITH BARELY ANY EFFORT ON HIS OR HER PART). AS THE COMPANY HAD GROWN IT HAD THEN USED ITS ENORMOUS FINANCIAL MUSCLE TO SIMPLY OUTPACE, CRUSH OR ABSORB COMPETITORS.

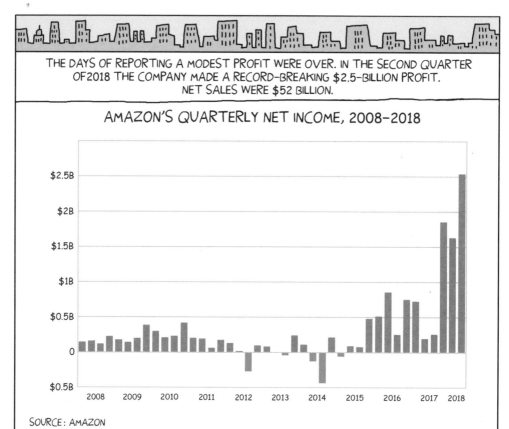

THE DAYS OF REPORTING A MODEST PROFIT WERE OVER. IN THE SECOND QUARTER OF 2018 THE COMPANY MADE A RECORD-BREAKING $2.5-BILLION PROFIT. NET SALES WERE $52 BILLION.

AMAZON'S QUARTERLY NET INCOME, 2008–2018

SOURCE: AMAZON

THAT SAME YEAR AMAZON BECAME ONLY THE SECOND TRILLION-DOLLAR COMPANY IN THE WORLD (AFTER APPLE) WHEN THE TOTAL DOLLAR MARKET VALUE OF ITS SHARES PASSED THAT ENORMOUS FIGURE.

CRASH!

THIS MADE JEFF BEZOS THE WORLD'S WEALTHIEST INDIVIDUAL, WITH AN ESTIMATED NET WORTH OF $150 BILLION.

HA HA HA HA HA HA HA HA!

HERE ARE A JUST A FEW OF THE MANY COMPANIES AMAZON OWNS.

IMDB, AN ONLINE DATABASE OF INFORMATION RELATED TO FILMS, TV, AND VIDEO GAMES, INCLUDING CAST/PRODUCTION/CREW/PERSONAL BIOGRAPHIES AND PLOT SUMMARIES.

AUDIBLE, THE WORLD'S LARGEST PRODUCER OF DOWNLOADABLE AUDIOBOOKS. AUDIBLE ALSO SELL PODCASTS AND AUDIO VERSIONS OF MAGAZINES AND NEWSPAPERS.

GOODREADS. AN ONLINE COMMUNITY WITH BOOK REVIEWS, RECOMMENDATIONS AND DISCUSSION GROUPS.

TWITCH.TV. A LIVE-STREAMING VIDEO PLATFORM THAT FOCUSES ON VIDEOGAMING AND OTHER GAME-RELATED EVENTS.

KIVA SYSTEMS (AMAZON ROBOTICS). A COMPANY THAT'S DEVELOPING DELIVERY DRONES AND ROBOTS TO WORK IN AMAZON'S WAREHOUSES.

WHOLE FOOD MARKETS. AN AMERICAN SUPERMARKET CHAIN THAT SPECIALISES IN SELLING ORGANIC PRODUCTS. BOUGHT BY AMAZON IN 2017 FOR $3.7 BILLION.

COMIXOLOGY. A CLOUD-BASED DIGITAL PLATFORM THAT OFFERS 40,000 COMICS AND GRAPHIC NOVELS.

HEH!

AND FINALLY, THROUGH NASH HOLDINGS (A PRIVATE COMPANY BEZOS OWNS), HE BOUGHT THE *WASHINGTON POST* IN 2013 FOR $250 MILLION.

HAHAHAHAHA!

ACCORDING TO THE LAND REPORT, A PUBLICATION THAT TRACKS LAND OWNERSHIP IN THE US, BEZOS IS THE 25TH LARGEST LANDOWNER IN THE COUNTRY. HIS PROPERTIES INCLUDE SEVERAL HOMES ON THE SHORES OF LAKE WASHINGTON IN WASHINGTON STATE, TWO NEIGHBOURING HOUSES IN BEVERLY HILLS, CALIFORNIA, A FORMER MUSEUM IN WASHINGTON DC, FOUR LINKED APARTMENTS IN AN ART DECO TOWER ON MANHATTAN'S CENTRAL PARK WEST, AND 300,000 ACRES IN VAN HORN, WEST TEXAS.

SUCH IS LIFE FOR JEFF BEZOS. BUT WHAT IS IT LIKE FOR THE THOUSANDS HE EMPLOYS?

WHAT ARE CONDITIONS LIKE IN AN AMAZON WAREHOUSE?

THE JOURNALIST JAMES BLOODWORTH WENT UNDERCOVER AT AN AMAZON WAREHOUSE IN STAFFORDSHIRE, UK, FOR A BOOK ON LOW-WAGE BRITAIN.

I HAD DONE WAREHOUSE WORK PREVIOUSLY WHEN I WAS YOUNGER, ALONG WITH A RANGE OF OTHER POORLY PAID, MANUAL JOBS.

IN OTHER WORDS MY SHOCK AT THE WAY WORKERS WERE TREATED BY AMAZON WAS NOT A PRODUCT OF SOME WET-BEHIND-THE-EARS NAIVETY.

I FULLY EXPECTED WAREHOUSE WORK TO BE TOUGH. YET WHAT I WITNESSED AT AMAZON WENT WAY BEYOND THAT. THIS WAS A WORKPLACE ENVIRONMENT IN WHICH DECENCY, RESPECT AND DIGNITY WERE ABSENT.

THE WAREHOUSE HAD THE ATMOSPHERE OF WHAT I IMAGINE A LOW-SECURITY PRISON WOULD FEEL LIKE.

YOU HAD TO PASS IN AND OUT OF GIGANTIC AIRPORT-STYLE SECURITY GATES AT THE END OF EVERY SHIFT AND EACH TIME YOU NEEDED A BREAK...

ON ONE OCCASION BLOODWORTH WAS LOOKING FOR ITEMS ON AN UPPER FLOOR OF THE WAREHOUSE WHEN HE CAME ACROSS A BOTTLE OF URINE.

HE LATER LEARNED THAT WORKERS OFTEN DIDN'T TAKE TOILET BREAKS BECAUSE THEY FEARED PUNISHMENT FOR MISSING PRODUCTION TARGETS. PEEING IN A BOTTLE WAS PREFERABLE.

AMAZON IS KNOWN TO TRACK HOW FAST ITS WAREHOUSE WORKERS CAN PICK AND PACKAGE ITEMS FROM ITS SHELVES, IMPOSING STRICTLY TIMED BREAKS AND TARGETS. IT ISSUES WARNING POINTS FOR THOSE WHO DON'T MEET ITS GOALS.

THE WORKERS' RIGHTS CAMPAIGN GROUP 'ORGANISE' SURVEYED AMAZON WAREHOUSE WORKERS ON THEIR EXPERIENCES. HERE ARE A FEW OF THEIR ANONYMOUS QUOTES.

I HAVE TO FINISH MY BREAK EARLY BECAUSE IF I CLICK ON ONE MINUTE LATE I'M ISSUED WITH A PENALTY. THREE PENALTIES AND YOU GET SACKED FROM YOUR JOB.

THERE ARE TWO FIFTEEN-MINUTE BREAKS, WHICH IS ACTUALLY LESS, AS IT TAKES ABOUT SIX MINUTES TO WALK TO WHERE I WORK IN THE FULFILMENT CENTRE...

AND ANOTHER SIX TO GET BACK. YOU HAVE TO BE QUICK OR YOU'LL GET A CONDUCT WARNING.

BREAKS ARE USUALLY SAD. WE ARE TRYING TO MAKE THE MOST OF IT, BUT NOBODY IS TRULY HAPPY.

YOU SEE PEOPLE STRUGGLING TO COME TO TERMS WITH THE DEMANDING ENVIRONMENT: SORE BACK, FEET, HANDS, HEADACHES.

FOR PICKING, THE TARGET IS AROUND 100 UNITS PER HOUR, WHICH MEANS WE HAVE TO PICK 100 UNITS WITHIN 60 MINUTES FROM ANYWHERE ACROSS ONE FLOOR OF THE FULFILMENT CENTRE.

THIS IS FOR A NORMAL DAY. DURING PEAK TIME, IT'S 120 TO 140 UNITS PER HOUR, WHICH IS NEAR IMPOSSIBLE.

IN 2011, THE *MORNING CALL*, A DAILY NEWSPAPER BASED IN ALLENTOWN, PENNSYLVANIA, REPORTED THAT AN AMAZON EMPLOYEE HAD CONTACTED THE US OCCUPATIONAL SAFETY AND HEALTH ADMINISTRATION TO SAY THAT THE HEAT IN THE AMAZON WAREHOUSE IN LEHIGH VALLEY, PA, HAD REACHED 102 DEGREES FAHRENHEIT (38.9 CELSIUS) AND THAT 15 WORKERS HAD COLLAPSED. THE EMPLOYEE ALSO CLAIMED THAT THE SICK WORKERS WHO'D BEEN SENT HOME HAD RECEIVED DISCIPLINARY POINTS.

THE PAPER ALSO REPORTED THAT AMAZON PAID CETRONIA AMBULANCE CORPS TO HAVE AMBULANCES AND PARAMEDICS STATIONED OUTSIDE THE WAREHOUSE DURING SEVERE DAYS OF EXCESS HEAT.

WORKERS WHO HAD BEEN EMPLOYED IN OTHER COMPANIES' WAREHOUSES SAID THAT, NORMALLY, LOADING-DOCK DOORS ON EITHER SIDE OF THE BUILDING WOULD BE LEFT OPEN TO LET FRESH AIR CIRCULATE, BUT THIS WAS NOT THE CASE AT AMAZON. MANAGERS TOLD STAFF THAT THE DOORS WERE SHUT BECAUSE THEY WERE WORRIED ABOUT THEFT.

ELMER GORIS, WHO HAD PREVIOUS EXPERIENCE IN WAREHOUSE WORK, WAS EMPLOYED BY AMAZON AT LEHIGH VALLEY FOR A YEAR.

I NEVER FELT LIKE PASSING OUT IN A WAREHOUSE AND I NEVER FELT TREATED LIKE A PIECE OF CRAP IN ANY OTHER WAREHOUSE. THEY CAN DO THIS BECAUSE THERE AREN'T ANY JOBS IN THIS AREA.

ABOUT THE HEAT ON THE UPPER FLOOR OF THE BUILDING, GORIS TOLD THE *MORNING CALL*...

I REMEMBER GOING UP THERE TO CHECK THE LOCATION OF AN ITEM. I LASTED TWO MINUTES BECAUSE I COULDN'T BREATHE UP THERE.

STEPHEN DALLAL WORKED FOR THE COMPANY FOR SIX MONTHS AS A PICKER BEFORE HE LOST HIS JOB FOR NOT MEETING PRODUCTION TARGETS.

IT JUST GOT HARDER AND HARDER. IT STARTED WITH 75 PIECES AN HOUR, THEN 125 AN HOUR. IT JUST GOT FASTER AND FASTER AND FASTER.

ONE ANONYMOUS EMPLOYEE IN HIS FIFTIES SAID HE WORKED FOR SEVEN MONTHS FOR AMAZON BEFORE HE WAS FIRED FOR NOT REACHING TARGETS. HIS JOB WAS AS A PICKER, TAKING ITEMS FROM SHELVES AND DELIVERING TO THE PACKERS.

AT THE BEGINNING I THOUGHT I WAS DOING REALLY WELL. I NEVER MISSED A DAY. NEVER CAME IN LATE. I WAS THE MODEL EMPLOYEE.

BUT AFTER A WHILE I COULD ONLY ACHIEVE A CERTAIN RATE AND I COULDN'T GO ANY FASTER. IT WAS JUST BRUTAL.

ANOTHER ANONYMOUS WORKER, WHO SPENT SEVERAL MONTHS UNLOADING BOXES OF BOOKS, SAID...

EVERYBODY GETS BACKACHE...

BUT IF YOU SLOW DOWN THEY REPRIMAND YOU. THEY'RE KILLING PEOPLE MENTALLY AND PHYSICALLY. THEY JUST PUSH, PUSH, PUSH.

IN APRIL 2018, THE NATIONAL COUNCIL FOR OCCUPATIONAL SAFETY AND HEALTH, A PRIVATE NONPROFIT WORKERS' ADVOCACY GROUP, NAMED AMAZON IN A REPORT ON WORKPLACE SAFETY. THE REPORT SAID...

AMAZON WORKERS SUFFER INJURY, AND SOMETIMES LOSE THEIR LIVES, IN A WORKING ENVIRONMENT WITH A RELENTLESS DEMAND TO FILL ORDERS AND CLOSE MONITORING OF EMPLOYEE ACTIONS.

THE REPORT THEN GOES ON TO DESCRIBE THE DEATHS OF SEVEN AMAZON EMPLOYEES SINCE 2013.

DEVAN MICHAEL SHOEMAKER, 28, WAS KILLED ON 19 SEPTEMBER 2017, WHEN HE WAS RUN OVER BY A TRUCK AT AN AMAZON WAREHOUSE IN CARLISLE, PENNSYLVANIA.

PHILLIP TERRY, 59, WAS KILLED ON 23 SEPTEMBER 2017, WHEN HIS HEAD WAS CRUSHED BY A FORKLIFT AT AN AMAZON WAREHOUSE IN PLAINFIELD, INDIANA.

KARLA KAY ARNOLD, 50, WAS HIT BY A CAR IN THE PARKING LOT OF AN AMAZON WAREHOUSE IN MONEE, ILLINOIS, ON 23 OCTOBER 2017.

JEFF LOCKHART, 29, DIED FROM A CARDIAC ARREST IN AN AMAZON WAREHOUSE IN CHESTER, VIRGINIA, ON 19 JANUARY 2013.

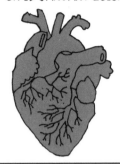

ROLAND SMITH, 57, WAS KILLED AFTER BEING DRAGGED AND CRUSHED BY A CONVEYOR BELT AT AN AMAZON WAREHOUSE IN AVENEL, NEW JERSEY, ON 4 DECEMBER 2013.

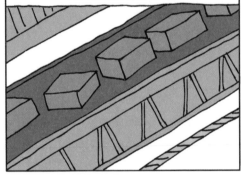

JODY RHOADS, 52, WAS CRUSHED AND PINNED BY A PALLET-LOADER AT AN AMAZON WAREHOUSE IN CARLISLE, PENNSYLVANIA ON 1 JUNE 2014.

ANTHONY CHARLES LEE, 39, WAS CRUSHED BY A FORKLIFT TRUCK AT AN AMAZON WAREHOUSE IN FERNLEY, NEVADA ON 4 NOVEMBER 2014.

NOT MENTIONED IN THE REPORT IS THE UNNAMED WORKER WHO DIED AFTER VOMITING BLOOD AT AN AMAZON WAREHOUSE IN SACRAMENTO, CALIFORNIA, ON 14 DECEMBER 2017.

ACCIDENTS HAVE CONTINUED TO TAKE PLACE. FOR EXAMPLE, IN ROBBINSVILLE, NEW JERSEY, ON 5 DECEMBER 2018...

TWENTY-FOUR AMAZON WORKERS WERE HOSPITALISED WHEN A ROBOT DROPPED A CAN OF BEAR REPELLENT.

CHOKE!

THESE ARE THE DAY-TO-DAY EXPERIENCES OF PEOPLE AT THE BOTTOM OF AMAZON'S CORPORATE STRUCTURE, BUT WHAT ABOUT THOSE FURTHER UP THE LADDER? WHAT ARE WORKING CONDITIONS LIKE FOR THE THOUSANDS OF WHITE-COLLAR EMPLOYEES WHO TOIL DAILY FOR THE WORLD'S LARGEST ONLINE RETAIL STORE?

AN AUGUST 2015 ARTICLE BY THE *NEW YORK TIMES* GIVES SOME INSIGHT INTO AMAZON CORPORATE LIFE. THE NEWSPAPER INTERVIEWED MORE THAN A HUNDRED CURRENT AND FORMER AMAZONIANS, INCLUDING MEMBERS OF THE LEADERSHIP TEAM, HUMAN RESOURCES, EXECUTIVES, MARKETEERS, RETAIL SPECIALISTS AND ENGINEERS.

WORKERS DESCRIBE HOW THEY TRIED TO RECONCILE THE OFTEN BRUTAL ASPECTS OF THE JOB WITH THE GENUINELY EXCITING OPPORTUNITY THEY WERE GIVEN TO CREATE SOMETHING NEW.

THE COMPANY USES A SELF-REINFORCING SET OF MANAGEMENT DATA AND PSYCHOLOGICAL TOOLS TO PUSH ITS TENS OF THOUSANDS OF WORKERS TO THEIR LIMITS.

EMPLOYEES ARE ENCOURAGED TO CHALLENGE ONE ANOTHER EVEN WHEN DOING SO IS UNCOMFORTABLE AND EXHAUSTING.

THIS FRICTION CAN MEAN THAT WORKERS' IDEAS ARE RIPPED APART IN MEETINGS AND THIS SOMETIMES LEADS TO OPEN CONFLICT.

THE INTERNAL PHONE DIRECTORY INSTRUCTS COLLEAGUES ON HOW TO SEND SECRET FEEDBACK TO ONE ANOTHER'S BOSSES.

HERE'S AN ACTUAL EXAMPLE OF TEXT OFFERED BY THE GUIDE.

I FELT CONCERNED ABOUT HIS INFLEXIBILITY AND OPENLY COMPLAINING ABOUT MINOR TASKS.

TECHNIQUES OF THIS SORT CREATED AN ATMOSPHERE OF INTRIGUE AND SCHEMING. WORKERS DESCRIBED MAKING PACTS WITH COLLEAGUES TO BURY A PARTICULAR INDIVIDUAL...

OR TO PRAISE ONE ANOTHER LAVISHLY.

YOU'RE GREAT.

NO, YOU ARE.

YOU WALK OUT OF A CONFERENCE ROOM AND YOU'LL SEE A GROWN MAN COVERING HIS FACE.

BO OLSON, MARKETING

NEARLY EVERY PERSON I WORKED WITH, I SAW CRY AT THEIR DESK.

NOT EVERYONE INTERVIEWED SAW THIS AS ENTIRELY NEGATIVE. SOME EX-AMAZON EMPLOYEES SAID WHAT THEY LEARNED AT THE COMPANY HELPED THEIR CAREERS TAKE OFF...

AND THEY HAD BECOME ADDICTED TO THE AMAZON WAY OF WORKING.

A LOT OF PEOPLE FEEL THIS TENSION. IT'S THE GREATEST PLACE I HATE TO WORK.

JOHN ROSSMAN, EXECUTIVE

AMAZON WORKFORCE TURNOVER IS HUGE. THE COMPANY IS CONSTANTLY HIRING.

WELCOME NEW WORKERS

THOSE WORKERS WHO PERFORM POORLY OR CAN'T TAKE THE PRESSURE ARE SOON SHOWN THE DOOR.

AMAZON IS OKAY WITH MOVING THROUGH A LOT OF PEOPLE TO IDENTIFY AND RETAIN SUPERSTARS.

VIJAY RAVINDRAM EX–MANAGER AT AMAZON.

THEY KEEP THE STARS BY OFFERING A COMBINATION OF INCREDIBLE OPPORTUNITIES AND COMPENSATION.

IT'S LIKE PANNING FOR GOLD.

ONCE A YEAR THERE IS WHAT AMAZON CALL AN ORGANISATIONAL LEVEL REVIEW, WHERE MANAGEMENT DEBATE SUBORDINATES' MERITS.

THE MEETING REVIEW STARTS WITH A DISCUSSION OF THE LOWER-LEVEL EMPLOYEES, WHOSE PERFORMANCE IS DEBATED IN FRONT OF HIGHER-LEVEL MANAGERS. AS THE DAY GOES ON, SUCCESSIVE ROUNDS OF MANAGERS LEAVE, KNOWING THAT THOSE WHO REMAIN IN THE ROOM WILL DETERMINE THEIR FATES.

MANY SUPERVISORS SAY THE PROCESS IS LIKE PREPARING FOR A COURT CASE. TO AVOID LOSING GOOD MEMBERS OF THEIR TEAM THEY MUST COME ARMED WITH REAMS OF PAPERWORK...

AND BE PREPARED TO INCRIMINATE MEMBERS OF OPPOSING GROUPS.

IT'S THEIR FAULT.

ANOTHER STRATEGY USED IS TO CHOOSE A SACRIFICIAL LAMB TO PROTECT MORE VALUABLE WORKERS.

IT'S HIS FAULT.

JIM

ONE ANONYMOUS MARKETEER SAID...

YOU LEARN HOW TO DIPLOMATICALLY THROW PEOPLE UNDER THE BUS. IT'S A HORRIBLE FEELING.

OTHER LARGE COMPANIES, INCLUDING MICROSOFT AND GENERAL ELECTRIC, HAVE ENDED THIS PRACTICE, BECAUSE IT CAN FORCE MANAGERS TO GET RID OF VALUABLE TALENT JUST TO MEET QUOTAS.

WHERE'S EVERYONE?

WE FIRED THEM.

MOLLIE JAY, A MEMBER OF THE KINDLE TEAM, SAID SHE'D BEEN GIVEN HIGH MARKS FOR YEARS.

BUT WHEN HER FATHER BECAME ILL WITH CANCER AND SHE STOPPED WORKING LATE NIGHTS AND WEEKENDS IN ORDER TO CARE FOR HIM, HER STATUS CHANGED. HER MANAGER TOLD HER THAT SHE WAS...

A PROBLEM.

JAY WASN'T ALLOWED TO TRANSFER TO A LESS DEMANDING ROLE. SHE EVENTUALLY TOOK UNPAID LEAVE AND NEVER RETURNED TO AMAZON.

GOODBYE!

EXIT

WHEN YOU'RE NOT ABLE TO GIVE YOUR ABSOLUTE ALL, 80 HOURS A WEEK, THEY SEE IT AS A MAJOR WEAKNESS.

THE *NEW YORK TIMES* ARTICLE QUOTES A NUMBER OF EX-AMAZON EMPLOYEES ANONYMOUSLY. A MOTHER OF A STILLBORN CHILD SAID...

I HAD JUST EXPERIENCED THE MOST DEVASTATING EVENT OF MY LIFE...

ONLY TO BE TOLD THAT MY PERFORMANCE WOULD BE MONITORED.

A WOMAN WHO HAD BREAST CANCER WAS INFORMED THAT SHE WOULD BE PUT ON A 'PERFORMANCE IMPROVEMENT PLAN'. WHICH IS AMAZON CODE FOR 'YOU'RE IN DANGER OF BEING FIRED.'

AN EMPLOYEE WHO MISCARRIED TWINS WAS OBLIGED TO GO ON A BUSINESS TRIP THE DAY AFTER SHE HAD SURGERY.

HER BOSS TOLD HER...

FROM WHERE YOU ARE IN LIFE, TRYING TO START A FAMILY, I DON'T KNOW IF THIS IS THE RIGHT PLACE FOR YOU.

JEFF BEZOS REACTED TO THE *NEW YORK TIMES* ARTICLE BY WRITING A LETTER TO HIS EMPLOYEES, SAYING...

THIS ARTICLE DOESN'T DESCRIBE THE AMAZON I KNOW OR THE CARING AMAZONIANS I WORK WITH.

BUT IF YOU KNOW OF ANY STORIES LIKE THOSE REPORTED, I WANT YOU TO ESCALATE TO HR. YOU CAN ALSO EMAIL ME DIRECT AT JEFF@AMAZON.COM.

EVEN IF IT'S RARE OR ISOLATED, OUR TOLERANCE FOR SUCH LACK OF EMPATHY NEEDS TO BE ZERO.

I STRONGLY BELIEVE THAT ANYONE WORKING IN A COMPANY THAT REALLY IS LIKE THE ONE DESCRIBED IN THE NYT WOULD BE CRAZY TO STAY. I KNOW I WOULD LEAVE SUCH A COMPANY.

BUT HOPEFULLY YOU DON'T RECOGNISE THE COMPANY DESCRIBED. HOPEFULLY YOU'RE HAVING FUN WORKING WITH A BUNCH OF BRILLIANT TEAMMATES, HELPING INVENT THE FUTURE AND LAUGHING ALONG THE WAY.

EVEN THOUGH BEZOS CLAIMED NOT TO RECOGNISE HIS COMPANY'S OFTEN RUTHLESS CORPORATE CULTURE, IT CLEARLY EXISTS.

AMAZON'S BUSINESS AND EMPLOYMENT PRACTICES ARE A DIRECT EXTENSION OF ITS FOUNDER'S WORKAHOLIC AND COMPETITIVE NATURE.

GET IT DONE.

IN RECENT YEARS BEZOS HAS ATTEMPTED TO ALLEVIATE SOME OF THE CRITICISM OF AMAZON BY RAISING THE MINIMUM WAGE OF ITS UK AND US EMPLOYEES.

EVERYONE GETS A RAISE.

THE COMPANY HAD COME UNDER FIRE FOR PAYING SUCH LOW WAGES THAT THOUSANDS OF AMAZON WAREHOUSE WORKERS IN THE US HAD TO APPLY FOR GOVERNMENT FOOD STAMPS. THIS EFFECTIVELY MEANT THAT TAXPAYERS WERE SUBSIDISING AMAZON'S WAGE BILL.

BEZOS HAS ALSO GIVEN TO CHARITY. UNTIL 2018 HE HADN'T ENGAGED MUCH IN PHILANTHROPY. HE IS THE ONLY AMERICAN AMONG THE WORLD'S FIVE RICHEST PEOPLE NOT TO JOIN THE GIVING PLEDGE.

WOULD YOU LIKE TO GIVE?

THE GIVING PLEDGE IS A CAMPAIGN THAT ENCOURAGES WEALTHY PEOPLE TO GIVE A MAJORITY OF THEIR MONEY TO PHILANTHROPIC CAUSES.

NO.

HOWEVER, IN JANUARY 2018 HE AND HIS WIFE MACKENZIE GAVE $33 MILLION TO THE NON-PROFIT ORGANISATION THEDREAM.US, WHICH PROVIDES SUPPORT TO CHILDREN WHO COME TO THE US AS UNDOCUMENTED IMMIGRANTS.

THE GRANT, THE LARGEST IN THE ORGANISATION'S HISTORY, GAVE 1,000 UNDOCUMENTED IMMIGRANT GRADUATES OF US HIGH SCHOOLS WITH DACA (DEFERRED ACTION FOR CHILDHOOD ARRIVAL) STATUS THE OPPORTUNITY TO GO TO COLLEGE.

MY DAD CAME TO THE US WHEN HE WAS 16 AS PART OF OPERATION PEDRO PAN, HE LANDED IN THIS COUNTRY ALONE AND UNABLE TO SPEAK ENGLISH. WITH A LOT OF GRIT AND DETERMINATION AND THE HELP OF SOME REMARKABLE ORGANISATIONS IN DELAWARE...

USA

MY DAD BECAME AN OUTSTANDING CITIZEN, AND HE CONTINUES TO GIVE BACK TO THIS COUNTRY THAT HE FEELS BLESSED HIM IN SO MANY WAYS. MACKENZIE AND I ARE HONORED TO BE ABLE TO HELP TODAY'S DREAMERS BY FUNDING THESE SCHOLARSHIPS.

ALSO IN 2018, BEZOS LAUNCHED A $2-BILLION FUND TO SUPPORT EDUCATION PROGRAMMES IN UNDER-SERVED COMMUNITIES.

GOT ANY SPARE CHANGE?

CALLED THE BEZOS DAY ONE FUND, IT FOCUSES ON CREATING RESOURCES FOR HOMELESS FAMILIES AND FULL-SCHOLARSHIP PRESCHOOL PROGRAMMES.

SOUNDS GREAT.

HOME-LESS

PREVIOUS TO THIS, BEZOS HAD GIVEN $15 MILLION TO PRINCETON UNIVERSITY, FROM WHERE HE AND HIS WIFE GRADUATED, TO HELP BUILD A CENTRE TO STUDY NEUROLOGICAL DISORDERS...

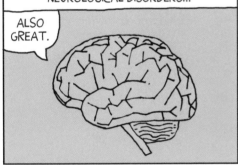

ALSO GREAT.

AND $35 MILLION TO THE FRED HUTCHINSON CANCER RESEARCH CENTER IN SEATTLE. THIS WAS THE LARGEST DONATION THEY HAD EVER RECEIVED.

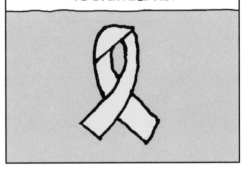

BUT ALL OF THIS GIVING STILL AMOUNTED TO A MERE FRACTION OF BEZOS'S $163-BILLION FORTUNE.

THE TIMING OF THE MAJORITY OF THIS CHARITY, COMING AS IT DID SHORTLY AFTER SUCH INTENSE CRITICISM OF AMAZON'S BUSINESS PRACTICES, DID SUGGEST TO SOME THAT IT WAS PARTLY DONE AS A PUBLIC-RELATIONS EXERCISE.

IT SHOULD BE POINTED OUT THAT FELLOW SEATTLE-AREA BILLIONAIRE BILL GATES HAS DONATED MORE THAN $40 BILLION OF HIS FORTUNE THROUGH HIS BILL AND MELINDA GATES FOUNDATION.

BEZOS COULD USE HIS WEALTH TO FIGHT HUNGER, IMPROVE AMAZON WORKERS' WAGES TO A SIGNIFICANT DEGREE OR PAY HIS FULL SHARE OF TAXES.

NO.

INSTEAD, HIS REAL PASSION IS SPACE.

THE ONLY WAY I CAN SEE TO DEPLOY THIS MUCH FINANCIAL RESERVES...

IS BY CONVERTING MY AMAZON WINNINGS INTO SPACE TRAVEL.

BEZOS HAD BEEN FASCINATED BY THE IDEA OF SPACE TRAVEL SINCE HE WAS A BOY WATCHING THE APOLLO MOON LANDINGS. IT HAD ENGENDERED A LIFELONG INTEREST IN SCIENCE FICTION AND ESPECIALLY STAR TREK.

THIS LED TO HIM HAVING A CAMEO, UNDER HEAVY MAKE UP, IN THE 2016 MOVIE STAR TREK BEYOND.

JEFF BEZOS FOUNDED HIS SPACE COMPANY, BLUE ORIGIN, IN 2000, BUT ITS EXISTENCE ONLY BECAME PUBLIC IN 2003. BLUE ORIGIN (THE NAME REFERS TO THE BLUE PLANET EARTH) WAS FORMED TO DEVELOP TECHNOLOGIES THAT WOULD ENABLE HUMAN ACCESS TO SPACE. THE AIM IS TO DRAMATICALLY REDUCE COSTS FOR MANNED SPACE FLIGHT. THE KEY TO THIS, ACCORDING TO BEZOS, IS RENEWABLE ROCKETS. BLUE ORIGIN'S FIRST ROCKET, *NEW SHEPARD* (NAMED AFTER THE APOLLO ASTRONAUT ALAN SHEPARD), HAS SUCCESSFULLY REACHED THE EDGE OF SPACE AND LANDED SAFELY MULTIPLE TIMES.

IN SEPTEMBER 2016, BLUE ORIGIN ANNOUNCED ITS SECOND ROCKET: *NEW GLENN* (NAMED AFTER APOLLO ASTRONAUT JOHN GLENN). MUCH LARGER IN SCALE, IT WILL BE ALMOST AS TALL AS NASA'S *SATURN V* MOON ROCKET, WITH 35 TIMES THE LIFTING POWER OF THE *NEW SHEPARD*. THE *NEW GLENN* IS DESIGNED TO GO INTO EARTH ORBIT AND THEN RE-ENTER THE ATMOSPHERE AND LAND TAIL-FIRST, DESPITE ITS ENORMOUS SIZE.

ROCKETS THE SCALE OF *NEW GLENN* AND LARGER COULD ONE DAY LIFT 100 OR MORE PASSENGERS, BEZOS CLAIMS, AND THESE FIRST TWO ROCKETS, HE SAYS, ARE MODEL Ts - EARLY EFFORTS THAT, LIKE FORD'S EARLY CARS, WILL SEEM CRUDE BY COMPARISON TO THEIR MORE CAPABLE SUCCESSORS.

I DON'T WANT TO LIVE IN A CIVILISATION OF STATUS. I WANT TO LIVE IN A CIVILISATION OF INVENTION AND GROWTH AND INCREDIBLE NEW THINGS, AND I'M VERY CONFIDENT IT'S THE ONLY WAY – YOU HAVE TO GO INTO SPACE.

I BELIEVE THAT WE ARE SITTING ON THE EDGE OF A GOLDEN AGE OF SPACE EXPLORATION. RIGHT ON THE EDGE. THE THING THAT I WOULD BE MOST PROUD OF, WHEN I'M 80 YEARS OLD, IS IF BLUE ORIGIN CAN LOWER THE COST OF ACCESS TO SPACE BY SUCH A LARGE AMOUNT THAT THERE CAN BE A DYNAMIC, ENTREPRENEURIAL EXPLOSION IN SPACE – JUST AS WE'VE SEEN OVER THE LAST 20 YEARS WITH THE INTERNET.

AS WHEN BEZOS BUILT AMAZON UP OVER THOSE EARLY YEARS, HE IS NOT CONCERNED ABOUT BLUE ORIGIN MAKING A PROFIT IN THE SHORT TERM.

HIS INVESTMENT OF A BILLION DOLLARS A YEAR IN THE COMPANY IS INTENDED TO GAIN MARKET DOMINATION IN THE LONG TERM.

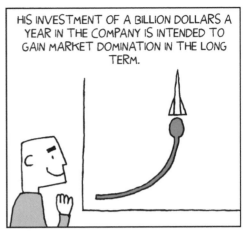

HOWEVER, BEZOS IS NOT THE ONLY BILLIONAIRE WITH AN INTEREST IN SPACE.

IN 2010, PAYPAL CO-FOUNDER AND TESLA CAR MANUFACTURER ELON MUSK'S SPACEX WAS THE FIRST PRIVATE COMPANY TO SUCCESSFULLY LAUNCH INTO ORBIT AND THEN RECOVER A SPACECRAFT.

RICHARD BRANSON'S VIRGIN GALACTIC IS DEVELOPING A COMMERCIAL REUSABLE SPACECRAFT FOR TOURISM AND SCIENCE MISSIONS.

BOEING ARE ALSO DEVELOPING A RECOVERABLE ROCKET, THE *STARLINER*, IN COLLABORATION WITH NASA.

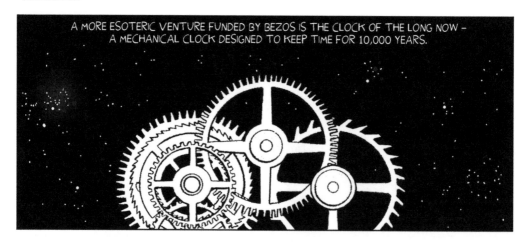

A MORE ESOTERIC VENTURE FUNDED BY BEZOS IS THE CLOCK OF THE LONG NOW – A MECHANICAL CLOCK DESIGNED TO KEEP TIME FOR 10,000 YEARS.

THE CLOCK IS A PROJECT OF THE LONG NOW FOUNDATION – A NON-PROFIT DEDICATED TO ENCOURAGING LONG-TERM THINKING AND RESPONSIBILITY. BEZOS DONATED $42 MILLION TO FUND THE CLOCK. THE PROTOTYPE IS BEING BUILT BENEATH A MOUNTAIN ON LAND BEZOS OWNS IN WEST TEXAS. THE FINAL VERSION WILL BE BUILT AT MOUNT WASHINGTON IN NEVADA.

INVENTOR DANNY HILLIS FIRST SHARED THE CONCEPT IN AN ESSAY FOR *WIRED* IN 1995. IN IT, HE DESCRIBED A TIMEPIECE THAT WOULD TICK ONCE A YEAR AND HAVE A CENTURY HAND THAT WOULD MOVE ONLY ONCE EVERY 100 YEARS. A CUCKOO WOULD EMERGE ONCE EVERY 1,000 YEARS.

OVER THE LIFETIME OF THIS CLOCK, THE UNITED STATES WON'T EXIST. WHOLE CIVILISATIONS WILL RISE AND FALL.

NEW SYSTEMS OF GOVERNMENT WILL BE INVENTED.

YOU CAN'T IMAGINE THE WORLD – NO ONE CAN – THAT WE'RE TRYING TO GET THIS CLOCK TO PASS THROUGH.

IN THE YEAR 4000, YOU'LL SEE THIS CLOCK AND YOU'LL WONDER, 'WHY ON EARTH DID THEY BUILD THIS?'

BEZOS IS A MAN WHO HAS HIS EYES ON THE FUTURE, BUT HE CAN'T ENTIRELY ESCAPE THE CONCERNS OF THE PRESENT.

IN JANUARY 2019, BEZOS AND HIS WIFE OF 25 YEARS, MACKENZIE, ANNOUNCED THAT THEY WERE GETTING A DIVORCE. IN THE EVENTUAL SETTLEMENT, MACKENZIE RETAINED 25 PER CENT OF THE COUPLE'S STAKE IN AMAZON, MAKING HER WORTH AROUND $25 BILLION AND THE WORLD'S THIRD WEALTHIEST WOMAN.

THAT STILL LEFT JEFF BEZOS THE WORLD'S RICHEST MAN, WITH
A FORTUNE WORTH $110 BILLION, ACCORDING TO *FORBES*.

HALF OF $117 BILLION IS STILL MORE THAN ENOUGH TO CONTINUE FUNDING HIS PET PROJECTS. IT'S WORTH REMINDING OURSELVES WHO REALLY PAYS FOR SUCH EXTRAVAGANCE.

IN THE WINTER OF 2016, HARD-PRESSED AMAZON WORKERS IN DUNFERMLINE, FIFE, SCOTLAND...

RESORTED TO SLEEPING IN TENTS NEAR THE COMPANY WAREHOUSE IN A DESPERATE ATTEMPT TO SAVE MONEY ON TRAVEL COSTS.

WILLIE RENNIE, LEADER OF THE SCOTTISH LIBERAL DEMOCRATS, SAID...

AMAZON SHOULD BE ASHAMED THAT THEY PAY THEIR WORKERS SO LITTLE THAT THEY HAVE TO CAMP OUT IN THE DEAD OF WINTER TO MAKE ENDS MEET.

AMAZON NEED TO TAKE A LONG, HARD LOOK AT THEMSELVES AND CHANGE THEIR WAYS.

THEY PAY A SMALL AMOUNT OF TAX AND RECEIVED MILLIONS OF POUNDS FROM THE SCOTTISH NATIONAL PARTY GOVERNMENT. SO THE LEAST THEY SHOULD DO IS PAY THE PROPER LIVING WAGE.

IT'S NOT UNUSUAL FOR GOVERNMENTS TO HAND OUT MONEY TO BIG BUSINESS IN RETURN FOR INVESTMENT AND JOBS. IN SCOTLAND, BETWEEN 2007 AND 2018, AMAZON WERE GIVEN AT LEAST £3.5 MILLION OF TAXPAYER-FUNDED REGIONAL SELECTIVE ASSISTANCE (RSA) GRANTS.

IT'S A WIN-WIN FOR COMPANIES LIKE AMAZON, WHO THEN MAKE HUGE PROFITS, DELIVERING VERY LITTLE TO LOCAL COMMUNITIES.

THANKS FOR NOTHING.

AMAZON HAS SUCH ENORMOUS FINANCIAL MUSCLE NOW THAT IT CAN MAKE ENTIRE COUNTRIES DANCE TO ITS TUNE. IN THE US, MORE THAN 200 CITIES SPENT A YEAR LAVISHING PROMISED TAX BREAKS AND OTHER INCENTIVES FOR THE CHANCE TO HOST THE TECH GIANT'S NEW HQ.

THE GAME-SHOW QUALITIES OF THIS BIDDING PROCESS DREW A GREAT DEAL OF CRITICISM.

RICHARD L. FLORIDA, PROFESSOR AND HEAD OF THE MARTIN PROSPERITY INSTITUTE AT THE ROTMAN SCHOOL OF MANAGEMENT AT THE UNIVERSITY OF TORONTO.

THE VERY IDEA THAT A TRILLION-DOLLAR COMPANY RUN BY THE WORLD'S RICHEST MAN COULD RUN AN *AMERICAN IDOL* AUCTION ON MORE THAN 230 CITIES ACROSS THE UNITED STATES (AND CANADA AND MEXICO) TO EXTRACT DATA ON SITES AND ON INCENTIVES, AND PICK UP A HANDY THREE BILLION DOLLARS OF TAXPAYER MONEY IN THE PROCESS, IS A SAD STATEMENT OF EXTREME CORPORATE POWER IN OUR TIME.

IN NOVEMBER 2018 AMAZON ANNOUNCED THE WINNERS OF THE BIDDING PROCESS. IT WOULD SPLIT ITS SECOND HQ IN TWO, ONE HALF BEING IN THE LONG ISLAND CITY AREA OF QUEENS, NEW YORK, AND THE OTHER AT CRYSTAL CITY IN ARLINGTON COUNTY, VIRGINIA, JUST SOUTH OF DOWNTOWN WASHINGTON DC.

TO LAND THIS DEAL AHEAD OF THE COMPETITION, NEW YORK STATE HAD TO OFFER AMAZON UP TO $1.7 BILLION IN GRANTS AND TAX BREAKS.

NEW YORK STATE GOVERNOR ANDREW CUOMO

I'LL CHANGE MY NAME TO AMAZON CUOMO IF THAT'S WHAT IT TAKES.

ON TOP OF THE STATE'S INCENTIVE PACKAGE, NEW YORK CITY PROMISED TO PROVIDE A FURTHER $1.3 BILLION IN TAX BREAKS.

NEW YORK MAYOR BILL DE BLASIO

IT'S AN EXTRAORDINARY DAY FOR QUEENS. IT'S SOMETHING THAT EVERYONE SHOULD BE PROUD OF.

AMAZON ALSO GOT A PROMISE OF BELOW-MARKET-PRICE LEASES ON BUILDINGS AND SPACES, PLUS A HELICOPTER PAD PROVIDED BY THE CITY.

IN RETURN, AMAZON PLEDGED TO BRING 25,000 HIGH-PAYING JOBS OVER A PERIOD OF TEN YEARS AND AN OVERALL INVESTMENT OF $5 BILLION, SPLIT BETWEEN THE TWO SITES

IN NEW YORK, OPPOSITION TO THE DEAL WAS FEROCIOUS. STATE SENATOR MICHAEL GIANARIS AND CITY COUNCILLOR JIMMY VAN BRAMER, BOTH QUEENS DEMOCRATS, VOWED TO FIGHT THE INCENTIVE PACKAGE. THEY ISSUED A JOINT STATEMENT.

GIANARIS

VAN BRAMER

WE ARE WITNESS TO A CYNICAL GAME IN WHICH AMAZON DUPED NEW YORK INTO OFFERING UNPRECEDENTED AMOUNTS OF TAX DOLLARS TO ONE OF THE WEALTHIEST COMPANIES ON EARTH FOR A PROMISE OF JOBS THAT WOULD REPRESENT LESS THAN THREE PER CENT OF THE JOBS TYPICALLY CREATED IN OUR CITY OVER A TEN YEAR PERIOD. WE WERE NOT ELECTED TO SERVE AS AMAZON DRONES.

ALEXANDRIA OCASIO-CORTEZ, THE DEMOCRATIC REPRESENTATIVE FOR NEW YORK'S 14TH DISTRICT, SAID...

THE IDEA THAT (AMAZON) WILL RECEIVE HUNDREDS OF MILLIONS OF DOLLARS IN TAX BREAKS AT A TIME WHEN OUR SUBWAY IS CRUMBLING AND OUR COMMUNITIES NEED MORE INVESTMENT, NOT LESS, IS EXTREMELY CONCERNING TO RESIDENTS HERE.

WHEN WE TALK ABOUT BRINGING JOBS TO THE COMMUNITY, WE NEED TO DIG DEEP. HAS THE COMPANY PROMISED TO HIRE IN THE EXISTING COMMUNITY? WHAT'S THE QUALITY OF JOBS AND HOW MANY ARE PROMISED? ARE THESE JOBS LOW-WAGE OR HIGH-WAGE? ARE THERE BENEFITS? CAN PEOPLE COLLECTIVELY BARGAIN?

DESPITE GOVERNOR CUOMO AND MAYOR DE BLASIO'S SUPPORT FOR THE AMAZON DEAL, A COALITION OF NEW YORK LAWMAKERS FOUGHT TO INJECT RESISTANCE INTO EVERY PART OF THE APPROVAL PROCESS.

PERHAPS THE LAST STRAW FOR AMAZON WAS WHEN SENATOR GIANARIS WAS APPOINTED TO SERVE ON THE PUBLIC AUTHORITIES CONTROL BOARD, WHICH HAD TO APPROVE ALL BUT A $500-MILLION CAPITAL GRANT FROM THE STATE TO THE TECH GIANT. THIS WOULD HAVE POTENTIALLY GIVEN THE SENATOR POWER TO VETO THE PROJECT.

I'M NOT LOOKING TO NEGOTIATE A BETTER DEAL. I AM AGAINST THE DEAL THAT HAS BEEN PROPOSED AND I DON'T BELIEVE THAT IT CAN FORM THE FOUNDATION OF A NEGOTIATION.

IN FEBRUARY 2019 AMAZON ANNOUNCED THAT IT WAS PULLING OUT OF THE LONG ISLAND DEAL AND INSTEAD WOULD MOVE ITS HQ TO NASHVILLE, TENNESSEE. IN A STATEMENT THE COMPANY WROTE...

WHILE POLLS SHOW THAT 70 PER CENT OF NEW YORKERS SUPPORT OUR PLANS AND INVESTMENT, A NUMBER OF STATE AND LOCAL POLITICIANS HAVE MADE IT CLEAR THAT THEY OPPOSE OUR PRESENCE AND WILL NOT WORK WITH US TO BUILD THE TYPE OF RELATIONSHIPS THAT ARE REQUIRED TO GO FORWARD WITH THE PROJECT WE AND MANY OTHERS ENVISIONED IN LONG ISLAND CITY.

THIS WAS A RARE DEFEAT FOR JEFF BEZOS AND AMAZON, AND ONE THAT SUGGESTS THAT THERE COULD BE THE BEGINNINGS OF A MOVEMENT AGAINST THE POWER AND WEALTH OF GIANT COMPANIES AND THEIR BILLIONAIRE OWNERS.

BECAUSE WHAT, AFTER ALL, DOES AMAZON CONTRIBUTE TO THE WORLD? THEY ARE A COMPANY, VALUED AT NEARLY $800 BILLION, THAT PAID THE US ZERO IN FEDERAL INCOME TAX IN THE YEAR 2017 TO 2018, DESPITE MAKING A $11.2-BILLION PROFIT.

NEW YORK WAS RIGHT TO PUSH BACK AGAINST AMAZON'S LONG ISLAND HQ, QUESTIONING THE TECH GIANT IS AN ATTEMPT TO DO SOMETHING BOLDER THAN ATTRACT THOUSANDS OF JOBS. IT'S AN ATTEMPT TO RESTORE POWER TO MILLIONS OF CITIZENS AND WORKERS. THERE IS A LINK BETWEEN CORPORATE CONCENTRATION AND RISING INEQUALITY. DOMINANT COMPANIES LIKE AMAZON EXTRACT WEALTH FROM THE MAJORITY AND FUNNEL IT TO A SMALL NUMBER OF PEOPLE AT THE TOP. BY REDUCING THE NUMBER OF COMPETITORS, THESE COMPANIES ALSO MAKE IT HARDER FOR WORKERS TO GET A FAIR WAGE AND FOR PRODUCERS TO GET A FAIR PRICE.

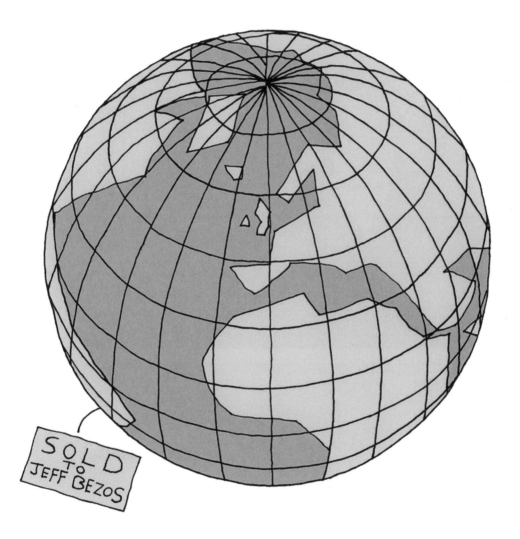

JEFF BEZOS HAS NOW GONE FAR BEYOND THE EVERYTHING STORE HE ORIGINALLY CONCEIVED. HE DOESN'T JUST WANT TO DOMINATE THE MARKET, BUT TO REPLACE IT. HE APPEARS TO BE AIMING FOR AMAZON TO BE THE UNDERLYING DEFAULT INFRASTRUCTURE THAT ALL COMMERCE RUNS ON. AMAZON'S WEBSITE IS ALREADY THE DOMINANT PLATFORM FOR ONLINE RETAIL SALES AND ITS AMAZON WEB SERVICE DIVISION PROVIDES 34 PER CENT OF THE WORLD'S CLOUD COMPUTING CAPACITY.

HOW MUCH POWER ARE WE AS A SOCIETY WILLING TO GIVE ONE MAN? NONE OF US HAVE TO BUY FROM AMAZON. IT ISN'T AGAINST THE LAW NOT TO CONTRIBUTE TO JEFF BEZOS'S FORTUNE. MILLIONS OF US ARE COMPLICIT IN THE TECH GIANT'S RISE. HE COULDN'T HAVE DONE IT WITHOUT US.

BUT EACH TIME WE BUY FROM AMAZON OR USE ONE OF ITS MANY SERVICES, WE UNDERMINE LOCAL BUSINESSES, IMPOVERISH WORKERS AND CONTRIBUTE TO THE GROWING INEQUALITY WE SEE ALL AROUND US.

IT'S LONG PAST TIME THAT WE ALL THOUGHT MORE CAREFULLY BEFORE HITTING THE 'BUY NOW' BUTTON.

END.

AFTERWORD

THIS PANEL
AFTER JAMES GILLRAY

CAN THE WORLD AFFORD TO HAVE A TINY GLOBAL ELITE SQUANDER RESOURCES AND HOLD UNDUE POLITICAL INFLUENCE OVER THE REST OF US? THE ANSWER MUST BE NO. I'VE FOCUSED IN THIS BOOK ON A SMALL NUMBER OF INDIVIDUALS WHO GENERALLY TAKE A CONSERVATIVE OR LIBERTARIAN POLITICAL STANCE, BUT I COULD HAVE EASILY PICKED THREE OR FOUR LEFT-LEANING BILLIONAIRES AND ARRIVED AT THE SAME CONCLUSION.

NO NO ONE SHOULD HAVE SUCH UNELECTED POWER, AND THAT INCLUDES MORE LIBERAL BILLIONAIRES LIKE GEORGE SOROS AND WARREN BUFFETT. AT SOME LEVEL OF EXTREME WEALTH, MONEY INEVITABLY CORRUPTS. WHETHER ON THE LEFT OR THE RIGHT, IT BUYS POLITICAL POWER, SILENCES DISSENT, AND SERVES TO PERPETUATE EVER-GREATER WEALTH, OFTEN UNRELATED TO ANY SOCIAL GOOD.

IN THIS BOOK I'VE TRIED TO DEMONSTRATE HOW EASY IT IS FOR THE SUPER-RICH TO DISTORT OUR ECONOMIES AND RUN OUR POLITICAL PROCESSES FOR THEIR OWN BENEFIT. MUCH HAS BEEN WRITTEN ABOUT VLADIMIR PUTIN AND RUSSIA'S INTERFERENCE IN THE POLITICS OF THE UNITED STATES, BRITAIN AND OTHER WESTERN DEMOCRACIES IN RECENT YEARS, BUT THE POWER THAT THE KOCH BROTHERS WIELD THROUGH THEIR NETWORK, OR THE INFLUENCE RUPERT MURDOCH HAS THROUGH HIS MEDIA EMPIRE, HAS BEEN AS DAMAGING.

PUTIN SHOULDN'T BE CONSIDERED SEPARATELY FROM OTHERS IN THE BILLIONAIRE CLASS, BUT AS PART OF A MUCH BIGGER GLOBAL OLIGARCHY PROBLEM. THE 'ONE PER CENT' HAVE LARGELY DISCONNECTED THEMSELVES FROM THE CIVIC LIFE OF THE WORLD AND FROM ANY CONCERN ABOUT ITS WELL-BEING, EXCEPT AS A PLACE TO EXTRACT PROFIT.

IT'S TRUE THAT MANY OF THE ONE PER CENT GIVE MILLIONS AWAY IN CHARITY EACH YEAR, BUT PHILANTHROPY FOR THE SUPER-RICH IS SIMPLY A WAY FOR THEM TO KEEP THE STATUS QUO, NOT CHANGE IT. THROUGH CHARITABLE GIVING THEY CAN USEFULLY REBRAND THEMSELVES AS SAVIOURS OF THE POOR, WHILE CONTINUING TO DO HARM IN OTHER AREAS OF THEIR BUSINESSES.

WHAT CAN WE DO TO REDUCE THE INEQUALITY WE SEE IN THE WORLD AROUND US? HOW CAN WE STOP THE VERY RICH FROM USING THEIR MONEY TO SUBVERT OUR DEMOCRATIC INSTITUTIONS? HERE ARE JUST TWO WAYS. FIRSTLY, WE COULD REDUCE THE TOP ONE PER CENT'S FINANCIAL POWER BY DIMINISHING THEIR INCOME WITH TAX AND PAY RULES, AND, SECONDLY, WE COULD RAISE INCOME FOR WORKERS AT THE BOTTOM WITH SUBSIDIES AND MINIMUM WAGE INCREASES. BOTH THESE MEASURES WOULD INVOLVE AGGRESSIVE GOVERNMENT INTERVENTION.

CRITICS OF THESE IDEAS WILL SCREAM THAT THIS IS SOCIALISM AND THEREFORE THE END OF FREEDOM. BUT IT'S MORE THAN POSSIBLE TO HAVE SENSIBLE RESTRICTIONS ON A FREE-MARKET SYSTEM AND STILL HAVE ROBUST CAPITALISM. FOR DECADES, FROM THE 1950s TO THE 1970s, IN THE UNITED STATES THE TOP FEDERAL INCOME TAX RATE REMAINED HIGH, NEVER DIPPING BELOW 70 PER CENT, AND IT DID THE COUNTRY NO HARM. IN FACT THE US ECONOMY BOOMED DURING THAT PERIOD. SUCH A POLICY WILL HARDLY BE PUNITIVE, SINCE IT WILL AFFECT SUCH A SMALL NUMBER OF PEOPLE AND BARELY MAKE AN IMPACT ON THEIR LIFE SATISFACTION. THEY WILL STILL BE RICH ENOUGH TO BUY WHATEVER THEY WANT.

THE CHOICE ISN'T BETWEEN UNRESTRAINED CAPITALISM OR SOME CENTRALLY PLANNED SOVIET NIGHTMARE. THERE IS A SENSIBLE MIDDLE ROAD. YOU DON'T NEED TO BE A MARXIST TO WANT DAY CARE, SCHOOLS, FIRE DEPTS, SANITATION, ROADS AND A CLEAN ENVIRONMENT, INSTEAD OF ANOTHER TAX BREAK FOR THE VASTLY RICH. THE PREVIOUS GILDED AGE CAME TO AN END AND THIS ONE COULD TOO. CAPITALISM DOESN'T NEED REPLACING, IT NEEDS REFORM. GOVERNMENT SHOULD BREAK UP MONOPOLIES LIKE FACEBOOK, GOOGLE AND AMAZON AND PROMOTE COMPETITIVE MARKETS.

IT'S LONG PAST TIME THAT THE UNELECTED POWER OF THE BILLIONAIRE CLASS WAS CURTAILED. FAILURE TO ACT NOW WILL ONLY LEAD TO A FURTHER WIDENING OF THE GULF BETWEEN RICH AND POOR, YET MORE ATTACKS ON OUR DEMOCRACY, AND RUNAWAY ENVIRONMENTAL COLLAPSE.

IS THIS THE WORLD WE WANT?

ACKNOWLEDGEMENTS:

I'm indebted to the many writers whose work I've drawn from while researching *Billionaires*. In particular *Dark Money* by Jane Mayer, *Dial M For Murdoch* by Tom Watson and Martin Hickman, *Murdoch's Politics* by David McKnight, *Rupert Murdoch: A Reassessment* by Rodney Tiffen, *The Sons of Wichita* by Daniel Schulman, *The Everything Store* by Brad Stone, and *Hired: Six Months Undercover in Low-Wage Britain* by James Bloodworth. All of these books are excellent and essential if you want to explore these subjects in further detail.

Thanks are also due to Graham Johnstone, Christine Quinn, Nick Abadzis, Simon Fraser, Jonathan Edwards, Louise Evans and my parents.

Thanks to Linda McQueen, Candida Lacey, Dawn Sackett and everyone at Myriad Editions.

Thanks especially to my excellent editor Corinne Pearlman.

And of course to Bonnie Millard for her love, support and encouragement.

R E F E R E N C E S :

MURDOCH

Watson T, Hickman M. *Dial M For Murdoch: News Corporation and the Corruption of Britain.* Penguin Books: London; 2012.

McKnight D. *Murdoch's Politics: How One Man's Thirst For Wealth and Power Shapes the World.* Pluto Press: London; 2013.

Folkenflik D. *Murdoch's World: The Last of the Old Media Empires.* PublicAffairs (Perseus Books): United States; 2013.

Brock D, Rabin-Havt A, and Media Matters For America. *The Fox Effect: How Roger Ailes Turned a Network Into a Propaganda Machine.* Anchor Books: New York; 2012.

Tiffen R. *Rupert Murdoch: A Reassessment.* University of New South Wales Press: Australia; 2014.

Gabler N. Roger Ailes: The Man Who Destroyed Objectivity. *Bill Moyers.* 2017 May 23. https://billmoyers.com/story/roger-ailes-destroyed-objectivity (accessed 2017 June 4).

Dickinson T. How Roger Ailes Built the Fox News Fear Factory. *Rolling Stone.* 2011 June 9. www.rollingstone.com/politics/politics-news/how-roger-ailes-built-the-fox-news-fear-factory-244652 (accessed 2017 June 4).

Evans H. How Thatcher and Murdoch made their secret deal. *The Guardian.* 2015 April 28. www.theguardian.com/uk-news/2015/apr/28/how-margaret-thatcher-and-rupert-murdoch-made-secret-deal (accessed 2017 June 5).

Oatridge N. Wapping Times. www.oatridge.co.uk/wapping.htm (accessed 2017 July 3).

Macintyre D. Wapping dispute 30 years on: How Rupert Murdoch changed labour relations – and newspapers – forever. *The Independent.* 2016 January 21. www.independent.co.uk/news/media/press/wapping-dispute-30-years-on-how-rupert-murdoch-changed-labour-relations-and-newspapers-forever-a6826316.html (accessed 2017 June 2).

Travis A. Murdoch did meet Thatcher before Times takeover, memo reveals. *The Guardian.* 2012 Mar 17. www.theguardian.com/media/2012/mar/17/rupert-murdoch-margaret-thatcher (accessed 2017 July 2).

Timms D. Fortress Wapping: a history. *The Guardian.* 2004 Oct 12. www.theguardian.com/media/2004/oct/12/rupertmurdoch.citynews1 (accessed 2017 July 12).

Gibson O. What the Sun said 15 years ago. *The Guardian.* 2004 July 7. www.theguardian.com/media/2004/jul/07/pressandpublishing.football1 (accessed 2017 July 13).

Siddle J. Hillsborough: The shameless smears, lies and cover-ups. *Liverpool Echo.* 2016 April 26. www.liverpoolecho.co.uk/news/liverpool-news/hillsborough-shameless-smears-lies-cover-11245354 (accessed 2017 July 15).

Bell M. The reporter who took on the 'News of the World' and won. *The Independent.* 2009 Nov 29. www.independent.co.uk/news/media/press/the-reporter-who-took-on-the-news-of-the-world-and-won-1830378.html (accessed 2017 July 15).

Ruddick G. Murdoch papers hid evidence of illegality, say phone-hacking victims. *The Guardian.* 2017 Oct 11. www.theguardian.com/media/2017/oct/11/murdoch-papers-hid-evidence-of-illegality-say-phone-hacking-victims (accessed 2017 Oct 12).

Steel E, Schmidt MS. Bill O'Reilly Settled New Harassment Claim, Then Fox Renewed His Contract. *New York Times.* 2017 Oct 21. www.nytimes.com/2017/10/21/business/media/bill-oreilly-sexual-harassment.html (accessed 2017 Oct 25).

Lyngar E. I lost my dad to Fox News: How a generation was captured by thrashing hysteria. *Salon.* 2014 Feb 27. www.salon.com/2014/02/27/i_lost_my_dad_to_fox_news_how_a_generation_was_captured_by_thrashing_hysteria (accessed 2017 Oct 21).

White M. Tony Blair and Rupert Murdoch: the deconstruction of a friendship. *The Guardian.* 2014 Feb 14. www.theguardian.com/politics/2014/feb/14/tony-blair-rupert-murdoch-deconstruction-friendship-wendi-deng (accessed 2017 Oct 26).

Mendick R. Phone hacking: Police chief Andy Hayman paid for champagne dinners with News of the World journalists. *The Telegraph.* 2011 July 24. www.telegraph.co.uk/news/uknews/phone-hacking/8656580/Phone-hacking-Police-chief-Andy-Hayman-paid-for-champagne-dinners-with-News-of-the-World-journalists.html (accessed 2017 Nov 2).

Laville S, Dodd V. News of the World paid bribes worth £100,000 to up to five Met officers. *The Guardian.* 2011 July 7. www.theguardian.com/media/2011/jul/07/phone-hacking-bribes-five-police-officers (accessed 2017 Nov 3).

BBC. News Corp officially splits in two. 2013 June 28. www.bbc.co.uk/news/business-23104822 (accessed 2017 Nov 9).

Rupert Murdoch reportedly prodded Trump to fire Steve Bannon days before Charlottesville erupted in violence. *Business Insider*, via AFP. 2017 Aug 14. www.businessinsider.com/afp-murdoch-urged-trump-to-fire-bannon-nyt-2017-8?r=UK. (accessed 2017 Nov 12).

Thomsen J. Trump called Murdoch to make sure Disney deal wouldn't affect Fox News: report. *The Hill.* 2017 Dec 23. https://thehill.com/homenews/administration/366335-trump-called-murdoch-to-make-sure-disney-deal-wouldntaffect-fox-news (accessed 2017 Dec 23).

Neustatter A. Murdoch's matriarch. *The Guardian*. 2009 Feb 21. www.theguardian.com/lifeandstyle/2009/feb/20/interview-elizabeth-murdoch (accessed 2017 Nov 19).

Meyer J. The Making of the Fox News White House. *New Yorker*. 2019 Mar 4. www.newyorker.com/magazine/2019/03/11/the-making-of-the-fox-news-white-house (accessed 2019 March 5).

THE KOCH BROTHERS

Meyer J. *Dark Money: How a Secretive Group of Billionaires is Trying to Buy Political Control in the US*. Scribe Publications: Victoria; 2016.

Schulman D. *Sons of Wichita: How the Koch Brothers Became America's Most Powerful and Private Dynasty*. Grand Central Publishing: New York; 2014.

Meyer J. Covert Operations:The billionaire brothers who are waging a war against Obama. *New Yorker*. 2010 August 30. www.newyorker.com/magazine/2010/08/30/covert-operations (accessed 2017 Dec 1).

Reiff N. Top 7 Companies Owned by the Koch Brothers. *Investopedia*. 2018 June 5. www.investopedia.com/insights/companies-owned-koch-brothers (accessed 2017 Dec 2)

Cassell W Jr. The Koch Brothers: America's 2nd Wealthiest Family. *Investopedia*. Updated 2018 June 5. www.investopedia.com/articles/investing/122915/koch-brothers-americas-2nd-wealthiest-family.asp (accessed 2017 Dec 2).

Confessore N. Father of Koch Brothers Helped Build Nazi Oil Refinery, Book Says. *New York Times*. 2016 Jan 11. www.nytimes.com/2016/01/12/us/politics/father-of-koch-brothers-helped-build-nazi-oil-refinery-book-says.html (accessed 2017 Dec 5).

Schulman D. The Making of the Kochtopus: How the billionaire brothers built a political network that rivals the GOP itself. *Mother Jones*. 2014 Nov 3. www.motherjones.com/politics/2014/11/history-of-koch-brothers-donation-network-money (accessed 2017 Dec 6).

Kopan T. Report: Think tanks tied to Kochs. *Politico*. 2013 Nov 13. www.politico.com/story/2013/11/koch-brothers-think-tank-report-099791 (accessed 2017 Dec 10).

Lipton E, Williams B. How Think Tanks Amplify Corporate America's Influence. *New York Times*. 2016 Aug 7. www.nytimes.com/2016/08/08/us/politics/think-tanks-research-and-corporate-lobbying.html (accessed 2017 Dec 11).

Levinthal D (Centre For Public Integrity). How the Koch Brothers Are Influencing U.S. Colleges. *Time*. 2015 Dec

15. http://time.com/4148838/koch-brothers-colleges-universities (accessed 2017 Dec 12).

Barakat M. Documents show ties between university, conservative donors. *AP News*. 2018 May 1. https://apnews.com/0c87e4318bcc4eb9b8e69f9f54c7b889 (accessed 2018 May 12).

PR Watch Admin. Charles Koch Ramps Up Higher Ed Funding to Fuel 'Talent Pipeline'. *PR Watch*. 2017 Feb 2. www.prwatch.org/news/2017/01/13210/charles-koch-ramps-higher-ed-funding-talent-pipeline (accessed 2017 Dec 12).

Cohen P. Professors' Liberalism Contagious? Maybe Not. *New York Times*. 2008 Nov 2. www.nytimes.com/2008/11/03/books/03infl.html (accessed 2017 Dec 12).

Harriot M. Millions of Students Are Quietly Being Taught the Koch Brothers' Whitewashed Version of Black History. *The Root*. 2018 Mar 14. www.theroot.com/millions-of-students-are-quietly-being-taught-the-koch-1823742091 (accessed 2018 May 23).

DeMelle B. Study Confirms Tea Party Was Created by Big Tobacco and Billionaire Koch Brothers. *Huffpost*. 2017 Dec 6. www.huffingtonpost.com/brendan-demelle/study-confirms-tea-party-_b_2663125.html (accessed 2018 May 23).

Ambrosz JS. Dark money boosts election TV ad buys: Spending up 90% over 2014 midterms. *Salon*. 2018 May 22. www.salon.com/2018/05/22/dark-money-boosts-election-tv-ad-buys_partner (accessed 2018 May 23).

Gertz M. How Years Of The Right-Wing Media's Obama Hatred Paved The Way For Trump. *Media Matters*. 2017 Jan 20. www.mediamatters.org/blog/2017/01/20/how-years-right-wing-media-s-obama-hatred-paved-way-trump/215059 (accessed 2018 May 25).

Broder JM. 'Cap and Trade' Loses Its Standing as Energy Policy of Choice. *New York Times*. 2010 March 25. www.nytimes.com/2010/03/26/science/earth/26climate.html (accessed 2018 May 23).

Haq A. Revealed: Donor's Trust is the Secret ATM Machine For Climate Deniers. *PolluterWatch*. 2013 Feb 15. http://polluterwatch.com/blog/revealed-donors-trust-secret-atm-machine-climate-deniers (accessed 2018 May 28).

Levy G. How Citizens United Has Changed Politics in 5 Years. *US News*. 2015 Jan 1. www.usnews.com/news/articles/2015/01/21/5-years-later-citizens-united-has-remade-us-politics#close-modal (accessed 2018 June 1).

Ruelas G. Koch Industries Pollution: Koch and the environment. *Greenpeace*. www.greenpeace.org/usa/global-warming/climate-deniers/koch-industries/koch-industries-pollution (accessed 2018 June 3).

Dickinson T. Inside the Koch Brothers' Toxic Empire. *Rolling Stone*. 2014 Sept 24. www.rollingstone.com/politics/politics-news/inside-the-koch-brothers-toxic-empire-164403 (accessed 2018 June 4).

Rice A. Wild Bill Koch Builds a Private Town Out West. *Architect Magazine*. 2012 Aug 22. www.architectmagazine.com/design/wild-bill-koch-builds-a-private-town-out-west_o (accessed 2018 June 6).

Ainslie G. Bill Koch: How a "hick from Kansas" won the America's Cup. *Boat International*. 2017 June 8. www.boatinternational.com/yachts/americas-cup/bill-koch-how-a-hick-from-kansas-won-the-americas-cup--33817 (accessed 2018 June 7).

Woodward R. Billionaire Bill Koch wins appeal over fake wine. *Decanter*. 2013 Oct 1. www.decanter.com/wine-news/billionaire-bill-koch-wins-appeal-over-fake-wine-276524 (accessed 2018 June 8).

Cascone S. Scientists Tell Natural History Museums to Shun Billionaire Donor and Climate Change-Denier David Koch. *Artnet News*. 2015 March 25. https://news.artnet.com/exhibitions/david-koch-natural-history-museums-281214 (accessed 2018 June 10).

Schulman D. The "Other" Koch Brother. *Vanity Fair*. 2014 May 9. www.vanityfair.com/style/society/2014/05/frederick-koch-brothers (accessed 2018 June 12).

Elliott P. The Koch Brothers Are Pushing for Criminal Justice Changes. *Time*. 2018 Jan 29. http://time.com/5123969/koch-brothers-criminal-justice-reform (accessed 2018 June 13).

Solomon B. Billionaire Charles Koch: Trump-Hillary Is Like Voting 'Cancer Or Heart Attack'. *Forbes*. 2016 July 11. www.forbes.com/sites/briansolomon/2016/07/11/billionaire-charles-koch-trump-hillary-is-like-voting-cancer-or-heart-attack (accessed 2018 June 13).

Meyer J. One Koch Brother Forces the Other Out of the Family Business. *New Yorker*. 2018 June 7. www.newyorker.com/news/news-desk/the-meaning-of-a-koch-brothers-retirement (accessed 2018 June 13).

JEFF BEZOS

Stone B. *The Everything Store: Jeff Bezos and the Age of Amazon*. Little Brown and Company: Boston; 2013.

Bloodworth J. *Hired: Six Months Undercover in Low-Wage Britain*. Atlantic Books: London; 2019.

Tobias M. Bernie Sanders says Amazon paid no federal income tax in 2017. He's right. *Politifact*. 2018 May 3. www.politifact.com/truth-o-meter/statements/2018/may/03/bernie-s/amazon-paid-0-federal-income-taxes-2017 (accessed 2018 June 16).

Hanbury M. Amazon CEO Jeff Bezos says working at McDonald's as a 16-year-old made him obsessed with automation and managing employees. *Business Insider*. 2018 April 17. www.businessinsider.com/amazons-jeff-bezos-worked-at-mcdonalds-2018-4? (accessed 2018 June 17).

Bernton H, Kelleher S. Amazon warehouse jobs push workers to physical limit. *Seattle Times*. 2015 Aug 17. www.seattletimes.com/business/amazon-warehouse-jobs-push-workers-to-physical-limit (accessed 2018 June 19).

Kim E. Amazon's first employee shares the biggest lesson he learned from losing his job there. *Business Insider*. 2016 Sept 12. www.businessinsider.com/amazon-first-employee-shel-kaphan-biggest-lesson-learned-2016-9? (accessed 2018 June 21).

Hartmans A. Here's where Amazon's first 21 employees are now. *Business Insider*. 2017 June 7. www.businessinsider.com/where-early-amazon-employees-are-now-2017-4? (accessed 2018 June 23).

Fottrell Q. Meet Amazon's first customer – this is the book he bought. *MarketWatch*. 2017 May 15. www.marketwatch.com/story/meet-amazons-first-ever-customer-2015-04-22 (accessed 2018 June 23).

Reiff N. Top 7 Companies Owned by Amazon. *Investopedia*. 2019 Mar 14. www.investopedia.com/articles/markets/102115/top-10-companies-owned-amazon.asp (accessed 2018 June 24).

If You Had Invested Right After Amazon's IPO. *Investopedia*. 2019 Feb 13. www.investopedia.com/articles/investing/082715/if-you-had-invested-right-after-amazons-ipo.asp (accessed 2019 Mar 1).

Perez JC. Amazon records first profitable year in its history. *Computerworld*. 2004 Jan 28. www.computerworld.com/article/2575106/amazon-records-first-profitable-year-in-its-history.html (accessed 2018 June 27).

D'Onfro J, Stone M. See what it's like inside Amazon's massive warehouses. *Business Insider*. 2015 Aug 17. www.businessinsider.com/what-its-like-in-amazons-massive-warehouses-fulfillment-centers-2014-11? (accessed 2018 June 28).

Kantor J, Streitfeld D. Inside Amazon: Wrestling Big Ideas in a Bruising Workplace. *New York Times*. 2015 Aug 15. www.nytimes.com/2015/08/16/technology/inside-amazon-wrestling-big-ideas-in-a-bruising-workplace.html (accessed 2018 July 3).

Bertrand N. How Amazon's Ugly Fight With A Publisher Actually Started. *Business Insider*. 2014 Oct 7. www.businessinsider.com/how-did-the-amazon-feud-with-hachette-start-2014-10? (accessed 2018 July 4).

Apple to pay $450m settlement over US ebook price fixing. *The Guardian*, via Reuters. 2016 Mar 7. www.theguardian.com/technology/2016/mar/07/apple-450-million-settlement-e-book-price-fixing-supreme-court (accessed 2018 July 5).

Taibbi M. Amazon's Long Game Is Clearer Than Ever. *Rolling Stone*. 2018 Nov 14. www.rollingstone.com/politics/politics-features/why-amazon-chose-new-york-virginia-756355 (accessed 2018 Nov 20).

Levy S. Jeff Bezos Wants Us All to Leave Earth–For Good. *Wired*. 2018 Oct 15. www.wired.com/story/jeff-bezos-blue-origin (accessed 2018 Nov 21).

Keates N. The Many Places Amazon CEO Jeff Bezos Calls Home. *Wall Street Journal*. 2019 Jan 9. www.wsj.com/articles/the-many-places-amazon-ceo-jeff-bezos-calls-home-1507204462 (accessed 2019 Jan 23).

Bloodworth J. I worked in an Amazon warehouse. Bernie Sanders is right to target them. *The Guardian*. 2018 Sept 17. www.theguardian.com/commentisfree/2018/sep/17/amazon-warehouse-bernie-sanders (accessed 2019 Jan 2).

Organise survey report. *Amazon: What's it like where you work?* https://static1.squarespace.com/static/5a3af3e22aeba594ad56d8cb/t/5ad098b3562fa7b8c90d5e1b/1523620020369/Amazon+Warehouse+Staff+Survey+Results.pdf (accessed 2019 Jan 2).

Soper S. Amazon workers cool after company took heat for hot warehouses. *Seattle Times*. 2012 June 6. www.seattletimes.com/business/amazon-workers-cool-after-company-took-heat-for-hot-warehouses (accessed 2019 Jan 3).

Sainato M. Accidents at Amazon: workers left to suffer after warehouse injuries. *The Guardian*. 2018 July 30. www.theguardian.com/technology/2018/jul/30/accidents-at-amazon-workers-left-to-suffer-after-warehouse-injuries (accessed 2019 Jan 3).

Green D. Seven people have died on the job in Amazon's warehouses since 2013–here's what happened. *Business Insider*. 2018 April 28. www.businessinsider.com/amazon-warehouse-safety-and-deaths-2018-4? (accessed 2019 Jan 3).

Diamond ML. Bear spray incident at NJ Amazon warehouse shines light on safety record. *APP*. 2018 Dec 5. https://eu.app.com/story/money/business/main-street/2018/12/05/bear-spray-incident-nj-amazon-warehouse-shines-light-safety-record/2215515002 (accessed 2019 Jan 5).

Cook J. Full memo: Jeff Bezos responds to brutal NYT story, says it doesn't represent the Amazon he leads. *Geekwire*. 2015 August 16. www.geekwire.com/2015/full-memo-jeff-bezos-responds-to-cutting-nyt-expose-says-tolerance-for-lack-of-empathy-needs-to-be-zero/(accessed 2019 Jan 6).

Green D. Data from states shows thousands of Amazon employees are on food stamps. *Business Insider*. 2018 Aug 25. www.businessinsider.com/amazon-employees-on-food-stamps-2018-8? (accessed 2019 Jan 8).

Kotecki P. Jeff Bezos is the richest man in modern history – here's how he spends on philanthropy. *Business Insider*. 2018 Sept 13. www.businessinsider.com/jeff-bezos-richest-person-modern-history-spends-on-charity-2018-7? (accessed 2019 Jan 10).

Fleishman G. Jeff Bezos Says Blue Origin Will Put People in Space in 2019. *Fortune*. 2018 Sept 20. http://fortune.com/2018/09/19/bezos-blue-origin-people-in-space-2019 (accessed 2019 Jan 22).

Gartenberg C. Construction begins on Jeff Bezos' $42 million 10,000-year clock. *The Verge*. 2018 Feb 20. www.theverge.com/tldr/2018/2/20/17031836/jeff-bezos-clock-10000-year-cost (accessed 2019 Jan 23).

Kentish B. Hard-pressed Amazon workers in Scotland sleeping in tents near warehouse to save money. *The Independent*. 2016 Dec 10. www.independent.co.uk/news/uk/home-news/amazon-workers-sleep-tents-dunfermline-fife-scotland-a7467657.html (accessed 2019 Jan 27).

Pulkkinen L. MacKenzie Bezos: divorce from Amazon CEO could make her world's richest woman. *The Guardian*. 2019 Jan 10. www.theguardian.com/us-news/2019/jan/10/mackenzie-bezos-jeff-amazon-divorce-worlds-richest-woman (accessed 2019 Jan 29).

Campbell J. Amazon HQ2: $3 billion in state, city tax breaks draws company to New York. *Rochester Democrat and Chronicle*. 2018 Nov 13. https://eu.democratandchronicle.com/story/news/politics/albany/2018/11/13/new-york-amazon-incentives-billion/1986979002 (accessed 2019 Feb 6).

Mitchell S. Amazon Doesn't Just Want to Dominate the Market–It Wants to Become the Market. *The Nation*. 2018 Feb 15. www.thenation.com/article/amazon-doesnt-just-want-to-dominate-the-market-it-wants-to-become-the-market (accessed 2019 Feb 17).

Hess A. Alexandria Ocasio-Cortez: Amazon headquarters in Queens is 'extremely concerning.' *CNBC*. 2018 Nov 13. www.cnbc.com/2018/11/13/alexandria-ocasio-cortez-amazon-queens-hq-is-extremely-concerning.html (accessed 2019 Feb 17).

Allen J, Shepardson D. Feeling unwelcome, Amazon ditches plans for New York hub. *Reuters*. 2019 Feb 14. www.reuters.com/article/us-amazon-new-york/amazon-pulls-plug-on-new-york-city-headquarters-idUSKCN1Q32F9 (accessed 2019 Feb 17).

A graphic milestone of investigative reporting, Cunningham's essays explode the lies, hoaxes and scams of popular science, debunking media myths and decoding some of today's most fiercely-debated issues: climate change, electroconvulsive therapy, fracking, the moon landing, the MMR (Measles, Mumps and Rubella) vaccine, homeopathy, chiropractic, evolution, and science denialism.

ISBN 978-1-908434-36-4
eISBN 978-1-908434-62-3

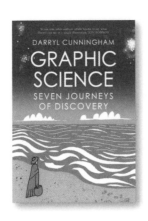

Much is known about scientists such as Darwin, Newton, and Einstein, but what about lesser known scientists – people who have not achieved a high level of fame, but who have contributed greatly to human knowledge? What were their lives like? What were their struggles, aims, successes, and failures? How do their discoveries fit into the bigger picture of science as a whole? Overlooked, sidelined, excluded, discredited: key figures in scientific discovery come and take their bow in an alternative Nobel prize gallery including George Washington Carver, Joyce Bell Burnell, Alfred Wegener and Nikola Tesla.

ISBN 978-0-9935633-2-4
eISBN 978-0-9935633-3-1

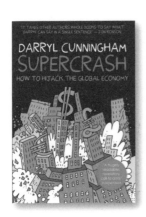

Darryl Cunningham takes us to the heart of the economic crisis, showing how the Neo-Cons hijacked the debate and led the way to a world dominated by the market. He traces the roots of the financial crisis of 2008 to the domination of right-wing policies and the people who created them, drawing a fascinating portrait of the New Right and the charismatic Ayn Rand. He examines the neurological basis of political thinking, and asks why it is so difficult for us to change our minds – even when faced with powerful evidence that a certain course of action is not working.

ISBN 978-1-908434-43-2
eISBN 978-1-908434-73-9